For Ju[...]

With all good wishes

Abram Leon Sachar

June 1944

For Gertrude & Julius Livingston
in old friendship —

Maurice Samuel

January, 1968

HARVEST
in the
DESERT

Maurice Samuel

B'NAI B'RITH HILLEL FOUNDATIONS
IN AMERICAN UNIVERSITIES

PHILADELPHIA
THE JEWISH PUBLICATION SOCIETY OF AMERICA
5704–1944

Contents

Also by MAURICE SAMUEL

NOVELS

    THE OUTSIDER

    WHATEVER GODS

    BEYOND WOMAN

PUBLICISTIC AND BELLES LETTRES

    YOU GENTILES

    I THE JEW

    WHAT HAPPENED IN PALESTINE

    ON THE RIM OF THE WILDERNESS

    JEWS ON APPROVAL

    KING MOB (pseudonym, FRANK K. NOTCH)

    THE GREAT HATRED

    THE WORLD OF SHOLOM ALEICHEM

Harvest in the Desert

CHAPTER ONE

The Haunted Land

❁

THE word "history" would be a little pretentious as
applied to this book. It is more in the nature of an extended lecture, made up of things seen, things taken from
records, things told me by observers, and accompanying
reflections of my own. I imagined someone saying to
me: "I know very little concerning what is called the
new Jewish Homeland in Palestine. You, I understand, have been tied up with the movement, for its
promotion, for a long time. Please tell me, as accurately
as you can, and without too much circumstantiality,
the story of the growth of that Homeland. How did
it begin? What were the forces making for it? Who
are the people involved? How has the present situation
arisen?"

What follows, then, is a fusion of research and report-
age, record and impression. It is all colored by my
positive attitude toward the enterprise, and to that
extent the reader will gather something regarding one
aspect of the forces engaged; nevertheless, the facts and
figures are objectively reliable. The "truth" about the
Jewish Homeland cannot be told by someone indifferent

or hostile to its fate, any more than a significant biography can be written by someone cold to its subject. The intellectual problem is at once subtle and simple; it is not solved by concealing or denying one's affection, since affection is a powerful instrument of research. It is solved by strengthening the affection so as to place it beyond the reach of bribery.

I begin with the land, which I saw for the first time some twenty years ago. In those days Jewish colonization and settlement were — after forty years of uncertain effort — in their preliminary stages. The Jews in the country were one-sixth of their present number, the Arabs less than one-half of theirs, and the total population was less than seven hundred thousand. Since the land is still comparatively empty, the effect at that time was one of extreme desolation.

It was, above all, a haunted land. The populational density in ghosts was out of all proportion to the apparent natural resources. For you asked yourself: "Where did they all live, and on what, when they were in the flesh?" They were extraordinarily important ghosts, too, with a world-wide reputation, and they oppressed the imagination by their stature and intensity not less than by their numbers.

I stood one day on a hilltop in Northern Samaria, and looked down into the Valley of Jezreel and across at the hills of Southern or Lower Galilee. Except for a few tiny points lost in the waste, the plain was uninhabited. Once — two thousand years ago and more — the area had swarmed with life. Cities and villages had filled it to the brim, and its fields had been a famous granary. Now I saw only the beginnings of a few Jewish colonies; I saw a few Arab villages, gray adobe huts like exhalations of the exhausted earth; and I saw here and there the black, square, three-sided tents of the Bedouins — *Oholei Kedar*, "the tents of Kedar," which Solomon mentions in The Song of Songs. Black they certainly were, but far from comely. The verses of the king were displaced in my mind by those of the prophet: "Your land is laid waste; your cities are burned with fire. Your soil, strangers consume it in your presence, and it is desolate as by the overthrow of strangers." Alas, not even strangers were now consuming the soil. The spoilers had disappeared with the spoiled, and only the desolation was left.

I was aware, however, of those great ghost presences. To the right rose Mount Gilboa, on which the first Jewish king had fallen in battle with the Philistines. Him the second king, the shepherd boy and singer, who was to be the forebear of the Messiah, lamented in unforgettable verse: "Mountains of Gilboa, let there be no rain and no dew upon you!" The curse had apparently stuck, for the head of the mountain was as barren as the palm of a man's hand, and at the foot of it the swamps stretched out, the paradise of the anopheles mosquito. To the left was the Carmel range, on which one day Elijah had conducted his bitter contest with the prophets of Baal. Before me wound a narrow ribbon of road, leading north first, and then east. Along this road Jeremiah had followed the exiles toward Babylon, and had gone down on all fours to kiss the bloody footprints of the little children.

It was so that the dead crowded out the living, and it was for the sake of the dead that thousands and tens of thousands of pilgrims came annually from all over

5

the world. It did not matter from what point of the compass the traveller entered the country; always he was accompanied or confronted by memories which interposed a heavy veil between him and the immediate. If from the south, he would say to himself: "Across this desert wandered the rabble of slaves which Moses welded into a people." If westward from Trans-Jordan: "Here Moses stood, forbidden to enter the land, and hereabouts he was buried in the unknown grave." Or coming down from the north: "This is the country of Elijah the Gileadite, the rebuker of kings and provider of widows." If he landed at Haifa it was under the shadow of Carmel, and if he landed at Jaffa he remembered: "From this point Jonah fled, reluctant to prophesy in Nineveh; hither he was brought back, to learn that a prophet's business is to prophesy, even if God plans to make a fool of him."

Within the country itself he could not move without constantly jostling the world's foremost immortals. In Nazareth and on the shores of Galilee he walked in the footsteps of the supreme teacher of the western world. In Hebron he saw, under the terebinths, the patriarchs of these ghostly generations, and the natural mausoleum which holds their bones. And lesser names crowded on him, of men, places and peoples which are fixed forever in the human mind as intense prototypes of experience, to be referred to as long as men are good and bad, weak and strong, wise and foolish — that is to say, as long as they are men. The heavy, metallic waters of the Dead Sea recall the cities they cover, eternal types of unredeemable corruption. In the eastern plain, across the hills, the Philistines labored to acquire their place in history as the representatives of the dull, the aggressive and the unspiritual; and there Samson dramatized forever the complex of the strong body and the weak will.

And what shall be said of the heart and center of the land, Jerusalem? Its summits, valleys and slopes could hardly accommodate the accumulation of sanctities and memories. The suggestion of first and last things, of the utmost range of human effort and hope, emanated from the scene. A thousand recollections struggled for the possession of the pilgrim's attention, and left him helpless. There is no comparable spot anywhere else on the face of the earth; nor is it likely that one like it will be created again.

Now I have not dropped into this vein of piety and sentiment simply because it is the proper thing to do in recalling a first visit to Palestine, and not even because I want to record my own emotions. I have done it because it is relevant to the story I have to tell. Palestine cannot be understood without its memories. They are as real and formative a part of it as its climate. The struggle of the Jews to rebuild the country is meaningless if those memories are eliminated; so is the world's interest in the struggle. Therefore they must be conjured up, in the appropriate mood, as a prelude. And they must be borne constantly in mind, even when we come down to the workaday, the secular, the trivial and the comical. There is much in the story which is quite incongruous with the exalted note I have tried to sound. We shall come down to politics, unemployment, strikes, agrarian credits, investments and chambers of commerce. We shall meet with low egotisms as well as high idealism. The story is human; it moves for the most part on an everyday plane; but it is unintelligible without the background of memories. For the people concerned is the one which stems from those former inhabitants of Palestine who are part of the world's consciousness wherever the Bible is read; and if the world at large always thinks of Palestine predominantly in connection with its ghosts, what shall be the relationship to it of the descendants of the ghosts?

It is one which cannot be described; it can only be shared, and one who does not share it cannot give a true account of the Return. A constituent element in the relationship was, for me, a great wonder and curiosity, which took the form of an apparently unanswerable question: What properties are there in this land, what features in its configuration, to account for its stupefying output of spirit presences? I made a special effort to shut out the past, and I considered only the men and women I encountered — those that were native to the country. I found no clue there. I saw ragged shepherds of lean flocks on stony hillsides; tumbledown cities given over to dirt and poverty; the picturesqueness of decay; a people sunk in listlessness and ignorance, unaware of the universal meaning of the land it inhabited. I accepted the hospitality of the tribe of the Halsa, near the Syrian border; primitive, courteous, illiterate, they might have been Afghanistans in deep Asia, or Soudanese of Omdurman, for all their awareness of great surroundings. By the melancholy wastes of the Huleh marshes, where the Jordan passes through a million reeds to the Sea of Galilee, I stayed awhile in an Arab village. A child playing in the shadow of a hut seemed to have two holes for eyes; but when I stepped closer the two holes burst into two clouds of flies, and the sick eyes were revealed. In the open square women sat weaving the swamp reeds into mats. I was taken into one of the huts: a single room, a hole in the roof to let out the smoke, an earthen floor with two levels, the upper for the family, the lower for the animals. What did these people know of the Palestine the world remembered? Nothing.

I went among the Jews of the old city settlements. *They* knew. They had a special relationship to the land. But their lives were untouched by it. They studied the sacred books, they prayed for the Messiah, not without conviction. Yet one looked among them in vain for a trace of the creative energies which the land had once possessed. Neither they, nor the shepherds, nor the tillers of the soil, nor the keepers of the bazaars, nor the smiths and potters in the booths, were in any way connected with the primordial strength of the country. A deadly inertia lay on the living; this might just as well have been a nameless territory without a record.

But when, still shutting out the past, I dwelt on the sheer physical characteristics of the land, as I saw them there and then, a hint of the unusual stole into my mind. Without a knowledge of history, I could have told that the desolation I surveyed was not native to the place. The crumbled terraces on the hillsides bore witness to a time when men had found their cultivation profitable. In certain areas the rich black soil stopped abruptly, not at a natural boundary of recalcitrant rock, but to disappear under a blanket of sands which wind and drift had spread over its fertility. There were gloomy marshes, habitations of disease, avoided even by birds in their flight, bearing similar witness to human neglect rather than the harshness of nature. Lonely trees in the valleys and on hilltops testified that forests had once stood there. All this spoke of the vanished habitability of the land.

There was something else — a hint concerning the sources of that strange capacity of the country, now gone with its habitability, to raise life to a fierce intensity.

An extraordinary degree of fantasy entered into the modelling of this territory. It is a land of contrasts and tensions. The southern base is soldered into the hot, forbidding wilderness of Sinai; the wedgelike northern extremity runs into the rich crescent which arches over toward Mesopotamia. A double range of hills, irregularly moulded, crossed by valleys, pitted by glens — as though a thumb had been pressed here and there into the heights before they had hardened and set — marks the length of the land. To the east it is cleft by a singular river bed, which burrows closer to the core of our planet than any other part of it still uncovered by the sea. This is the Jordan, the little river which, starting from the slopes of Hermon, descends so precipitously that they named it *Yardein,* the "Descender." The heights towering above its source are covered with eternal snow; less than two hundred miles away, the shores of the Dead Sea, where the river ends, have never been touched by snowfall. Right of the Jordan and the Dead Sea, the land rises again, and offers rich pasture to shepherds; but left of the Dead Sea, the hills are incredibly desolate, mile beyond mile of bulging shale rock, heartbreaking to look at. This is the Wilderness of Judaea. No other land of comparable size experiences such a variety of climates and scenic effects. No other land offers such a multitude of exposed plateaus and isolated retreats, of loving intimacy and devastating loneliness, within so small a compass. It is a land, then, which spurs to action and lulls to meditation, fit for extremes of wilfulness and inwardness.

The sunlight is strong, and for the greater part of the year continuous. The nights are so clear that it seems as if even the air had vanished with the day. The multitudes of the stars are then as it were within reach, and the infinity of space takes hold of the human spirit. It is impossible to sojourn in this land and escape the spell of its purely physical character. A chance visitor, wholly ignorant of its history — if such could be found — but sensitive to form and space, must exclaim: "Something has happened here, or will yet happen. It is a land with a destiny."

But that something had happened, of course, and was known to all the world. This was in a sense the curse of Palestine. Those that thought of it from afar, or made the pilgrimage to see it for themselves, were incapable of contemplating it under any other aspect than that of its past. The land was burdened with a reputation which blotted out its present and denied it the possibility of a future. Its inhabitants were regarded as irrelevant apparitions among the true tenants, the ghosts. Enough for the former if they managed to exist as the attendants of the ghosts. If they served any purpose it was to accentuate by their presence the dedication of this land to the dead.

╔══════════════════════════════════════╗

CHAPTER TWO

The Descendants of the Ghosts

❀

╚══════════════════════════════════════╝

Aʟʟ travellers returning from Palestine said the same thing: the country as such, in physiognomy and atmosphere, proclaimed itself as set apart for the unusual, as if one should stumble, in a waste, across a ready-made theater, equipped with every variety of scenery, and even with lighting effects. The landscape was one which exercised a peculiar compulsion on the spirit; it was not made for commonplace occupants.

But if this was so, there was a riddle to be solved. How was it that only one people, the Jews, had responded to the compulsion? How was it that only one Bible had been written there, and that its figures, which still haunted the hills and plains, were exclusively Jewish? There were nations in Palestine before the Jews — the Amorites, the Canaanites, the Jebusites, the Girgashites and the rest of them. There were occupying nations after the expulsion of the Jews — the Greek, the Roman, the Saracen, the Arab, the Turk. Why had they not established the compulsive affinity with the country?

Well, as to the first, we might say they never got their chance. They came too early in the history of the race.

Or — this is barely possible, if somehow quite implausible — they *did* have their Isaiahs and their Elijahs, whom no one now remembers. That is hard to believe; Isaiahs and Elijahs have a knack of impressing themselves on the generations. But what shall be said of the latter inhabitants, who followed the Jews? *Their* records are copious and explicit. They lie open to our scrutiny. They are not lacking in evidence of great gifts. But they are completely devoid of the particular relationship which Palestine calls for or leads us to expect. Only the Jews clicked with Palestine.

And if we examine the matter more closely, we begin to understand why. Palestine may be a land of destiny, but only to those who submit to it completely. The latter occupants entered the country under the wrong auspices and without the proper predisposition. To all of them Palestine was peripheral; the center of their consciousness remained in Athens, or Rome, or Mecca, or Constantinople. Palestine was an annex, an outpost, a province, not the heart of their world. And this made all the difference.

To the Jews Palestine was, from the beginning, everything. The surrender was complete, premeditated and preordained. It became an incurable fixation. It does not matter if we challenge the historicity of the Bible in regard to the accounts of the first Jewish ascent to the country. What matters is that every surviving record tells of the belief in those accounts. We cannot find anywhere else, in legend or mythology, a people which regarded itself as having been created in order to live a certain life in a certain country by divine command. Driven from it once into the Babylonian exile, the Jews achieved the impossible: they returned, and reconstituted themselves a people, in the tradition. That settled it, so to speak. Once is an accident; twice is a habit.

They never got over it. That is the all-important point of Jewish history. I do not mean to say that there were not Jews who did not liberate themselves from the connection. Within the last century or century and a half considerable numbers of them have, in effect, declared: "Enough is enough! After eighteen hundred years we are entitled to forget, and to come to terms with reality. There will be no Return." They even made a virtue of it, saying: "It was never intended that we should return," and adding: "God wants us to be scattered throughout the world, to set an example." But they were a minority. The others remembered.

Their whole life was a remembering, a vivid and tenacious remembering. On the day which commemorates the destruction of the Temple, they fasted and mourned, after the lapse of a thousand, two thousand years, as though they had been the witnesses and victims of the catastrophe, as though they had themselves escaped from the blazing ruins, leaving behind them their nearest and dearest. I have sat on the floor in stockinged feet among fellow-mourners, listened to the sobbing recital of the Lamentations of Jeremiah and, by the light of the commemorative candles, seen the tears run down the cheeks of grown men. This was no mechanical ritual. It came from the heart of a frustrated people. It was real, poignant and terrifying, a Fourth of July in reverse.

The eternal presentness of Palestine in their minds cannot be conveyed without a description of the texture of their life. Three times a day, and oftener on special occasions, they prayed for the Restoration. Even when they prayed for timely rains and abundant harvests, it was in Palestinian terms. Morning and evening, at the daily services, they exhorted themselves to be good, for then God would send the *yoreh* and *malkosh,* the "former" and the "latter" rains, in due season. They might be living in a northern country, where there are no former or latter rains; they might be living in a tropical belt where the rains are a curse. No matter. As far as they were concerned, Palestine set the standard. Perhaps they felt that what was good for Palestine must be good for the rest of the world.

Long after they had been driven from the soil, and had become an urban people, they continued to celebrate the harvest. They did not sow, in tears or otherwise; but they pretended to reap in joy; and the symbols of the celebration had nothing to do with the locality. When the harvesting comes in Palestine, the sun is at its hottest. In ancient days the reaper used to put up a booth in the middle of the field, and there he took shelter between spells of work. Jews living in the Arctic Circle continued to put up the booth, or *Sukkah,* at the time of the Palestinian harvest, to protect themselves from the rays of the Aurora Borealis.

They refused, likewise, to relinquish the language of ancient Palestine. Moving from land to land, they acquired and used in ordinary converse, a variety of languages, Arabic, Spanish, Yiddish. Hebrew remained the language of prayer and study, of hope and scholarship. Even when it had become largely unintelligible to the unlettered, the sound and flavor of it were retained by repetition; and when they wrote Spanish or Yiddish, at least they used the Hebrew letters.

15

The scholar was always their highest ideal of a man; but his scholarship had to mean a mastery of the ethical and religious principles which had been formulated in Palestine, and of the legal code which had governed Jewish life there. To live mentally in Palestine was the purpose of such scholarship.

It was all a retention of the machinery of Palestinian life. Some day they would return. They would be ready to slip into the Palestinian landscape. They would have no difficulty — they thought — in adapting themselves. They would have the proper intellectual and folkloristic equipment. Thus the act of "remembering Zion" was not a single and special gesture. It was a total art. It was the constant rehearsal of the mode of Palestinian life.

They said that merely to live in Palestine was equivalent to the fulfilment of all law. To be buried in Palestine was a wise precaution. For the resurrection could take place only in Palestine, and they shuddered at the thought of their bones having to roll underground to the last assembly. It was best to be on the spot. Failing this provision, they asked that a handful of Palestinian earth be placed under their heads when they were buried in the exile.

The world changed, and Jewish life changed, too, in many ways. The peoples with whom the Jews had dealt of old passed away. The course of empire took its westward way, dominion shifted from continent to continent. The Jews settled in Babylon, in Spain, in Russia, in America. They created centers and traditions of the exile. They established dynasties of scholars and rabbis. They had their rich and poor, their aristocrats, their snobberies, their saints, their internecine quarrels. They were split into warring sects. They were driven from land to land, lived a few hundred years here, a few hundred years there. The affinity with Palestine remained undiminished. So much so, that the rest of the world was compelled to acknowledge it. Mobs attacking the Jews incited themselves with the cry: "*Hep! Hep!*" The syllable, some say, is made up of the first three letters of the words: *Hieroselyma est perdita!* Jerusalem is lost! My father heard that cry in Roumania, in his boyhood, seventy years ago. Why should Roumanian peasants taunt the Jews with the destruction of Jerusalem, if Jerusalem was nothing to the Jews? But the truth is that the rioters really doubted what they said. Jerusalem was not lost; only its people had been mislaid.

It was not an easy thing to maintain and transmit the technique of this discipline of remembrance. It did not have the support of the legal machinery of the state. It did not have the sympathy of the surrounding population. On the contrary, there was every worldly temptation to defection. In fact, there were defections and failures; but they only emphasized the wonder of the persistence. For if the Jews had been incapable, through a sort of fossilization, to do otherwise than they did, if they had been as it were deprived of choice, the phenomenon would have been without moral meaning, something like the turtle's carapace. But they were free; free, that is, in the ordinary sense that a man may choose to be true or untrue to his character. And having chosen, he must renew the choice, beginning anew each day. This they did, days and years and centuries.

17

CHAPTER THREE

Waiting for the Messiah

❀

Thus the Jews maintained themselves in a state of instant preparedness for the Return; at least, as far as was humanly possible. Twice a year — on the first two evenings of Passover — they had a special ritual, a sort of *alerte*. They sat down to the ceremonial meal, all ready, in theory, to get up, put their bundles on their backs, and answer the trumpet call. For eight days they ate no bread, but, in its place, a flat, unleavened biscuit called the *matzah*. This was to remind them in what haste their forefathers had scrambled out of Egypt and set forth for Palestine, without time to bake bread for the journey. They might be called on to do likewise, so the reminder was also a rehearsal. But in the course of centuries the rehearsal became an end in itself, so elaborate that it defeated its own purpose. In the end it took much longer to bake the *matzot* according to prescription than to bake bread, and they could have made two journeys to Palestine in the time they spent on preparing for the Passover.

Thereby hangs a tale. The Jews were waiting for the Messiah to appear and lead them back to their Homeland. This was part of their religion. And like all people who learn to depend on charity, even if it is divine charity, they ran the danger of pauperization. The Messiah might, indeed, appear any moment; this too was part of the religion. But until he came they would make no attempt at a mass Return. They kept in fairly good order the machinery for living in Palestine, but they set up no machinery for getting there. They developed no technique for the transition, and we shall see that this was to cost them dear.

There were always individuals, and even groups of Jews, who became impatient and left the exile for Palestine. This was not considered rebellious. It was meritorious for the people as a whole to wait for the Messiah; but it was equally meritorious, or more so, for individuals to anticipate him. Thus the national contact with Palestine never became wholly imaginary. There was a constant coming and going between the diaspora and the Holy Land. The mass redemption, however, had to be initiated by God's special messenger; and it would herald the general judgment day.

We are confronted with a very interesting question which bears on the modern rebuilding of Palestine. Did the Jews really want to take up again their national existence in Palestine, or was their Palestino-centric ritual just mummery, or (quoting Toynbee) a species of fossilization? Back of this question lies another. Was there ever a time in history when they could have undertaken the mass Return with some chance of success? Was there ever a favorable constellation of worldly circumstances? There are some who say yes, and point to specific dates; but I believe that a closer examination of these instances, and of the picture as a whole, yields a negative answer.

There was, for instance, the incident of the Roman Emperor, Julian, known as the Apostate, in the middle of the fourth century. This queer and fascinating ruler nurtured, among other ambitions, that of playing Cyrus to the Jews. In a famous proclamation he offered them the privilege of restoring Jerusalem and rebuilding the Temple, "even as you have for so many years desired it to be restored." Julian's motives were dubious, without a touch of benevolence for the Jews, regard for justice, or even vague reverence. He hated Christianity and dreamed of restoring the old gods to their former hegemony. Among them he numbered the God of the Jews. It would be a neat trick, he thought, to play on the Christians, this restoration of Jewish rule in Palestine. But whatever his motives, he died shortly after issuing his proclamation to the Jews, and that ended the incident.

There is no evidence that the Jews took the offer seriously and accepted the paganizing emperor as a substitute for the Messiah. Of course the Christian writers of that time were anxious to prove otherwise. Julian had tried to spite them by getting the Jewish Temple rebuilt; they tried to spite him, or rather his memory, by asserting that a great effort had been made to carry out his plan, and that God had intervened to bring it to nought. The historian Gibbon, who detested Christianity only less than he detested Judaism, which he held responsible for Christianity, plays the story up. He transcribes, in his incomparable style, the account of an ancient historian whom no one takes seriously — not even Gibbon himself — and relates: "At the call

of the great deliverer, the Jews, from all the provinces
of the Empire, assembled on the holy mountain of their
fathers; and their insolent triumph alarmed and exas-
perated the Christian inhabitants of Jerusalem. The
desire of rebuilding the Temple has, in every age, been
the ruling passion of the children of Israel. In this
propitious moment the men forgot their avarice, and
the women their delicacy; spades and pickaxes of silver
were provided by the vanity of the rich, and the rubbish
was transported in mantles of silk and purple . . . The
commands of a great monarch were executed by the
enthusiasm of a whole people."

Such are the dangers of eloquence when the factual
does not coincide with the romantic. The description is
without foundation in truth. The assembling on Mount
Moriah of Jews from all the provinces of the Roman
Empire is pure invention. There is no record, in Jewish
or non-Jewish sources, of such a movement. There
were Jews in Palestine, of course, as there have always
been. The academy which had been founded three
hundred years before by Yohanan ben Zakkai — that
same academy which the short-sighted Vespasian had
authorized, never suspecting that it would organize the
spiritual forces which would outlive his Empire — still
existed. But no such signal was given as had once rallied
the Jews to the banner of Bar Kochba. And among the
Jewries of the diaspora there was no such excitement as
attended the call of the false Messiah, Sabbathai Zevi,
more than a thousand years later. The time was, in
fact, utterly unpropitious for the enterprise, and the
Jews knew it.

When the Roman Empire split up, and the eastern
half broke away from the western, Jerusalem became

21

a center of *Real-Politik* in the internal struggles of the Christian Church. Palestine, which lay within the territory of the Byzantine emperors, was covered with monasteries and churches. The rebuilding of a Jewish Homeland, that is to say, a mass Return, was completely out of the question. It might just as well have been attempted in the time of Hadrian the Destroyer. The Byzantine emperors sought the conversion of the Jews, not their restoration.

The rule of Byzantium over Palestine ended when the Persians, with the help of the Arabs, overran the country, and all but wiped out every vestige of Christianity. Was this the moment for which the Jews had waited? Had not another Persian, a millennium before, given them the right to rebuild?

There were, indeed, some Jews who thought they saw a parallel, but they were a handful, and only of the locality. Persian rule in Palestine lasted just fourteen years, and there was no thought of a Jewish kingdom. Then came a tide of conquest out of the deserts of interior Arabia. Mohammed had appeared, with a mission of conquest and conversion to the new faith. Jerusalem became a secondary sanctuary for Mohammedanism, but not in connection with the Jews and their religion. The Return, as a worldly enterprise, was hopeless.

It was no better when the western world surged back over Palestine in the time of the Crusades. Whatever the real causes of the Crusades — whether they were really religious, and aimed at nothing more than the liberation of the holy places, or whether they represented the break-up of the frozen condition of the Middle Ages — they were interpenetrated with a great hatred of the Jews; their name has become synonymous with mass slaughters of our people. A Latin Kingdom was set up, with Jerusalem as its capital, and maintained itself for a time. The story of its intrigues, ferocities and corruptions is in horrifying contrast with the ostensible religious motif of its foundation. What chance was there, in those days, for the Return?

The era of the Crusades was followed by a wild eruption in Asia, and the appearance of a strange and terrible tribe of Mongolians from the eastern shores of the Caspian Sea. For two hundred years Palestine was blotted out under the rule of the Mamelukes. And after them came the Ottoman Turks, whose empire lasted until our own time. The hand of the Turk lay heavy on the inhabitants of Palestine, Arab and Jew alike. An attempt to rebuild a Jewish Homeland would have foundered in blood.

We look in vain along this vista of conquests and re-conquests, for a fissure, a plausible and propitious interval, through which anyone but a Messiah could have poured the Jewish people in a grand restoration. And so we begin to understand that the Messianic idea served a practical purpose over and above the perpetuation of the hope. It was a protective device to restrain the Jewish people from making the effort as long as effort was futile. It is true that the device operated so long that it acquired an independent existence, like a vestigial organ which outlives in a species the environment for which it emerged, and becomes a hindrance where it was once a help. It was only after a painful internal struggle that the effect of the Messianic attitude, the reluctance to be set in motion when the right time had arrived, was overcome.

But there are wheels within wheels. A rigid Messianism was to some extent counteracted by the encouragement of individual resettlement in Palestine. Throughout the history of the exile the real Palestine, the Palestine of this world, was linked to Jewish communities everywhere in flesh and blood communication. Men who sang the lovesong of Palestine set out for the shores of the country, at least to end their days there. The sweetest singer in Israel since biblical days, Yehudah Halevi, abandoned, in his latter years, home and family, ease and worldly honor, to go up to Jerusalem where, according to the story, he was slain by an Arab. There are records of lesser-known men, Italian Jews, who grew sick of vain-longing and went home. They beheld the desolation of Jerusalem, they saw the jackals and the foxes inhabiting the empty lion's lair, and they lamented for the glory that was gone. Their words came back to the diaspora, to remind the Jews that the soil of Palestine was waiting, here below, and not in heaven.

In the time of the Spanish persecutions, which culminated with the mass expulsion of 1492, thousands of Spanish Jews found their way to Palestine. Indeed, in those days the calamities of Jewry led many to believe that the Messianic moment was at hand. In the city of Safed a strange community of mystics, dreamers, adepts in the Book of the Splendor, called the *Zohar*, grew up, first round the person then round the memory of the Ari. Pilgrims and settlers came from every corner of Europe; and four Holy Communities developed, in Jerusalem, Safed, Tiberias and Hebron.

Still, it was not the Return, and the Messianic spell was not broken. It was not broken even when, in the middle of the seventeenth century, one, Sabbathai Zevi, gave out that he was the Messiah, and Jewish merchants of London and Amsterdam began to sell their possessions in preparation for the exodus. Before the movement became general, Sabbathai Zevi, not being the Messiah, and therefore not being able to obtain the right to the return from the Turkish authorities, converted to Mohammedanism.

Before him there was a Prince of Naxos, Joseph, a Disraeli of the sixteenth century, who served a Moslem ruler, as Disraeli served a Christian. Unlike Disraeli he did not have to be prepared through apostasy for the privilege of advancement; indeed, he went through the opposite process, for, born of the Marranos, or enforced converts, he reverted to Judaism. Joseph Nasi had dreams of the Restoration, and encouraged the rebuilding of the city of Tiberias, by Jews. But the attempt came to nothing, nor did Jewry in exile abandon their Messianism.

But there were communities in Palestine, and from these emissaries went to every corner of the diaspora. They collected funds for the Cabalists and Talmudists. It was necessary to wait for the Messiah before the Return could be attempted, but it was also necessary to maintain a worldly bond with Palestine. The hasidic movement, in the eighteenth century, sent another ripple of emigrants to Palestine. Many of them, like the Cabalists with whom they had a strong affinity, were engaged in studying methods of precipitating the advent of the Messiah. They believed that a special kind of spiritual pressure could be put on the Almighty to compel Him to advance His cosmic schedule. Meanwhile they had to live; they had to be supported while they pursued these arduous researches. We of this generation remember out of our childhood how, in every pious Jewish home, there used to hang the collection box of Reb Meir *Baal ha-Nes*, Reb Meir the Wonder-worker, in which coins were deposited for the sustenance of the holy communities of Palestine. It was a good custom in its time, but we must recall Tennyson's lines:

> God fulfils Himself in many ways,
> Lest one good custom should corrupt the world.

The time was to come when this curious system of a subsidized Jewish representation in Palestine would, like the Messianic idea, need reinterpretation. And in both cases the reinterpretation was resisted. That is part of the history of the rebuilding in our day.

CHAPTER FOUR

In the Fulness of Time

◉

ONE more matter remains to be discussed before we get down to the body of our narrative, which is devoted to Palestine and the modern return of the Jews. I have said that the Messianic attitude toward Palestine, though quite genuine, seems in retrospect to have been a historic device to forestall any premature attempt at the rebuilding of the Jewish Homeland. That no doubt sounds like a bit of mysticism. If, for the sake of argument, we reject it, we shall have to consider a singular coincidence — the breakdown of the Messianic attitude when the practical chance presented itself.

The breakdown was by no means complete; nor was its effect uniform. Where it occurred, it did not always lead to secular activation of the old religious *motif*. Very often it meant the complete abandonment of the idea of the Return, and this on various grounds. And where the breakdown did not occur, where the Messianic attitude persisted — it still does in some circles — there was strenuous objection to the new movement (which came to be known as Zionism) for religious reasons. So divisions arose in Jewry; and since they are still operative, and have their influence on what is happening in Palestine, we must take account of them.

The most striking feature of the "coincidence" was, paradoxically, the discord in the element of time. The necessary changes began to take place in the attitude of the Jewish people *before* the political outlook for a Jewish Homeland in Palestine became favorable. This was extremely fortunate for the enterprise. The greatest internal obstacle to the fulfilment of the Zionist program proved to be not the opposition of certain groups of Jews — though this too was an important adverse factor — but the difficulty of overcoming the exile habit. The longing for Palestine was real; the belief in the ultimate restoration deep-rooted; but eighteen hundred years of intermittent homelessness had created a psychological machinery for a life in exile, and the dismantling of this machinery was a complicated business.

We may allow ourselves a parallel. When Moses led the Israelites out of Egypt they were unfit for self-government. Forty years of training, and the emergence of a new generation, were needed before the land could be occupied. But the Israelites had been in Egypt only four hundred years — and according to some accounts much less. This time they had been in various exiles for eighteen hundred years. The proportionate period of preparation, of awakening to self-reliance and self-emancipation, might be expected to stretch over a century.

When the preparation began, however, there was no sign of an opening into Palestine. The successive occupying nations, Roman, Greek, Saracen, Arab, Turk, had done their best, and their worst, with the country. Or, rather, it had become evident that they could not do a thing with it. Palestine lay there, all but emptied of the living, abused, exhausted, impoverished. It was one of the provinces of the Turkish Empire, and, like all empires in decline, the Turkish dreaded the development of the provinces. A strong province breaks away from a feeble capital. This had happened in the case of Egypt, which under Mehemet Ali became practically independent. So Constantinople was not simply indifferent to Palestine; its attitude was almost malevolent. The taxes it laid on the country were designed to repress its growth; the officials sent to administer it were corrupt and inefficient, or efficient only in wringing from the wretched population the maximum income consistent with a policy of repression. The taxes were farmed; that is to say, a speculator paid the imperial treasury a stated sum for the right to squeeze a maximum of return from a given *jiftlik*, or district. The largest income was derived from pilgrims. It was inconceivable, under these circumstances, that Constantinople should ever consent to the development of Palestine as a vigorous Jewish Homeland.

Yet among the Jews the preparation for the undertaking of such an enterprise had in fact begun. The details of the preparation are complicated and confused. To get a glimpse of them we must examine briefly the picture of Jewish life in the last century or century and a half.

The cat-and-mouse game of the Emancipation had entered on its first stage. A great promise had come to the Jews with the French Revolution, which sounded the death-knell of feudalism in Europe. The Age of Reason had dawned. Superstition, intolerance, discrimination, persecution, were on the way out. The divisions between Jew and Gentile were fading away. Religious disabilities in the field of government and of civic rights belonged to the vanishing past.

What a pity that certain great figures, initiators of the new era, had happened to harbor such an intense dislike of Jews. Gibbon was one, Voltaire another, Katherine the Great of Russia, an "enlightened" monarch, a third. What a pity that the man who gave the Age of Reason its name, Thomas Paine, should have had such a low opinion of Jews, and cited them as an example of the degeneration which is the result of inbreeding. Well, it did not matter; these were survivals of the old even in the heart of the new.

So it was believed by increasing numbers of Jews, who rushed forth joyously from the ghettos to enter into the heritage of modernity. They dropped, *en masse*, the paraphernalia of the Palestinian hope, so carefully conserved, and kept in working order, for eighteen centuries. They dropped the Messianic prayers in so far as they alluded to the old Homeland, and they dropped the language in which those prayers had so long been rehearsed. Paris, Vienna, Berlin, London were to become their Jerusalems. The theme interwoven with the Jewish religion, that of the recreation of a Jewish Palestine, was pulled out from the tapestry, thread by thread; if what was left was a trifle colorless, it could at least be described as "universal."

There were thousands who went much further, of course. Conversions to Christianity became frequent, and with them intermarriage, the only effective plan for the dissolution of the Jewish people. Others did not bother to formulate a new creed; they drifted with the tide. The memory of their origin grew weaker from generation to generation, as they diffused "out into the world."

Only the core of the people, the majority, held back, in part distrustful, but much more out of affirmative loyalty. They were suspicious of the offer of freedom, the more so as it was accompanied by an implicit demand — not always merely implicit, either — for a *quid pro quo*. That was nothing less than the abandonment of their particular way of life. The offer was, after all, not wholly disingenuous; at any rate, it seemed to be conditional. It sounded like: "Freedom of religion, if you consent to drop your religion."

The distrust which looked so churlish over a century ago has taken on by now the aspect of prophecy. But not even the most standoffish of the pietists, in his blackest moments, would have dared to forecast the extent of the swindle. Eighteen centuries of extrusion and persecution do not vanish from the memory of a people as a whole because of a proclamation. Still, they were inclined to believe that the abominations of the Crusades, of a Torquemada, or of a Chmelnitzky, would never be visited on them again. Prophetic to this degree they were not. They did not foresee a Petlura, much less a Hitler.

Yet, in the middle of the nineteenth century, there were signs aplenty that the promise of the Emancipation had been a check drawn on insufficient funds. Naturally those who had staked everything on the promise refused to read the signs. Always it was: "Wait a while. These things will pass." They did not pass. On the contrary, they multiplied. It was the nineteenth century which set the stage for the denouement of the twentieth. The

new anti-Semitic theories which are the spiritual sustenance of Nazism were carefully worked out two and
three generations ago.

Within the Jewish people, however, changes were
taking place which were to affect profoundly the relationship to the Return. I have called the Emancipation
a cat-and-mouse game. So it was. But there were great
affirmations in the nineteenth century, too, and these
had their repercussions in the unassimilating mass of
Jewry. An impulse of democracy was communicated
to the interior. Ever since their dispersion, the Jews had
entrusted the problems of their relations with Gentiles to
Shtadlonim, to individuals of wealth, importance, learning or influence. Entrusted is perhaps not the right word.
Shtadlonim of this type were not elected by anybody, nor
were they accountable to a public body. They simply
took it upon themselves, by virtue of their connections,
to represent the Jews to the Gentiles. They were self-
appointed Ministers of Foreign Affairs. They meant
well. At least, they meant as well as they could, for
human beings can mean well only within the limits of
their outlook. Their record is as good as that of any
similar body of autocrats among any other people. They
negotiated for the mitigation of severe decrees against
the Jews, and for the privilege of immigration. They
defended the reputation of the Jews against accusations
of anti-social practices. They were apologists, memori-
alists, spokesmen and representative figures, and they
have an honorable place in Jewish history. But the
middle of the nineteenth century saw the beginning of
their decline.

For it was about then that there became manifest in

the Jewish masses a stirring from below, and a dissatis-
faction with this system of representation. The limita-
tions of the *Shtadlonim*, inherent in their class position,
slowly grew more obvious. Their relation with the
Gentile world and its rulers placed them in a position
which was equivocal. There was a great struggle in the
nineteenth century between emergent democracy and
unyielding autocracy, and the Jewish question became
one of the battlegrounds. Or it might be called one of
the pawns in the game. Democracy promised the Jews
real emancipation; autocracy warned the Jews against
an alliance with democracy. Autocracy, while thus
warning the Jews, maintained an anti-Semitic attitude.
It did this because emancipation of the Jews was of
course a democratic measure. But it had an additional
reason. The propagation of anti-Semitic sentiment was
a potent antidote to the spread of democracy. Where
social discontent was ignorant of its own origins, it could
be deflected against the Jews, the more easily since
anti-Jewishness was part of the folklore of the western
world.

Thus, paradoxically, the rise of democracy has proved
to be, at least transitionally, calamitous for the Jews.
Yet they were, and are, aware that there is no hope for
them except in the triumph of democracy. To a considerable extent, but by no means wholly, the view was
shared by the upper Jewish classes, from which the
Shtadlonim were drawn. Their position, however, was
much more ticklish than that of the masses. They had
their vested interests in the social system generally, and
a particular kind of relationship with the ruling classes
among the Gentiles. They likewise had their position
of power among the Jews to maintain. In this complex

of forces, they lost the representative quality they had once possessed. It became increasingly clear that they were impotent to obtain, from Gentile rulers, any genuine mitigation of anti-Semitic policies. Yet, in exercising their function, they had to influence the Jewish masses against making common cause with the forces of democracy. This, *vis-à-vis* the Gentile rulers, was their chief *raison d'être*.

The inner revolt of the Jewish masses took two forms. One was a loosening of the Messianic complex with regard to Palestine; the other was an alliance with general democracy. Both were expressions of a will to action; both were obnoxious to the *Shtadlonim*. The awakening of Jewish nationalism came from below. It was anonymous and instinctive. It did not ask the permission of the heads of the communities. It was in effect a declaration that the masses did not trust the *Shtadlonim* to defend them; and since they had no faith in the Emancipation, they began to throw off the paralysis of Messianism and to consider the Return for the here and now. It need hardly be said, then, that the upper Jewish classes were from the beginning opposed to Zionism even in its earliest and most nebulous forms.

The other half of the revolt, the Jewish alliance with general democracy, meant, not the loosening of the Messianic complex with regard to Palestine, but — for the most part — a rejection of the whole idea of the Return. In this manner an odd relationship was established between the anti-Zionist Jewish democratic movement and the Jewish upper classes. They were on the whole opposed to each other on the question of democracy as such. The anti-Zionist masses wanted a change in the social system; the classes wanted the elimination of anti-Semitism. In this regard they had a partial unity of purpose. But they were wholly at one in their opposition to Zionism; the masses because they wanted all the energies of the Jews to be concentrated on the social revolution; the classes because they had accepted new Jerusalems. If we see today, here in America, some very strange instances of Jewish rightists and Jewish leftists acting in concert against Zionism, we shall be less astonished if we are acquainted with the history of Jewish life in the last hundred years.

It came about, then, that when the opportunity presented itself for the building of the Jewish Homeland, the masses which had remained faithful to the ideal were in part freed from two negative influences: the Messianic attitude and the dependence on *Shtadlonim*. This was not all. The nationalist and Zionist masses had been affected to some extent by the social theories of democracy. They were beginning to think of the Return in connection with these theories. The religious and the modern democratic were at work side by side in the new nationalism. It is true that the Messianic concept of the Return had always been linked to a vision of social justice; but there is a difference between a vision and the development of instruments for the realization of the vision. "Zion shall be redeemed in righteousness," Isaiah had said. The new Zionists repeated the verse in their own way: "Not just a Jewish Homeland, but a Homeland which by its character shall justify the long waiting. We will not let two thousand years of anticipation culminate in the anticlimax of a Jewish State which incorporates all the failures of modern society."

35

In this account of the preparation for the Return I have telescoped a long process which is in fact not yet completed. I have anticipated developments which did not set in until late in the story. It will be seen that both the will to Palestine and the clarification of a social purpose were slow to ripen, that they received setbacks, that many calls went unheeded, that contrary influences had their way at times. There were times when the prospect seemed hopeless, in Palestine as in the diaspora. In the latter there was, it seemed, no response; in the former the social ideal seemed to be fading out. We shall have to bear in mind the parallel quoted earlier in this chapter, the preparation of the Israelites who went out of Egypt for the purpose of creating a civilization in Palestine.

CHAPTER FIVE

First Gropings

❀

IN SPITE of its explosions, history is continuous, and it is as hard to fix the first symptoms of a revolution as it is to trace a folk-saying to its source. We would like to know: Exactly when did world politics begin to push Palestine as a Jewish Homeland into the pattern of contemporaneous realities? Exactly when did the idea of the creation in Palestine of a Jewish commonwealth by natural rather than supernatural instruments make its appearance among non-Jews? And about when did the change from the religious Messianic attitude in regard to this fulfilment begin to show itself among the Jews?

We shall never get a satisfying answer to these questions. But we do know that about a hundred years ago the change had become recognizable. For a long time the Restoration of Israel had been a leading motif in English religious sentiment and prophecy. The rebellion against papal sovereignty of the Church had been attended by a popular concentration of interest on the Bible, particularly, strange as it may seem, on the Old Testament. A group of English scholars had produced what is undoubtedly the greatest translation in the history of literature — the King James Version of the Bible. So magnificently was this work done, so superb was the style, that a popular feeling arose that the Bible had originally been written in English. (One thinks of the Germans who, having produced a perfect translation of Shakespeare, were wont to speak of *Unser Shakespeare*.) The peculiar predilection of the English for the Old Testament had two sources. One was the revolt against Rome, which prompted them to identify themselves with the Israelites being liberated from Egypt — a theme repeated in our own day in Negro spirituals. The other was the revolt against the House of Stuart. The identification was so emphatic that it gave birth in time, among the oversensitive, to positive hallucinations which made the English the Lost Ten Tribes. In any case, the divine promise of an Israel restored became part of English thinking. For a long time the concept was as eschatological, or Messianic, as among the Jews. But round the middle of the nineteenth century the change we are speaking of was already in evidence.

The political position of Palestine had something to do with it. A hundred years ago, Palestine, at the nadir of its worldly fortunes, had again become, after a lapse of many centuries, an object of international concern and rivalry. The Turkish Empire was dying on its feet, supported in that posture by the European powers who were afraid of the scramble that would take place for the carcass. In the midst of these ghoulish anticipations, Englishmen were giving utterance to the thought that, as far as Palestine was concerned, the best disposition that could be made of it was its restoration to the Jews.

Lords Palmerston and Shaftesbury were among the

leading proponents of the thesis. The language they used was still heavily weighted with biblical terminology, but it already had about it a ring of the twentieth century. In Lord Shaftesbury's records the following passage appears: "I am anxious about the hopes and destinies of the Jewish people. Everything seems ripe for their return to Palestine." And again: "Dined with Palmerston. Propounded my scheme, which seemed to strike his fancy . . . How singular is the order of Providence! Palmerston had already been chosen by God to be an instrument of good to His ancient people, to do homage, as it were, to their inheritance . . . But though the motive be kind, it is not enough. I am forced to argue politically, financially, commercially."

In the London *Times* of August 17, 1840, an article on the same subject appeared, beginning thus:

"The proposition to plant the Jewish people in the land of their fathers, under the protection of the Five Powers, is no longer a mere matter of speculation, but of serious political consideration."

So it was already a proposition! And of serious political consideration! Since when? And how had it become so? We cannot tell. But other articles of a similar character appeared in the London *Times* and other publications, and echoes of the discussion came back from abroad. In 1841, the year after the shocking blood-libel case in Damascus, the Jews of Palestine were placed, semi-officially, under the protection of the British consul in Jerusalem. Undoubtedly this move was in part related to the creation of a sphere of influence, then one of the international games in the Near East. In part it was due to the role which Sir Moses Montefiore had played in the blood-libel case, and his

39

interest in Palestine. Of him we shall have to speak at some length. Meanwhile we can see a far-off anticipation of the First World War, when Zionism came to be regarded as an important item in the reordering of the world. But we must note that no pressure had come from the Jewish people, which was still sunk in its Messianic dreams as far as the Return was concerned. Also, it was still without movements. There was no Zionist Organization, no B'nai B'rith, no Jewish Congress, to give expression to the popular will; to organize protests against incidents like the Damascus affair; or to advise the world in general of the feelings of the Jewish masses. External affairs were still in the hands of *Shtadlonim*.

The greatest of these, perhaps the greatest and best in Jewish history, was Sir Moses Montefiore. The mention of his name tempts us to a long digression. We shall resist; but he cannot be by-passed in this account. To begin with, he was a fascinating figure; not at all by virtue of extraordinary and dazzling qualities, like Disraeli, for example, but by virtue of a life which was very long, very active and unbelievably edifying. He was like a copy-book of moral maxims translated into reality. He has to be considered a bit at a time, lest the uniformity of his virtues and his oppressive respectability provoke us to unworthy protest. He belongs to this story because he illustrates excellently how the best intentions of the *Shtadlonim* — and their intentions were frequently of the best — were unavailing as long as the Jewish masses were not prepared for self-emancipation.

Moses Montefiore became one of the legendary figures

among the Jews of all countries. His picture hung in poor Jewish homes in Russia, in Roumania, in Galicia, in forlorn villages of the Carpathians. He was credited, during his lifetime, with a degree of power and influence which no Jew of any age has ever possessed. And no wonder. In the course of his long life he had interviewed, on behalf of the Jews, two Russian Czars, two Turkish Sultans, a King of France, a King of Prussia, a Shah of Persia, a Khedive of Egypt, an Emperor of Morocco, a prospective Emperor of France — not to mention the Queen of his own country and a host of princes, prelates, diplomats, statesmen and aristocrats at large. He had a genuine and unquenchable love for Palestine. He made seven pilgrimages to the country, the first in 1827, when he was forty-three, the last in 1875, when he was ninety-one. One reads almost with stupefaction a passage in his diaries, entered as the boat was taking him from Alexandria to Jaffa on the last trip. This nonagenarian, already twenty years beyond the normal allotment of three-score and ten (but with another decade before him!) wrote, like a vigorous and sentimental youngster: "As we were steaming out of the harbor, my spirits became buoyant in the extreme."

He was a hundred years old when the Kattowitz Conference for Palestine — to be described later — was held in 1884, and sent him its respectful congratulations. He was ninety-seven when the first modern colonies were founded, and he sent his contribution to Rishon le-Zion and Zichron Ya'akov. He died at the age of a hundred and one. The extra year was probably a gesture of defiance, the only touch of the flamboyant we can discover in his life.

In spite of his love of Palestine, his desire for its welfare and that of the Jewish people, his considerable influence, his prestige and his sixty years of — admittedly — intermittent activity for the country, he left behind him, as far as its annals of achievement are concerned, nothing besides his name. Attempts have been made to represent him as the first modern Zionist, the first to come out openly for the Return. The case has some evidence in its favor, but it cannot be sustained. It is certain that he wanted the poverty-stricken Jews of Palestine to combine, with their studies and pieties, the pursuit of handicrafts and agriculture. He negotiated with Mehemet Ali, the able, ferocious and picturesque Khedive of Egypt, for the purchase of lands in Palestine, and projected a colonizing company with a capital of $5,000,000. On his second visit to Palestine, in 1838, he wrote:

"I am sure that if the plan I have in contemplation should succeed, it will be the means of introducing happiness and plenty into the Holy Land. In the first instance I shall apply to Mehemet Ali for a grant of land for fifty years; some one or two hundred villages; giving him an increased rent of from ten to twenty per cent . . . The grant obtained, I shall, please Heaven, on my return to England, form a company for the cultivation of the land and the encouragement of our brethren in Europe to return to Palestine. Many Jews now emigrate to New South Wales, Canada, etc., but in the Holy Land they would find a greater certainty of success; here they would find wells already dug, olives and vines already planted, and a land so rich as to require little manure. By degrees I hope to induce the return of thousands of our brethren to the land of Israel. I am sure they would be happy in the observance of our holy religion, in a manner which is impossible in Europe."

He had little understanding of the land, and less of the heartache and labor connected with the encouragement of a national awakening. He had illusions about the condition of Palestine. He wrote: "There are groves of olive trees, I should think, more than five hundred years old, vineyards, much pasture, plenty of wells and an abundance of water; also figtrees, walnuts, almonds, mulberries, etc., and rich fields of wheat, barley and lentils; in fact, it is a land that would produce almost everything in abundance, with very little skill and labor." But he was quite wrong. He had seen a few patches of fertile soil. If the land was to be made to sustain millions, it would need the application of infinite skill and labor. He cannot, therefore, have considered what a task it would be to transform the ghetto dwellers of Europe into agricultural workers, on a soil that had been reduced to barrenness by centuries of neglect. He cannot have understood that nothing could bring about this transformation but a great democratic upheaval from within the people.

He said, toward the end of his life: "I do not expect that all Israelites will quit their abodes in those territories in which they feel happy, even as there are Englishmen in Hungary, Germany, America and Japan; but Palestine must belong to the Jews, and Jerusalem is destined to become the seat of a Jewish commonwealth." This is the clearest Zionist note in his record. It is remarkable enough, the more so as it comes from a typical *Shtadlan*. But Zionism is not day-dreaming; it is a mass movement, and from mass movements Montefiore was remote.

It was, nevertheless, something that might be called

43

proto-Zionism. Montefiore was not caught up passionately in the idea of the Return. He did not press it on the world, on the potentates and statesmen he interviewed. With them he discussed local Jewish grievances. No doubt he would have considered it impolitic to raise the question of a Jewish Homeland in Palestine; and this, precisely, is what made him a *Shtadlan*. Though he entertained the idea of the Return, he conceived it as something rather genteel, a blessing conferred by the benevolent rich on the grateful poor, a phenomenon which released no passions, but unfolded respectably while the world stood by and nodded approval.

But he was not without some influence on the remoter course of events. It was probably through him that Adolphe Crémieux, the French Jewish statesman, turned his attention to the oriental Jews. They worked together on the Damascus Affair in 1840, and when in 1860 Crémieux founded the *Alliance Israélite Universelle*, an organization — more exactly a committee of upper-class Jews — to promote the welfare and defend the rights of Jews everywhere, but particularly in the East, he remembered Palestine. Or he might have remembered it in any case. Again, an American Jew by the name of Judah Touro remembered it, and left Montefiore the sum of $50,000 to administer for the poor of Jerusalem. An Englishman by the name of Laurence Oliphant, one of those eccentric characters who from time to time inject a touch of fantasy into the rather depressing practicality of their nation, conferred with Montefiore, and gathered from him increased devotion to the idea of the Redemption. Possibly Montefiore had more to do with the imponderables of later Zionism than the record establishes.

The *Alliance Israélite* left a permanently identifiable mark on the life of Jewish Palestine. In 1871 it commissioned Charles Netter to establish the agricultural school of Mikveh Israel, which is still in existence. It was intended as a purely local institution. No propaganda for the Return, or even for a considerable influx of Jews from the exile, attended its creation. It had no Jewish national purpose. Neither did the modern schools which the *Alliance* founded for the children of Palestinian Jews, where French was the language of instruction. It was philanthropy pure and simple, such as was practiced by the *Alliance* and similar organizations among Jewish communities in other Mediterranean countries. Nevertheless, this work, once begun, linked up later with the Zionist movement. All sorts of motives and activities go into the fulfilment of a historic process.

CHAPTER SIX

Bilu

❁

FOR a long time nothing happened, nothing tangible that is. The slow changes proceeded below the surface, and here and there, visible above the surface, came scattered individual manifestations. A man called Moses Hess, who had been an early colleague of Karl Marx's in the socialist movement, broke away from his revolutionary preoccupations to write a book on the Jewish question, *Rome and Jerusalem*. It was a book remarkable in itself, and more so by contrast with what Marx himself wrote about the Jews, in one of the most anti-Semitic essays in modern literature. *Rome and Jerusalem*, published in 1862, was a repudiation of assimilationist theory and an exposé of the failure of the emancipation. It called for the establishment of a Jewish Homeland in Palestine, and — this is perhaps the most important feature of the book — it dealt with form and social purpose. Another man, Rabbi Zvi Kalischer, a German subject, like Hess, began to agitate shortly afterwards for the founding of a society to undertake the transference of Jews to Palestine and their settlement on the soil. A third, Perez Smolenskin, in Russia, published, among other studies of the same kind, a little book called *The Eternal People*.

These men struggled against the current of the time; for in so far as there was a dynamic of Jewish life, an active policy, it was toward assimilation. The dynamic of counter-assimilation had not yet been released. In the largest center of Jewish life, Russia, a temporary spell of tolerance created an illusion of permanent security. Where assimilation failed to take hold, the Jewish masses were inert, and the pre-consciousness of the Return to Palestine glimmered fitfully and uncertainly at isolated points. The books of Hess, Kalischer, Smolenskin created a little stir, and then seemed to be forgotten.

Then came, in 1881, the assassination of Alexander II of Russia, and with it the abrupt reversal of the seeming trend toward the emancipation of the Jews. From that time on, until the Revolution of 1917, the condition of Russian Jewry sank from level to level of humiliation and frustration. A wave of pogroms passed over the Jewish communities in 1881 and 1882. A series of "Temporary Enactments" to restrict freedom of movement, of education, of economic activity, for the Jews of Russia, poured from the capital. The Pale of Settlement, a sort of super-ghetto, was re-confirmed by the powerful minister, Ignatiev. The Jews became the focus of a conscious policy of general reaction.

But now, for the first time in the long history of their persecutions, Jews responded with a sudden and immediate interest in Palestine. We must be careful not to exaggerate the response. It was as yet a minority response. We must, however, understand the significance of its character. It was a practical matter; not divested of its religious background, but not primarily religious, not Messianic and eschatological. On the other hand, its practicality was limited to intention only. It was, in the sense of preparation and plan, eminently impractical.

While the great migration of Russian and East European Jewry generally took the westward course, across the Atlantic, a secondary stream moved southeastward. In 1882 seven thousand Jews entered Palestine, until then the largest number recorded in one year since the dispersion. But of these seven thousand, again, only a tiny minority could be called, in the modern sense, self-conscious, purposeful Zionists. This chapter will describe what happened to them.

The majority, though it was undoubtedly suffused with a pre-Zionist outlook, had not undergone the internal change of preparation. As to the country, it possessed no mould into which newcomers could be poured to undergo the transformation locally. Of the thirty thousand Jews then in Palestine, two per cent were working on the land. A colony had been established near Jerusalem, at a place called Motza. It failed, and was abandoned. Another had been established — this was in 1878 — near Jaffa, at Petah Tikvah. It failed, and was abandoned, to be taken up later, successfully. A few other colonies had just been started, primitive places, in which ghetto Jews were making their first contact with the soil. There was the agricultural school, Mikveh Israel, southeast of Jaffa; it had workers attached to its lands, but they were mostly Arabs. And so, of the Jews who entered Palestine in 1882, ninety-five per cent poured into the cities, Jerusalem, Jaffa, Haifa and Hebron. A few opened shops; others were artisans.

Most of them lived on what they had brought with them, and what they received from the *Halukkah*, or distribution system, of which more hereafter. A very poor beginning indeed for a practical Return.

But there was one tiny group in that secondary stream of migrants which incorporated a complete Zionist consciousness. It consisted of students, with a tiny sprinkling of artisans. They assembled in Kharkov, in 1882, and took an oath to proceed to Palestine, and to work *only* on the land, and *only* as a cooperative body. They adopted for their organization a dramatic name, *Dabyu*, from the first letters of the Hebrew biblical verse: "Speak to the Children of Israel, that they go forward." They changed it, soon after, to another name, equally dramatic — by which they are now remembered — *Bilu*, from the Hebrew biblical verse: "House of Jacob, come, let us go!"

To sensible people they looked more than a little ridiculous: twenty youngsters, one woman among them, without training, without money, talking big. It was not enough that they had decided in favor of Palestine rather than America, which was drawing the majority of migrants; and not enough that, having chosen Palestine, they were going to become farmers; and not enough that, having chosen to be farmers, they were exalting the status of the laborer. On top of all these absurdities, they were preparing to set an example to the world in the type of society they were about to establish.

They knew very little about manual labor, less about agriculture, even under Russian conditions. They had not the foggiest notion of Palestinian conditions, climate, soil or population. They only knew that life was no longer tolerable for the Jewish people in Russia; that

49

migration to other countries than Palestine only opened
the prospect of a repetition of the old cycle; that it was
time for the Jewish people to turn homeward; and that
in returning to its home the Jewish people should do
something better than reproduce, on its ancestral soil,
all the errors, defects and injustices of the social system
prevalent in the western world.

So they set out, and from one of the stations on their
trek, Constantinople, they issued, in Hebrew, a manifesto
to the Jewish people. It read thus in part:

What we want:

1. A home in our country. It was given to
us by the mercy of God, it is ours as registered in
the archives of history.

2. To beg it of the Sultan, and if it be impossible to obtain this, to beg that at least we may be
allowed to possess it as a state within a larger
state; the internal administration to be ours, to
have our civil and political rights, to act with the
Turkish Empire only in foreign affairs, so as to
help our brother Ishmael in his time of need.

We hope that the interests of our glorious nation will rouse our national spirit in rich and
powerful men, and that everyone, rich and poor,
will give his best labors to the holy cause.

Greetings, dear brothers and sisters.

Hear, O Israel, the Lord our God, the Lord is
one, and our land, Zion, is our only hope.

One does not know whether to laugh or to weep over
this naive document. "To beg it of the Sultan . . . or
to beg that at least we may be allowed to possess it as
a state within a state . . ." As if governing nations hand
out such precious privileges just so. As if "the national
spirit" is roused in rich and poor by nothing more than

an obscure manifesto issued from a boarding house by a handful of beggarly immigrants. And if the manifesto of the *Bilus* leaves us bewildered, we are not less staggered by the Hebrew diary left us by one of the original group, Chaim Chissin, who stayed with it through its early years of labor and disillusionment.

This diary has about it, in spite of the bright Palestinian sun which shines upon its pages, something of the nightmarish. Having landed, after many delays, at the port of Jaffa, the young enthusiasts proceeded to the farm-school of Mikveh Israel, the institution founded eleven years before by the *Alliance Israélite*. A man called Hirsh was then in charge of Mikveh Israel. He seems to have been the hardboiled type of administrator, utterly unresponsive to exalted slogans, and concerned only with the practical details of his job. National revivals, states within states, imperial concessions, were outside his competence. The *Bilus* asked for work; he looked at them and decided that they were unusable. Forty Arabs were employed on the lands of Mikveh Israel, but they were natives, born to the climate and inured to agricultural labor. What was he to do with twenty Russian students suffering from hallucinations — soft-handed university graduates and urban dwellers? He was for turning them back. But they were insistent. So he decided to give them a chance, and make it harder for them than it needed to be.

There were no quarters for them at Mikveh Israel, so they took lodgings in Jaffa and went out every morning to the school lands. They rose every morning at five, and at six o'clock they were digging under the hot sun. This was their first assignment — ditch-digging. Their hands became blistered, their feet raw, their backs stiff.

They received, of course, the same pay as the Arab laborers — but the Arab laborers did not have to pay for their lodgings; the Arab laborers had homes, and little garden plots; moreover, they had a very different standard of living. The young *Bilus* soon found that if they were to keep a roof over their heads, they would have to cut down on their food. There came a time when they had to start out for the day's work without breakfast. By unanimous resolution, they also deprived themselves of cigarettes. Before long fourteen of the group were out. They could not go on with the work. They stayed all day in their lodgings, demoralized. Six of them returned to Russia, four left the soil and went into the cities. Four of them recovered, somehow. In the end the group of *Bilus*, what with four local additions, numbered fourteen.

These hardier spirits accustomed themselves to the gruelling labor; but they could not carry on without some prospect of realizing their ideal. They had not come to Palestine to remain hired workers; they wanted to found a cooperative colony, and set an example for the *Bilu* societies which had sprung up in various Russian Jewish communities. That could not be done without money, of course. On the other hand, they were not beggars. They were offering up their youth in an idealistic enterprise which was nothing less than the regeneration of Israel. They expected Israel to meet them half way with financial support. They were insistent on this point. When a rich apostate Jew who was living in Jerusalem offered them help, as he did to many Jews whom he hoped to win over to Christianity, they rejected it contemptuously. So they waited, wrote letters to Russia, and waited again. Their friends back home seemed to have forgotten them. Sir Laurence Oliphant, the Zionist Englishman who was advocating the Restoration of the Jews at the Sublime Porte, had ideas, but not money. As far as ideas were concerned, they were more than adequately provided. Charles Netter, the founder of Mikveh Israel, came to Palestine, met the *Bilus*, took a liking to them, and promised them support. But he died soon after.

Then began a period of wanderings and of fruitless experiments. It was about this time that the colony of Rishon le-Zion was founded by Jews of Jerusalem. It was not a social experiment; it was a straightforward individualist enterprise. Like all the colonies of that period, it fared badly, even though it had no social idealism. When it was on the point of dissolution, an anonymous benefactor appeared, a *deus ex machina*. He turned out to be Baron Edmond de Rothschild, of Paris, of whom we shall hear more later. Rishon le-Zion took on a new lease of life. The *Bilus*, despairing of a future at Mikveh Israel, went in a body to Rishon le-Zion, again as hired laborers. The welcome they received was not one degree warmer than the one extended to them by Hirsh at Mikveh Israel. For the *Bilus*, besides being inferior as landworkers to the Arab fellaheen, were not inclined to look upon themselves as a "lower" class. Moreover, they had brought with them, from Russia, a new attitude toward Judaism. The Rishon colonists were orthodox Jews. The *Bilus* were not. The Rishon colonists were intent on bringing back all the Mosaic laws — including even the *Shemitah*, or seventh year during which a piece of land must lie fallow. One reads with a feeling of unreality, in Chissin's diary, and in later sources, of the long and passionate disputes which

53

centered on the attempted revival of this piece of biblical legislation. The *Bilus* could not understand its purpose. To them the ideal of the Restoration was associated with the spirit, not with the form, of the biblical laws.

Two years passed, during which the Russian students grew leaner and hungrier. Their numbers had increased to thirty. Fifteen were at Rishon le-Zion, fifteen had gone back to Mikveh. It was a long, bitter trial — the beginning of many similar trials in the growth of the cooperative ideal. Just when it seemed that the Mikveh Israel group was about to dissolve, and perhaps the Rishon le-Zion group after it, a new leader of the *Bilus* came to Palestine — Yehiel Michael Pines, a Hebrew scholar, a man of action and, oddly enough, an orthodox advocate of the Sabbatical Year.

Pines was the representative of one of the Jewish colonizing societies in the diaspora. There were several of these — little independent groups of enthusiasts in various cities. They were not organized in a federation. They had no program of action. Often they were ignorant of each other's existence. They differed from the *Halukkah* organizations, which had maintained the old Jewish communities, in their insistence on a new and practical approach to the Jewish settlements. But they seldom had more than a few thousand roubles to dispose of, and expert advice was beyond their reach.

Pines brought out some money, bought a parcel of land for the *Bilus*, and in December 1884, the cooperative colony of Gederah was founded.

The record tells us that ten men (nine of them original *Bilus*) went up to Gederah, to occupy the single wooden shack. They took with them nine mattocks, one gun, one donkey, a pot, a samovar — and a few books. They had neither ploughs nor oxen nor horses. Moreover, the land placed at their disposal was fit only for vines; four years would have to pass before they could gather their first harvest. In the meantime they would have to live on grants from the colonizing agencies. Diversified farming was unknown. Fruits, vegetables and eggs were purchased from neighboring Arab villages. The colony did not even have an adequate or reliable water-supply.

We must bear in mind — we shall constantly have to recall — that we are telling the story of children of the ghetto. They did not come of a long line of farmers, workers, craftsmen. They came of merchants, peddlers, scholars and rabbis. They were not handy at doing things. They had to learn to saw a piece of wood, drive in a nail, wield a spade and draw a furrow. All their lives they had been accustomed to the city and its conveniences. Water came from the faucet, milk from a pail, bread from the baker, vegetables from the store. Here they were in a wild country, a semi-tropical climate, an isolated, forlorn patch of wilderness far from the world's highroads. They had left the Russia of Tolstoi and Nekrassov and Dostoievsky and Turgeniev, the Russia of the populists, where thousands of young people were banded together in a revolutionary movement, going out to the simple folk in the villages to teach them the rudiments of liberty. They were alone here. Even their own people, the Jews, for whose sake they had broken with civilization, were for the most part indifferent to their bitter plight. True, the Russia they had left was also the Russia of the Pale, of Alexander III and of the secret police, the Russia of repression and obscurantism. Was Palestine any better? Turkish reaction was of an earlier vintage than Russian; it had not even reached the stage of a popular counter-movement. The *Bilus* had their troubles with the Turkish police, but on a low, even disgusting level. It was not a fight round the high principle of universal liberty; it was a continuous skirmish for little conveniences.

The Turkish law had some very queer provisions. For instance, no house could be built without a government permit. On the other hand, no house could be pulled down without a special decree; and for the purpose of this second law, a house was a roof held up by corner posts. So, if you could not get a permit to build a house, you put up a roof hastily in the night, and if the police came round next morning you defied them to do anything about it. Meanwhile you could fill in the walls and floors. You didn't fight the oppressors, as one did in Russia; you sneaked past the law. It was an unpleasant business, without any of the high conspiratorial excitements of life in Russia. No defiance. No proclamations. Just tricks. The *Bilus* of Gederah learned them, and became adepts. They put in a chicken coop first; stables afterwards. As money dribbled in for implements, seed and draft animals, they expanded the settlement, sneak by sneak. Between bribes, subterfuges and night work they managed to erect the minimum number of buildings.

Their position was different from that of the individualist colonists working at Petah Tikvah, Rishon le-Zion, Zichron Ya'akov and the other points being occupied by Jewish settlers. The latter were not under the pressure of a social ideal; and since they were not experimentors and doctrinaires, they came to terms more easily with local conditions. The hand of Baron Roth-

schild was always open with subsidies. The economy
they adopted was that of businessmen. They used Arab
labor, very cheap and very docile, for the more exhaust-
ing work of digging and planting. We must not imagine
that their lot was particularly easy at first, either. They
too had climate, want and isolation to contend with.
They too, though they employed Arab labor, found the
surrounding population a problem. Still it must be
said in fairness that they had taken on a less exacting
task than the *Bilus*.

The Arabs about Gederah derived some benefit from
the settlement; but not enough to keep them quiet.
For that matter no amount of benefits received ever
seemed to suffice for that. They were not exactly hostile
either. They only wanted their bit of loot; a chicken, a
spade, an occasional hand-out of *baksheesh*, so that they
would not report to the police the preparations for the
putting up of a roof. Or else they wanted to graze their
animals on the Jewish colony. They were not vicious
about all this; they merely resented interference. There
were quarrels, and sometimes fist-fights. Once, in later
years, when Gederah was already on its feet, with stone
buildings, with filled stables, and milch cows, there was
a regular pitched battle, with gunfire. In between,
there were friendly contacts, too, ceremonial gatherings,
and even some degree of cooperation in outwitting the
common enemy, the Turkish police.

Thus years passed, in melancholy procession. There
were crop failures, droughts, sicknesses. The colony
always needed financial assistance; for the fundamental
evil — this pursued Jewish colonization for a long time
— was that help came in sufficient quantities to keep

them alive, but never in sufficient quantities to enable them to plan intelligently and effectively. The *Mazkereth Montefiore*, one of the colonization funds, sent them money. The *Hoveve Zion*, when they were organized in Russia, sent them money. So did Baron de Rothschild. Slowly they overcame their ignorance of farming; learned when to plough and what to plant; for the winter sowing wheat and barley (for they extended their land and added to their vineyards fields of grain), for the summer sowing durra, the coarser kind of wheat. They lacked expert direction. There was no veterinary at that time, either in Jaffa or Jerusalem. They worked, on the average, ten hours a day. As a rule they were shockingly undernourished. For long periods the midday lunch would consist of radishes, potato soup and doughballs, the evening supper of tea and bread. And yet they held out, at any rate physically. But there was nothing to sustain their morale, and the old ideals began to fade. The dream of a successful cooperative of workers on equal terms yielded to the individual struggle. Gederah finished up as an individualist colony. The boys who had come out from Russia to create a model colony became disillusioned men who followed the example of Rishon and Petah Tikvah. They too found themselves compelled to employ cheap Arab labor, and to refuse employment to Jewish newcomers.

They knew, of course, that this was no way to build a Jewish homeland. If land was going to be owned and managed by Jews, but worked by native labor, a Jewish majority could never be established. Back of the partial failure — we must so qualify it — of the *Bilus* was a simple fact: the national revival of Jewry had not yet reached the right stage. Immigrants were coming in.

Jaffa was growing. Colonies were being founded. Land was being purchased. Rishon took on the appearance of a little townlet. Some sort of intellectual activity emerged, as the more successful farmers found themselves with free time on their hands in the evenings. A library was opened in Jaffa. It became the custom, in the colonies, to hold meetings on Friday and Saturday evenings, to listen to lectures, to conduct discussions. But there existed neither the instruments nor the predisposition among the *Ikkarim*, the farmers, for the systematic absorption of Jewish workers into the economy of the colonies. The prevalent attitude toward labor was, on the whole, typically capitalist. Thus, when an *Agudath Po'alim*, or trade union of landworkers, the first of its kind in the history of Palestine, was founded, the colonists fired the workers at once, and took in Arabs in their place. The disunity of the Jewish people in the diaspora was reflected in the tiny Jewish settlement in Palestine.

CHAPTER SEVEN

The First Wave

⚙

THE *Bilu* movement was to modern Zionism what Wycliffe was to the Reformation — a morning star which was eclipsed before the full flood of daylight washed over the horizon. For a time it seemed that the men and women who had tried to initiate a mass return to the soil of Palestine had been a historic "sport." It was only later, when the Second Wave of immigration toward Palestine set in, around nineteen hundred and four, that the inspiration of the *Bilus* bore fruit. By then the original protagonists of the ideal had grown old and disillusioned. Others took their place, remembered what they had been, and began where they had left off.

The foregoing passage is, however, somewhat unjust toward the First Wave of modern migration into Palestine, that which was contemporaneous with the *Bilus*. The thousands who came out of Russia, and did not go on the land, did nevertheless bring into the country human material which was later to be integrated with the national renaissance. And the hundreds, other than the *Bilus*, who did go on the land, were even more obviously a contribution to the internal transformation of the Jewish economy, and the awakening of the dormant national strength. It is customary, it is perhaps natural, to compare them with the *Bilus* and to regret their short-comings. They seem, superficially, to have been moti-vated by too personal an impulse; they had no social vision; their desire to become farmers on Palestinian soil was, according to this view, just one form of the normal drive for the improvement of one's economic status. But even if all this were granted, and even more — such as the obstacles which their form of colonization set up (as we shall see) to future growth — it must be ad-mitted that they did not choose the easiest path.

They were middle-class, these colonists of the First Wave or, as they call it in Hebrew, *Aliyah*, Ascent, or going up. Some of them had a little money when they set out; the others were middle-class in outlook if not in means — a frequent Jewish failing. In agricultural experience and in knowledge of the country all of them were the same paupers as the *Bilus*. If the physical trials they encountered were less cruel than those of the *Bilus* — for after all they did not want to become landworkers, and they employed Arab labor from the beginning — the heartache, the loneliness, the disillu-sionments of the first years were more or less of the same kind. There is not much sense in blaming middle-class people for being middle-class, and capitalists for being capitalists. It is possible, as a matter of fact, to find, in the middle-class initial colonization of Palestine, a parallel to the initial capitalist modernization of the western world, and to say of the former, as even socialists say of the latter: "Given the circumstances, it could not have been done otherwise." Today it is hard to find an economist or statesman who does not regard un-controlled capitalist enterprise as an outlived and obstructive approach to the problems of production and distribution. It is just as hard to find a communist who does not admit that, when it emerged, uncontrolled capitalist enterprise was a force for progress. The *Bilus* may have come too soon; it does not make them the less heroic in retrospect, but it does mitigate the blame, if we may so put it, which attaches to those who took up a hostile attitude toward them at the time.

The progressive factors in these middle-class colonists were their belief in the immediacy of the Return and their obstinate intention to contribute to it by settling on the land. In both of these respects they were a minority in the Jewish people, which speaks for their courage and imagination. The Zionist movement was still a-borning. It was only in 1884 that the Jews of Russia held their first pro-Palestinian conference, at Kattowitz. By the standards of later Zionist demonstrations it was a very small affair. The moving spirit was Leo Pinsker, another of the men who has left us a classic statement of the Zionist case, in his little book *Auto-Emancipation*. Pinsker, like Hess, Kalischer and the others, found few to heed him. The *Hoveve Zion*, the Lovers of Zion, were still rather queer, isolated groups of enthusiasts. The call of the Kattowitz Conference fell on deaf ears. We have a simple and pathetic measure of its effectiveness, or lack of it. In the year that followed the Conference, all of Russian Jewry contributed less than $25,000 toward the upbuilding of Palestine.

To understand the interaction between Palestinian development and the evolution of the Zionist movement, we shall be compelled, every so often, to shift our attention to the diaspora; and in the early stages we shall be concerned almost exclusively with Russia, the great reservoir of modern Jewish life. At the time of which we are now speaking, the eighties of the last century, the awakening toward self-redemption through the Return to Palestine was barely perceptible. It is true that the Zionist movement, such as it was, had no legal status. The Kattowitz Conference therefore was called ostensibly for the purpose of promoting a philanthropic enterprise. Zionist meetings were secret affairs. They were held in synagogues, as an adjunct to prayers; or in homes, under the pretext of family celebrations. Shmarya Levin, who became one of the tribunes of the movement, describes how a "betrothal" would be solemnized in one home after another; the same bottle of whiskey was held in reserve as evidence of a festivity. At the approach of the police, the whiskey would be poured into the glasses; at their retreat, it would be poured back into the bottle; partly because the Jews were not drinkers, and partly because the movement could not afford a bottle of whiskey for every "betrothal." But it was not the repressive attitude of the government which accounted for the slow progress of Zionism. It was the torpidity of the masses. Collections were made kopeck by kopeck, rouble by rouble. The thing was new, queer, dangerous and unrespectable. More than a generation was to pass before the movement took hold. The youngsters who used to go from door to door asking for donations — a certain Chaim Weizmann, a schoolboy in Pinsk, was one of them — were to grow up, the hopelessness of the Jewish situation in Russia, and in Europe generally, was to be made more clear, the colonists in Palestine were to go through a long period of probation, before Zionism would achieve the status of a world movement.

So those colonists who settled in Petah Tikvah, and Rishon le-Zion, and Zichron Ya'akov, and Rosh Pinah and Yesod Hamaalah could not count on a solicitous Jewry to see them through the hard time. Or if they did, it was a sad miscalculation. Had it not been for Baron Edmond de Rothschild, they would have gone under.

Some of the colonies were started with the capital of the settlers. Others, at least in part, with money collected outside of Palestine. Eliezer Rokeach, of Safed, set out on a pilgrimage to Russia, to raise funds. He did not get to Russia. I have already mentioned, more than once, the *Halukkah* system of collections for Palestinian Jews. It was an old institution, a religious philanthropy, which maintained the European Jewish communities in the cities. It had a tradition, and it had thousands of dependents, pauperized Jews who made no effort to earn a living. The *Halukkah* representatives in Palestine and Europe saw in the Zionist collections a dangerous rival activity. Their economic hostility was reinforced by their religious convictions; they would not have Israel redeemed by anyone but the Messiah. Rokeach was kept out of Russia, so he turned to Roumanian Jewry. There he persuaded a sufficient number of Jews, and collected a sufficient initial fund, to start the colonies of Rosh Pinah and Zichron Ya'akov, the former east of Safed, the latter at the northern end of the Plain of Sharon.

We recall how Petah Tikvah, in Judaea, or Southern

Palestine, was started, abandoned, and started again. I repeat: we must not imagine that the *Bilus* had a monopoly on hardship. Petah Tikvah was a swamp in those days, a forbidding, uninhabited, uninhabitable desolation on the banks of the Auja, or Yarkon. *Petah Tikvah*, the name chosen by the colonists, is Hebrew for "Gates of Hope." Never did gates open on a drearier prospect. The Arabs, who gave the district a wide berth, warned the Jews against the attempt. Neither man, nor beast, nor bird could live there, they said. And so it seemed, at first; for the settlers succumbed, one after another, to malaria; and the shacks, the stables, the half-prepared fields were abandoned. But only for a time. The attempt was renewed a few years later, and was sustained long enough. Petah Tikvah was conquered; it became, after some decades, the showplace of individual enterprise in Palestine; and today it is a rich center of orange, vine, grain and dairy production, a rural town of twenty thousand inhabitants. But that first period, in the early eighties, confronts us with a monotonous record of hunger, inexperience, sickness, loneliness and patience.

The more one considers the endurance of the individualist colonies, the more one is disinclined to allow the distinction between "conscious Zionists," the name which tradition confers on the *Bilus*, and "pre-Zionists," which is the grudging designation allowed the farmers of Petah Tikvah and Rishon and the other first settlements. It is quite certain that the economic drive alone, the will to personal security and advancement, does not account for their achievement. We know that they too — or at least the majority of them — talked of the Return; that they were vividly conscious of the magic of the land, and of a mission to which they were pledged; that they looked on themselves (again for the most part) as the forerunners of thousands and tens of thousands of others; and that these convictions contributed to their final success. Nevertheless the distinction cannot be wholly disallowed. It is the distinction which the tradition also makes, properly, between Baron Edmond de Rothschild in his early Palestinian work, and the program of the Zionist movement; and it will become clarified in the course of this narrative.

Meanwhile, what had become of Montefiore's naive anticipations: "It is a land that will produce almost everything in abundance, with very little skill and labor"? The few fertile spots which misled Montefiore were of course occupied. To buy out the occupants was beyond the means of the colonists, and not to the purpose. The rest of the land had to pass through a parallel transformation with the ruralizing Jews, and so it has been in most of the history of Palestinian colonization. And it is quite certain that if the first stage, the one now under examination, had depended on the resources of the Zionist movement, it would have been delayed by two decades; it might, in the opinion of some, have come too late. That this fatal or near-fatal delay did not intervene, that the work went on while the Zionist movement was finding itself, is due to the appearance on the scene of two men, Baron Maurice de Hirsch of Hungary, and Baron Edmond de Rothschild of Paris.

They were alike in their wealth, their aristocratic tastes, their dictatorial characters and their earnest preoccupation with the Jewish problem. They were very different in their attitude toward Palestine. As far back as the seventies of the last century de Hirsch was a generous supporter of the *Alliance Israélite* and its school system. But his mind was not Palestino-centric, as Edmond de Rothschild's was. De Hirsch did come to the conclusion, however, that the Jewish problem could not be solved *in situ*, that is, by changes on the spot. At first he conceived the notion that the maladjustment of Russian Jewry could be cured locally by a process of modernization, both in education and in occupational redistribution. He was ready to spend ten or fifteen million dollars for this purpose; he discovered that the Russian government had other views. It was by no means interested in solving the Jewish problem if that implied, as de Hirsch intended it should, the absorption of the Jewish masses into the economic and cultural life of the country. It was perhaps not interested at all in solving the Jewish problem. But even if it had co-operated with de Hirsch, it is improbable that an occupational transformation of any significance could have taken place among the Jews under such a general regime. De Hirsch shifted his ground. He conceived another plan. He would transfer vast numbers of Jews from eastern and central Europe to other countries (the Argentine became the center of the experiment, with peripheral enterprises elsewhere), and in the transference carry out the occupational redistribution. What was impossible in an old country with fixed forms would be possible in a new country, where a fresh start could be made.

The story of the ICA (the Jewish Colonization Association) concerns us only as an illustration of the inherent weakness of paternalistic philanthropy. Tens of thou-

sands of Jews were transferred to the Argentine and
other countries and settled on the soil. For a time they
took to the new life; some of them even became very
successful farmers. But no general enthusiasm grew
up round the enterprise. There was no over-all ideal
to resist the pull to the cities. De Hirsch's colonies were
planted in countries which, though marked by a large
proportion of rural life, were urbanizing — as indeed all
modern countries are; and the urban impulse was strong
in the Jews. De Hirsch did not consult the character
of the Jewish masses which he genuinely desired to help.
He could not know that to carry out a great plan of
redemption he would have to harness to his philanthropic
machinery the powerful element of the Jewish tradition,
which pointed to Palestine. It is enough to recall that,
for two thousand years, the Jews had repeated, not
le-shanah ha-ba'ah b'-Argentine ("Next year in the Argentine"), but *le-shanah ha-ba'ah bi-Yerushalayim.* Without
the prospect of a recreated Jewish Homeland, in the place
designated by Providence and memory, the transplanted
groups could not coalesce, the individuals could not
derive strength from each other, the settlements could
not stabilize and grow organically.

Palestine was one of the peripheral countries for de
Hirsch. He helped Jews there as he helped them wherever help was needed. To this extent his benefactions
crossed the Zionist field.

Edmond de Rothschild made Palestine *his* center. His
benefactions, too, illustrate some of the weaknesses of paternalistic philanthropy, but in another manner than de
Hirsch's. Rothschild was an exception among rich Jews
in his instinctive sympathy with the popular longing

for Palestine. He was not an exception among rich men in other respects of his public activity. He wanted to do good, but in his way only. De Hirsch did not consult the national inclination of the Jewish masses; Rothschild did not consult democratic necessity. He thought in terms of a Jewish home in Palestine, but not in terms of agitation, demonstration, propaganda and renaissance. He was cold to Theodore Herzl. He was repelled by the social-minded *Bilus*. He thought — at first — that money and direction from above could fill Palestine with Jewish farmers. He changed later; but in the time of the First Wave he relied on money and experts.

He was so generous with the first that he partly overcame the handicaps of the second. No one knows the exact amount Edmond de Rothschild put into his Palestinian plans. It has been estimated at upward of fifty million dollars, spread over forty years. A good proportion of that sum was expended in the first period, and it was needed. For the system worked against itself. The initiative of the farmers was discouraged by the domination of the administrators and the generosity of the great benefactor. The experts of the Baron made the decisions for the colonists, chose the crops to be planted and determined the form of the economy. The Baron wanted a money economy. He believed that this would yield quicker results in the creation of an independent farmer class. He encouraged, or rather ordered, a concentration on vines, possibly because he was doing so well with his own very extensive vineyards in the south of France. For years he paid the colonists twenty and thirty per cent more than the market price for their grapes. He constructed enormous wine cellars — they

were said to be the second largest in the world — at
Rishon. When the futility of this method became obvious, most of the vines had to be uprooted. The Baron
bore the cost. The colonists obeyed orders; if the results
were not what had been expected, they turned to the
Baron for help; and they received it.

A money economy such as the Baron first adopted
had another disadvantage. It confirmed the farmers
in the habit of getting the cheapest labor available,
which of course was Arab. This blocked the flow of
Jews from city to soil, and therefore the flow from the
diaspora into Palestine. The Zionist movement, still
crystallizing slowly, understood this danger; but it was
not yet strong enough to do more than enter a protest.
It was not until 1890 that Zionism was legalized, after
a fashion, in Russia; the Zionists were allowed to operate
publicly as a Society for the Support of Agricultural
Laborers in Syria and Palestine. A centralizing committee was set up in Odessa. But the funds at its disposal were exiguous. In 1896 it collected $24,000; in
1897, $29,000. It was all very well for them to criticize
the Baron's methods; but he was paying the piper, and
he would not let them call the tune.

One of the oddities of that period of Zionist history
is the role played by Ahad Ha'am. Under this, his
pen name, Asher Ginsberg is remembered only as the
Hebrew essayist, stylist, philosopher, and protagonist
of a school of Zionist thought. He is remembered as the
founder of the B'nai Moshe, the exclusive organization
of Zionist leaders which trained, among others, Menachem Mendel Ussischkin, Yechiel Tschlenov and
Shmarya Levin. It is not remembered that Ahad
Ha'am was also endowed with an eminently practical

mind. He was an important executive in the great tea firm of Kalonymos Wolf Wissotzky, and for many years the manager of the English branch, as well as Wissotzky's executive for Jewish cultural enterprises. It was Asher Ginsberg, the theorist, who first published a critical analysis of the methods of colonization pursued in Palestine by Baron de Rothschild. It was a courageous thing to do, at a time when the Zionists had little more than advice to offer. But it was well done; and in the long run not without effect. Baron Edmond was dictatorial, but not stupidly so. In time he recognized the validity of the criticism. A change came over the spirit of his administration. The defects persisted for a long time; they were transferred, in some measure, to the PICA (Palestine Jewish Colonization Association) in which the Baron concentrated his Palestine work after 1899. But they were in a considerable measure remedied before the Baron's death in 1925.

With all these defects, however, the philanthropy of the Baron kept the colonies alive, and extended the network. By 1897, the year of the First Zionist Congress, the First Wave was exhausted, but it had left its mark on the country. There were now twenty-two Jewish colonies, with some five thousand inhabitants. Few of the colonies were yet self-supporting, but some progress had been made. At least more Jews were living on the land. The total Jewish population was estimated at about seventy thousand. In the cities sixty per cent of the Jews were still dependent on the *Halukkah* doles. Taken as a whole, the Palestinian picture was not an encouraging one in the year when the World Zionist Organization was created.

CHAPTER EIGHT

Theodore Herzl

WHEN a great man is born, history opens up a little to accommodate him. This is not a courtesy but a come-on. Once trapped, the great man is seldom consulted. He is made to play one role when he thinks he is playing another; and he is taken off the stage in accordance with the needs of the plot.

Scores of biographies will illustrate these points, and few better than Theodore Herzl's. To all appearances this man, born in Budapest in 1860, was destined for a moderately distinguished career as a journalist and man of letters in the Central Europe of Francis Joseph I, the *Wiener Neue Freie Presse*, Johann Strauss and Arthur Schnitzler. His Jewish education was fragmentary, his attachment to his people, in spite of occasional spurts of sentiment, rather casual. His interests and gifts inclined him to literature. He wrote charmingly — feuilletons, reviews, plays and sketches. Those who knew him in his thirty-fifth or thirty-sixth year found him charming, attractive, able, cultured — obviously a man with quite a future. Then history beckoned to him in the Dreyfus affair, which he was reporting for his paper, the *Wiener Neue Freie Presse*, from Paris. The element of greatness in him was set in motion. The famous trial shook him to the soul. He perceived the Jewish problem, and said to himself: "I must do something about it." He thought he would meet his obligation by writing a book advocating a Jewish state. And he wrote it, to the sound of invisible eagle's wings beating above him. That, he believed, was all he had to give — for he was a writer, nothing more. He was mistaken. He was not a writer, but a maker of history, and he would give nothing less than his life. Literally so; for he killed himself in the seven years of overwork between his thirty-seventh and forty-fourth years. He died with his task completed, though he did not know it; for while he was pursuing a phantom objective, he was unconsciously achieving a real one.

Herzl is often spoken of as the creator of political Zionism. He was not that. If political Zionism means the promotion of political conditions favorable to the creation of a Jewish state in Palestine, the concept existed before Herzl's time. There were hundreds of political Zionists in the eighteen eighties and nineties. In Russia, in the Jewish student colonies of Berlin, Vienna, Berne, Geneva, Paris and Montpellier, there were young men and women thinking of the political constellation which would point the way to the creation of a Jewish state. We have seen that the *Bilus*, in their manifesto from Constantinople, took up a political attitude. It is true that they did little about it; but we shall see that what Herzl did in that direction was of no importance by comparison with what he did within the Zionist movement. For he gave it organization, form and *élan*; he set up the first Jewish parliament in the history of the exile;

73

and he enabled it to bring forth the instruments which were to make the movement effective.

Nothing was further from his initial plans of action. For that matter, we have seen that he planned not to take any action at all. He would present the idea to the world; let others carry it out. When he found that the fever of inspiration which attended the writing of the *Judenstaat* had become a permanent condition which literary expression would not assuage, he looked for a few Jewish multimillionaires to take over. He had a notion that the very simplicity of his solution of the Jewish problem would sweep people off their feet. Discovering that the rich and powerful were afflicted with a high degree of stability, he turned to the masses, and issued the first call to a Congress. But even then the Congress was secondary or auxiliary in his purpose.

This was the gist of his intentions: a Jewish state (whether in Palestine or elsewhere, and it did not matter at first) could be created only by large action, in the full light of day; if that state was to be in Palestine, then the piddling activities of the early Zionists, the *Hoveve Zion*, and even the larger enterprises of Baron Edmond de Rothschild, were meaningless: a Jewish state could not be sneaked into existence. First had to come a Charter for a Jewish Homeland, granted by the Turkish Government and recognized in international law. Then would follow vast, systematic action.

Money would be the lever with which the Charter would be pried out of the Turks. Turkey was chronically in need of money; the Ottoman debt was the happy hunting ground of European financiers. Suppose, said Herzl to himself, I could persuade Jewish financiers to take over the Ottoman debt, and ease the burden of the

Sultan, would not the Sultan, in exchange, grant us the Charter for a Jewish Homeland in Palestine? In an interview with Abdul Hamid he put the matter in his charming feuilletoniste manner. Abdul Hamid was the lion in the fable (a sorrier specimen of a lion never sat on the throne of Suleiman the Magnificent); the lion had a thorn in his paw; Herzl was Androcles, who would withdraw the thorn — and the reward would be the Charter.

Naive as it sounds here in the telling, the reality was even more so. For nearly seven years Herzl dreamed day and night of the Charter. He thought up the wildest combinations, interviewed the strangest variety of people. A Polish international adventurer by the name of Nevlinski, publisher of a newspaper with a circulation of seven copies, became his expert and *homme de confiance vis-à-vis* the Sublime Porte; a sweet old English religious crackpot, the Reverend Hechler, who believed in the Jewish Return on the basis of cabalistic calculations relating to the Book of Daniel, was Herzl's link with provincial German royalty. His diplomatic negotiations extended in every direction. He became a sort of protégé of the Grand Duke of Baden, through whom he sought the beneficent intervention of the German Emperor. He interviewed the German ambassador in Vienna. He wrote to Bismarck. He visited Count Witte in Russia, hoping to get the Russian ambassador at Constantinople to put in a good word for the Zionist idea. He interviewed the Sultan twice, and hinted at great financial possibilities when there wasn't enough money in the Zionist treasury to support a modest weekly newspaper. He was received by the German Emperor in Palestine. When, in 1903, the British Government offered the

Zionists Uganda, in East Africa, for a Jewish Homeland,
Herzl was all for acceptance. It is a much debated
question whether Herzl really intended to swing the
movement from Palestine to Uganda, or whether he
wanted to use Uganda as a pawn — to show the Turks
that there were other possibilities, and that they had
better hurry up and give the Zionists a Charter, or else.
But all these maneuvers, hopes, negotiations, came to
nothing.

Nor would it have helped if Herzl had commanded
the resources at which he mysteriously hinted in his
conversations with the Sultan and high Turkish officials.
The Turkish government was incapable of action, or
even of decision. A hundred million dollars would not
have sufficed to cover the preliminary bribes to an
action of this kind. It hurts one to read, in Herzl's
diaries, of the days when he sat waiting for the Charter
to arrive. It hurts one to follow the futile and devious
devices by which he tried to keep the Zionist Congresses
in line with his diplomatic stunts. If only someone had
been able to show him that he was building much
greater than he knew, that the auxiliary to his plans (as
he thought it to be), the Zionist Congress, was primary
in his historic service, that his struggles with his followers were part of the process of growth for the Zionist
movement!

The World Zionist Organization, founded by the
Congress, did not immediately draw in the scattered
societies which were interested in the promotion of
Palestinian colonization. The Odessa Committee, for
instance, carried on separately until the beginning of the
First World War. But Congress became the accepted

76

forum of the movement, its front to the world and, in increasing measure, the dominating authority. The Russian Zionists, led by Menachem Mendel Ussischkin, resisted longest; they defeated the proposal to make Uganda a half-way station to Palestine, they criticized most consistently Herzl's exclusive preoccupation with the Charter, his indifference to the coral-insect practical work in Palestine. The young Zionists, with Chaim Weizmann at the head, constituted an opposition based on the cultural and practical program of Ahad Ha'am. But all cooperated devotedly in the creation of the instruments of the Organization.

The first of these was the Congress itself. The essence of its democratic character may be expressed thus: a body of men and women elected by popular vote was to control the disposition of funds contributed toward the colonization of Palestine irrespective of the source of the contributions. The smallest contributor had no more and no less representation at the Congress than the largest. This, a new principle in Jewish life, was the corrective to the paternalism of philanthropists and of *Shtadlonim*. If Baron de Rothschild of Paris, or Felix M. Warburg of New York in later years, directed — as they did — a large part of their benefactions for Palestine through the Zionist Organization, they had to submit to the decisions of the Zionist Congresses in regard to the uses made of those benefactions. The relinquishment of the big contributor's right to do what he thought best with his money did not come easily, of course. In the nineteen-twenties, for instance, when the American Jewish community emerged as the largest contributor to the Zionist funds, there was not a little heart-burning over the fact that the American delegations to the Congresses were not proportionately influential. But Congress decisions remained binding; and many individuals saw their moneys disbursed in social experiments with which they did not sympathize. Rich men have played no part to speak of in the leadership of the Zionist movement. Poor men have been very much to the fore. Salaried office-holders have helped to direct policy, as they do in national governments.

The first instrument created by the Congress was the Jewish Colonial Trust. Herzl intended this to be the great central fund of his projected "Jewish Company;" with it he was to swing the purchase of the Charter. He set as his first modest objective the sum of $10,000,000. At the end of three years, in 1902, not much more than a tenth of that sum had been contributed in shares! But out of that modest beginning there developed the Anglo-Palestine Company, which, in years to come, was to play a leading role in the development of the country.

The second instrument was the Jewish National Fund, concerning which we shall have much to tell in the sequel. No other Zionist institution has embodied the specific character of the Zionist movement in the same degree as the Jewish National Fund, and it is therefore relevant to note that the essential idea was already present in the earliest practical suggestions for colonization in Palestine. At the Kattowitz Conference of 1884 the plan of Professor Hermann Schapira for the creation of a fund to buy land in Palestine *as the inalienable property of the Jewish people* was favorably discussed. In the years that followed the proposal cropped up at various points. At the First Congress, in 1897, it was submitted officially, and referred to the Second Congress. The sum contemplated was $50,000,000. The actual launching of the Jewish National Fund did not occur until the Fifth Congress (December 1901), and with the experience of the Jewish Colonial Trust before them, the Zionists set their sights a little lower. The resolution called for the collection of $1,000,000 before any land purchases were made. In the year 1907, when official Zionist colonization operations — as distinguished from those of earlier organizations — began, the Jewish National Fund had only $300,000! Again and again we shall see gigantic proposals bring forth tiny beginnings; again and again we shall see the tiny beginnings grow into gigantic proportions.

Several corollaries flowed from the principle of land redeemed as the perpetual possession of the Jewish people. As national property, such land was withdrawn from the market, and could never become an object of speculation. Since it could only be leased, and never purchased, all increases in value accrued to the Jewish people as such. Since it was acquired by the Jewish people on the widest possible subscription basis, it came to be regarded as the special domain of the common man, and this expressed itself in the provision that on no land of the Jewish National Fund was labor to be employed for profit. Land of the Jewish National Fund must be worked by the lessee and his family. Thus the Jewish National Fund has evolved into the instrument for the great social experiment of the cooperative colonies; without it the colonization of Palestine would not have developed its most distinctive feature.

In later years, and long after the death of Herzl, other instruments were created by the Zionist Organization, the largest being the Keren Hayesod, or general colonizing fund. The first were the most important in that they fixed the constitution; what followed was extension and amendment.

Herzl devoted immense energies to the creation of the Jewish Colonial Trust, but considerably less to the Jewish National Fund. He understood the social values of the National Fund, but inasmuch as his mind and heart were fixed on the Charter, he gave first attention to the implements which he held to be necessary for his diplomatic work. His imagination could not stoop to details not connected with a grand, immediate vision; but where such a vision was involved his patience and his capacity for drudgery were overwhelming. He was not successful with the Jewish Colonial Trust; he was successful with the Congress in the special sense we have noted, which was another than he had originally intended.

It is useless to speculate what form the Zionist movement would have taken if Herzl had not come from the west to collaborate with the forces of the east. But the collaboration expressed itself in tensions as well as in agreements. Herzl complained that the Zionists presented him with an official opposition before he had a government. The majority of the *Hoveve Zion* were in disagreement with the leader's relegation of practical work in Palestine to second place, even though the practical work was utterly unimpressive. Ahad Ha'am, preacher of perfectionism, was concerned with the qualitative aspect of the Jewish resettlement. His followers believed that, as the appetite comes with eating, so activity is encouraged by action. They were not satisfied with the pitiful performance in Palestine, but they were less concerned than Herzl with the impression that made on the outside world. In any case, they said — and these views were best set forth by Weizmann in what came to be called "synthetic Zionism" — Congresses as demonstrations would acquire value only as, in Palestine itself, a body of achievement gave reality to Jewish claims. Herzl, haunted by the Jewish tragedy, and almost crushed by it when the pogroms broke out in Russia, in 1903, said that without the Charter the trifling settlements in Palestine would never expand to anything like the needed proportions; the Russian Zionists, who were living the Jewish tragedy, said that without the expansion of the settlements there would never be a Charter.

This was the deadlock which was resolved only after the death of Herzl. The struggle between Political Zionism and Practical Zionism is by now an almost forgotten phase of the history of the movement. The argument was never settled; it was resolved by the course of events. But the Congress as an institution survived all stresses, was even strengthened by them, and emerged finally as the Jewish parliament in exile.

Its status as such is of course moral; its "enactments" have only the force of suggestion. Its authority is recognized only by believers in a Jewish Homeland in Palestine, and not by all of those. But a curious light is cast on Herzl's achievement by the history of the Uganda struggle and the subsequent split in the ranks of the Zionists.

In 1903 the British government offered the Jewish people, through the Zionist Organization, a territory in East Africa. The offer was rejected. It turned out, later, that the project was impractical; most of the land was unsuitable; and the opportunities were further diminished by the protests of non-Jewish white settlers in the territory. But the passionate debate in the Zionist Congress centered on other considerations. For the majority of the Zionists it was Palestine or nothing. It was inconceivable to them that a Jewish Homeland should re-arise elsewhere than on its original site, that the Jewish people should thus relinquish formally its associations with the country which had moulded its character, its culture and its tradition. We need not stop to ask here to what extent Herzl meant Uganda as a substitute for Palestine, as a half-way station to Palestine, or only as a diplomatic maneuver *vis-à-vis* the Turks. It is certain that the Zionists feared the Uganda proposal as an attempt to deflect the historic purpose of the movement.

They demonstrated there and then that such a deflection was impossible. The paraphernalia of a Jewish life in Palestine, which the Jews had carried with them across the centuries, could not be remodelled by the attachment of a label, "For Use in Uganda." The Jews simply would not build a national homeland in Uganda. The obvious retort, that they were not building one in Palestine either, left the anti-Ugandists unmoved. The Jewish people was still in the paralysis of the exile, they said. It *would* build the Jewish Homeland in Palestine.

The upshot of the struggle was that, when the movement was split, the Zionists, not the Ugandists, remained in possession of the Congress. It was Herzl who had created the Congress; it was he who had introduced the Uganda proposal; his closest followers supported him. But it was they who broke away, to found another organization, and to seek another territory. Most of them returned afterwards, and these testify perhaps more than the old guard to the solidity of the structure erected by Herzl.

Herzl died, on July 3, 1904, in the midst of the struggle. It has been said that he was killed by the recalcitrance of the Zionists, whose opposition blocked his diplomatic efforts. But when we consider, at this distance, the complete picture of the period, it appears that his death was hastened by something quite different, namely, by the contradiction between his conscious aim and his historic purpose. He thought that, because the Charter for Palestine was further from his grasp than when he had started out, he was a failure; he did not know that he was the most successful leader the Jews have had in the history of their exile. We cannot guess what services he would have rendered if he had lived on, any more than we can guess what more Lincoln would have achieved if he had not been assassinated; but it is clear that Herzl fulfilled completely his historic mission. Perhaps his very death, in the prime of his manhood, was a necessary part of it. In any case, the legend of his personality dominates, in perfect expression, the idea of the Jewish Homeland. Sometimes we may regret that this legend eclipses the record of his actual achievement and has taken on a touch of the mythical. It might be better for us, and juster to him, to evaluate his work objectively. But perhaps it is necessary that the contradiction should continue even after his death.

CHAPTER NINE

Digression on an Astronomer

❀

FOR many years I was puzzled by some of the arguments which the opponents of the Uganda proposal had urged against its feasibility. I could understand them when they said: "The Jewish people won't put its heart into the project. It isn't enough that need should drive them. The creative power of need is limited. It does not tap the same deep sources as affirmation. Men and women don't do their best under compulsion; they must have the encouragement of a free ideal. A homeland will blossom only where Jews experience, in addition to need, an opening up of the play impulses." I could understand them, but I could not get a picture of what they meant. And when I asked them to paint it for me, as part of their concept of the future, they said:

"That's just the point. You can't paint it. Its details are unpredictable. In colonizing Palestine we shall have plans in many ways identical with plans for the colonizing of Uganda, or of the Argentine. We shall foresee so much and so much of the growth, no doubt inaccurately, but at least on the basis of calculable factors. The essential feature in the release of a national movement is the emergence of incalculable creative factors; of personalities and enthusiasms which cannot be hired, contracted for, or organized. It's like dealing with a genius. You can encourage him by providing him with a favorable environment of freedom; but you can't tie him to a schedule. One of the differences between Uganda, or Baron de Hirsch's Argentine, and Palestine is this: the former will be the point toward which oppression will *thrust* Jews; the latter will be the point toward which sentiment will also *attract* Jews. The former will be only an expression of frustration; the latter will also express liberation. Only those Jews will go to Uganda who can't go anywhere else; many will go to Palestine who could go elsewhere, but who choose Palestine because it sets off in them a certain excitement, with deep reverberations in the folkways, and with constructive values which cannot be tapped otherwise. You'll see!"

A time came when I began to see, and now I must try to convey to others, who may be as puzzled on this point as I was, exactly what I saw. I have chosen, out of my notes and recollections, one central incident, a rather odd and even trivial one, as symbol and illustration.

On one of my early visits to Palestine, a long, long time ago, I got into a public conveyance to take the trip from Tel Aviv to Jerusalem. I had been by that road before, the winding, ascending road which follows more or less the route of the camel-drivers, from the plain to the mountain heights. But neither on my tenth nor my fiftieth trip had I lost my delight in the journey, and I look forward still to watching the levels drop away behind me, and the rugged hills come sailing to meet me in swinging semi-circular motion as we take the hairpin bends to left and right. The ancient terraces on the slopes, the gray villages in the valleys or on the summits, the clusters of cacti, the alternations of the desert and the sown — they are much the same now as they were thousands of years ago. The scenery is wild and exhilarating, the air lucid. I sat on that trip, as I almost always do, in a trance of astonishment — astonishment that the journey is really lovelier than my recollection of it. On this occasion, however, we had barely traversed the foothills when I was brought to by a slap on the knee and a joyous exclamation. A book was thrust under my nose, and a voice exclaimed: "*Re-eh et zeh*, look at this!"

The man who had broken into my enchanted mood was a little, middle-aged, bespectacled fellow, with a wizened face, a bald head and childlike eyes which, as I saw in the brief glance I gave him, were flooded at the moment with something like ecstasy. I turned my attention to the book. It was a Hebrew geography; not of the kind already in use in the Palestinian schools, but a hundred years old, written by one of the *maskilim* whose name I have forgotten. A curious work, certainly, but not one to warrant the violent demonstration of which I had been the victim. The first thirty pages or so consisted of letters of commendation, from scholars, rabbis, philanthropists, men of affairs, communal leaders, poets, biblical commentators and educators, addressed to the writer, apparently in response to the prospectus on the work sent out before it was begun. All of them were moved, edified and delighted that he should have undertaken the enterprise. The last thirty pages consisted of letters of congratulation from the same rabbis, philanthropists, scholars, biblical commentators, etc., addressed to the writer on the occasion of the completion of the work. Once again they were

86

moved, edified and delighted; this time that he should have carried the enterprise to a successful conclusion. In between the layers of commendation and congratulation was sandwiched the geography.

A hasty examination revealed that the writer had drawn his information largely from Marco Polo, Benjamin of Tudela and other "recent" medieval explorers. An astronomical addendum seemed to have been taken from the *Almagest* or Maimonides. But not these had caused my companion to jump almost out of his skin. He directed my attention once more to the page he had first shown me. It contained, in one column, a table of latitude and longitude for the principal cities of the world. In the second column it gave the comparative times of day. But this man, who had written in Russia, had not used, as the Russian geographies did, the city of Poltava as the zero point, saying: "When it is midday in Poltava, it is eleven a. m. in Berlin, ten a. m. in London, five a. m. in New York, four p. m. in Bombay." He had not used Greenwich, as the British did, or Paris, like the French. Instead he had made the city of Jerusalem his zero point. "When it is midday in Jerusalem it is this and this hour in the other cities of the world."

I smiled, and said: "The funny things Jews do!"

"No, no," exclaimed my companion. "That isn't the point. Don't you understand that this man was anticipating the time when Jewish children would be going to a modern school in a rebuilt Palestine, and would have to orientate themselves geographically by Jerusalem?"

"He might at least have put in a word for Vasco da Gama and Copernicus," I objected.

"He did the best he could," said my companion. "There's no satisfying some people. Don't you think it's enough that he at least tried to contribute something to our school system? And that he foresaw, even if he couldn't properly meet, one of our requirements?"

I felt a pang of remorse for my seeming coolness, and it suddenly occurred to me that no one had ever prepared, for a future generation of Jewish schoolchildren, a list of comparative times of day with Juba, the capital of Uganda, as the zero point. I warmed up to my companion (I have forgotten his name; it was something like Hillel, and I will use that), and we spent the rest of the trip in friendly conversation. He told me that he was a secretary in some institution, but that his avocation was astronomy. Moreover, he was at work compiling and creating a modern Hebrew astronomical terminology, inasmuch as the classic language came into existence when things like binaries, nebulae, spectroscopic analysis, lunar librations, asteroids, solar coronas, stellar parallaxes and solar transits were unknown. He grew understandably excited when he discovered that, having a smattering of astronomy in addition to a smattering of Hebrew, I could appreciate some of his etymological ingenuities. In those days Hebrew was receiving all sorts of extensions: for of old there had been (for instance) no automobiles, therefore no clutches, differentials, spark plugs, gear shifts and the like; nor telephones, nor telegraphs, nor any of the modern appliances. Though, to be sure, for some of these, Hebrew adaptations had been devised before my friend Hillel came to Palestine.

I parted from him in Jerusalem, promising him, as I promised hundreds of interesting people I met, to look him up again. I never did. But this is not the whole of the story, not the complete symbol which I promised the reader. The rounding off came years later.

I was in Tel Aviv again, after a tour of the colonies of the Valley of Jezreel (always called, in Palestine, "the Emek," *the* Valley), of Galilee and of the Sharon plain. An immense gulf of time separated the land from the early struggles I have described, and others yet to be described; immense not by the count of days, but by the volume of change. Tel Aviv itself was as good an instance as any of this relativity of time. In less than thirty years the tumultuous city on the sand dunes already had its periods, in architectural styles, in economic tendencies and in types of immigrational problem: the crenellated — and somewhat dilapidated — High School, or *Gymnasium*, at the foot of Herzl Street, belonged to the early, silly, functionless romantic of the (first) pre-war period; the older houses on the Ahad Ha-'am Street were taken over from the Arab city style; the jerry-built homes on the side streets of the Allenby Road belonged to the feverish Fourth Wave episode; the well-to-do section called Lev Tel Aviv ("Heart of Tel Aviv") was reminiscent of Brownsville; and in the newer sections German architecture suggested little annexes to provincial world fairs. Economically the first residential period (now practically forgotten) had been succeeded by the mixed commercial and industrial; there had been the dangerous boom of the Fourth Wave; there had followed the stabilization, the expansion of labor, the building of the fair, the creation of the harbor. The streets of Tel Aviv had received and had swallowed the predominance of Yiddish and of Russian. They were now slowly engulfing German, and digesting it, as they had digested the others, into Hebrew. You had to forget fast, and learn fast, in Tel Aviv.

On the evening of my return from the Emek I went to see a performance of Stefan Zweig's *Jeremiah* by the *Habimah* players. Surely Stefan Zweig, the uprooted Jew who was to take his own life in exile when the world to which he had given himself crumbled about him, never dreamed, when he wrote this play, that some day it would be given, in the original language of the prophet he portrayed, in the land where the prophet had lived, by and for the returned descendants of the prophet and his contemporaries. I might perhaps have made this circumstance — and for that matter many others — the illustration of the unpredictable, creative evocations which distinguish a national from a sociological movement. For who could have foreseen a Stanislavsky and a Zemach in Moscow preparing a dramatic troupe of the first order which would prove to be one of the spiritual constituents of a Jewish Homeland? But I have not yet reached the point of this chapter.

I went out of the theater, along streets thronged with Tel Avivians, among crowds of gay young people, past cafés jammed with customers. The movie-houses and meeting halls were emptying. At the corner of Allenby Street and the seafront I ran into an American journalist, fresh from the west, and we walked to and fro along the beach while the crowds dwindled and the lights in Jaffa across the bay were extinguished one by one. In a pause of the conversation I happened to stop and look up at the sky, which was, as always between the rainy seasons, marvelously clear. I noticed then that an astronomical event, of minor significance but of great beauty, was in preparation. The gibbous and brilliant moon was close to Spica, a star of the first magnitude in the constellation of Virgo. The whole sky was revolving, against the diurnal motion of the earth, to the right; but the moon, in her slower motion about the earth, was crawling leftward through the constellations. The illumined half of the moon pointed right, toward the long-vanished sun, the unilluminated and invisible half, or rather less than half, pointed left. Some time that night an occultation would take place; this is to say, the invisible bulk of the moon would blot out, at a given instant, and with startling, instantaneous effect, the star Spica. Now that, as every amateur astronomer will attest, is something to be seen, especially through a telescope.

I explained all this to my friend, and told him that I had a telescope at home; and if I only knew what time the occultation would take place, I would treat him to the celestial spectacle at my expense. Very much at my expense, since only one of us could have his eye glued to the telescope at the climactic moment. Such are the enthusiasms of Zionists and amateur astronomers. But how was I to know when the occultation would take place? And where, in God's name, was I to find out? Now if this were only New York, I would surely be able to ring up someone with a Nautical Almanac. And failing that, there was always some newspaper information service. But we were in Tel Aviv, a great city no doubt, but after all . . .

My friend said: "The other day, walking through the *Shechunat ha-Po'alim* (the Workers' Quarter at the seaward end of the Rothschild Boulevard) I saw a telescope mounted on a roof. If you're so set on the occultation, let's go there. The owner of the telescope may know."

"At this hour of the night?" I answered, dubiously. "If he's as hipped on the subject as you are, he'll be up right enough."

So we set out along the Yarkon Street, parallel with the beach, and came to the Workers' Quarter. There, sure enough, on the flat roof of one of the single-storied houses, a telescope was mounted on a tripod. No one was standing beside it, but a light was shining in one of the windows below.

"*Vive Tel Aviv!*" I exclaimed. But the best was yet to come.

We knocked timidly at the door, and a woman came out. I asked whether the *ba'al ha-bayit*, or whoever else it was owned the telescope, was in. She shook her head. The *ba'al ha-bayit*, the householder, her husband, was the owner of the telescope. But he was a night-worker, and was away till morning.

What a pity! I was about to apologize and withdraw, when the woman said:

"Before he went out, an hour ago, he left a message with me. He said: 'It may be, it *may* be, though it is not at all likely — and still one can't tell — it may be, and one must always be prepared, that someone will come to the house because there's a telescope on the roof, and ask you what time a certain event will take place."

She produced from her pocket a slip of paper, and continued:

"What that event is, he did not tell me, as I know nothing about the stars. But whatever it is, I was to advise anyone who asked about it, that it will take place" — she looked closely at the paper in the light streaming out from the kitchen — "it will take place at eleven seconds and fifty-three minutes after one o'clock. If anyone wanted to use the telescope at that time, he was welcome to it."

When I was able to catch my breath, I thanked her. No, we did not want to use the telescope. I had one at home. I only wanted the information. I asked her also to convey our thanks to her husband — to *Adon* — "Hillel," she said.

It was my man of the geography book.

But by now the excitement of the occultation had been displaced in me by another excitement.

"The absurdity of it!" I said, exultantly, as we walked back. "The utter, delicious and heartening absurdity of it! That's what makes a homeland. Not just land, agriculture, funds, factories, experts, administrators and blueprints, but cranks, mystics, vegetarians, bibliophiles, poets — and amateur astronomers who remember that someone might want to know the minute and split second of an occultation. A thing like this couldn't have happened in Uganda."

"No, it couldn't," said my astonished friend. "Why should it?"

CHAPTER TEN

Men from Nowhere

❀

THE essential difference, then, between a philanthropic enterprise like Baron de Hirsch's, large though
it was — probably the largest of its kind on record —
and a nationally rooted movement, lay in the capacity
of the latter to mobilize men from nowhere. No name
other than de Hirsch's is now associated in Jewish memory with the history of the ICA. It is highly probable
that no name other than Herzl's would have survived
in connection with Uganda, if that territory had developed a settlement of the same size as the Argentinian —
which it is not likely to have done. But a great gallery
of names, of quite extraordinary men, already adds to
the human interest of the Jewish homeland. They are
worth knowing for their own sakes. They are universal
types of creative genius.

Just as interesting and provocative were countless men
and women from nowhere who were drawn into the
Jewish homeland by its suggestive and evocative power,
but whose names have been absorbed into the national
anonymity. There is not room in this book for honorable
mention of more than a fraction of the known and the
obscure. The subject is raised at this point because we

are now on the threshold of the transformation of the Palestinian enterprise from the philanthropic to the national; we are on the eve of the long-delayed mass awakening. Only one more interval separates us from it, to be covered in the next chapter. Meanwhile I have chosen, almost at random, a few more illustrations of "unpredictables," confining myself to those I have known in person.

There was a man called Joshua Chankin living in Palestine when I first came there. He was then already in late middle age. No matter whom I asked for a guide, or for someone who would make up the best itinerary for a tour of the country, the answer always was: "Joshua Chankin! There isn't a nook or cranny in the country he doesn't know. There isn't a stone he doesn't remember. He's your man."

An extraordinary man this Chankin turned out to be. Tall, gaunt, bearded, with hair falling abundantly over his neck, and with a Christlike face. For all his nearly sixty years, his frame was powerful, his eyes alert, his spirit unquenched. He was an old-timer, a contemporary of the *Bilus*, with whom he and his family had come out. There were other Chankins in Palestine, brothers and sisters of Joshua, but he was *the* Chankin. From the first day of his arrival he had set himself a special task, among others: to become the land buyer of the Jews. An important and difficult task, for it entailed two qualifications at least. You had to know the land, and you had to know the Arabs. You will read in the early records of the pioneers how, through lack of these qualifications in the negotiators, more than one deal and more than one settlement came to grief. To acquire these qualifications Chankin began, from the moment

95

of his arrival, to acquire a knowledge of the land, the language and the inhabitants. Over and over again he traversed the land, north to south, east to west, diagonally, criss-cross, zigzag and in labyrinths, till he had covered every lost valley, every peak and *wadi* and wilderness, every village and townlet, every settlement of fellaheen and every grazing-ground of the Bedouin. He travelled on foot, on horseback and by carriage. He went usually alone and always unarmed, except for a big stick, which became in time as famous as himself. "How are you, Joshua?" they asked. "And how's your stick?"

He got to know the Arabs, perhaps better than they knew themselves; the Arabs of the coastal cities, the effendis and muftis and moneylenders, the tillers of the soil, the half-wild tribes of the Jordan valley. They liked him, because he spoke their language in more than the literal sense of that phrase. They called him affectionately, *Abu Saar*, "Father of Hair," because of his beard and locks. They welcomed him to their homes, their huts and their tents. It was always a delight to converse with him.

The secret of negotiations with the Arabs, he told me, was not merely patience, though Chankin was inexhaustibly, almost inhumanly patient. It was, rather, a trick of deriving pleasure from negotiation as such. "You westerners," he said to me, "think that the purpose of a business deal is the business deal itself. You don't think of a business deal as an exercise in human relations, pleasurable for its own sake, whether the deal is consummated or not." And Chankin could carry on the palavers in the preliminaries to a purchase over a period of years. A sale was a ceremonial, a cultural exercise, almost a religious service, to be prolonged even when the understanding had been reached. You approached the subject with ingenious indirectness; the remoter the opening from the intention, the more it was liked and admired. It was unbecoming, among decent folk, to fall at once into a business conversation. You exchanged greetings; you offered a little dissertation on the goodness of God; you discussed the crops; you listened to a lyric on horses; you praised the beauty of the sky. And then if, with no intention on anyone's part, one happened somehow, to the mutual astonishment of both parties, to be talking about the high value of a certain piece of land (this from the putative seller), or its unfortunate defects (this from the putative buyer), you suddenly came to, hastily changed the subject, and returned to Providence, horses, crops and the celestial panorama.

You parted, with noble salutations and flourishes, and met again a few weeks or months later; and again, most annoyingly, the piece of land cropped up in the middle of an edifying exchange of lofty sentiments. That piece of land, now; it must probably be superfluous to its present owner. It was uncultivated, perhaps uncultivable, was it not? Indeed? No one had ever said that before. As to its being superfluous, who could tell? After all, the owner had lived there, he and his father and his fathers' fathers, since el Burak set his hoof on the rock in the Aksa. Superfluity was a matter of sentiment not less than of utility — not that, Allah forbid, the utility of this piece of land had ever been called in question before. And so the conversation drifted away once more to indifferent matters — and was resumed at the next accidental encounter.

Quiet, soft-spoken, dignified, shrewd, with a *Litvak* sense of humor (though he was no *Litvak*, his home having been Krementchug, in deep Russia), Chankin had the manner of it down to the last flourish of the hand, the last good-humored shrugging of the shoulder. He bought more land than any other agent in Palestine, perhaps as much as all the other agents put together. He bought land in the Valley of Jezreel from the absentee Sursuks, whose fathers had obtained, by graft, and for a song, great stretches of good but abandoned soil from the Turkish administration of 1870. They sold it for millions of dollars. He bought land in the swampy Huleh and on the heights above Haifa, where Hadar ha-Carmel grew up, the new Jewish suburb. He negotiated for Arthur Ruppin (of whom more below) the purchase of the first stretch of sand dunes north of Jaffa, where the city of Tel Aviv was to grow. He bought for the PICA, for the Zionist Organization, for the National Fund, for associations and for private individuals. He had other achievements to his credit; he founded colonies, he fought Baron de Rothschild's misdirected philanthropies in the days when these philanthropies were threatening to become an obstruction, to the national development, he helped establish an agricultural bank, and he threw himself into the struggle for the introduction of Jewish labor into the old colonies. But he is remembered as Chankin the land-buyer; and he was that until his death in 1941.

He is the representative of the romantic time, though he lived well on into the scientific time, of which the chief representative was Arthur Ruppin. The two men are linked by their association in the history of Zionist colonization, and by the perfect contrast of their personalities. Ruppin did not come to Palestine until 1907. Nor was he brought to the country on the wings of a picturesque fantasy. His enthusiasm was of the cool, determined and methodical kind. In appearance, too, he might have been "typed" by a dramatic director as a foil to Chankin, with whom he worked closely for more than three decades. He was a small, neat, clean-shaven, dapper man, wholly unpicturesque. He carried, instead of a big, gnarled stick, a portfolio full of statistics. He had behind him, when he came to Palestine, a successful academic and business career. His first book on the sociology of the Jews — which was to be followed by many others — was already a standard work, though he was not yet thirty years of age. He looked and talked like a typical German official of the old school. He was of course interested in the Jewish people. He had begun to weigh in his mind the possibility of performing a useful task in Palestine. He did not throw himself headlong into the enterprise. He came out first on a visit; he made a careful survey; he satisfied himself that he could do a good job; and he accepted the offer of the Zionist Organization to become the director of the Palestine Department which was about to be opened.

The reports of Ruppin to the Zionist Congresses, and his papers on the progress of Palestinian agriculture, are models of calm, objective, statistical method. They are dull to the point of anaesthesia. At the same time they are as exciting as the catalogue of the days in the first chapter of Genesis. They deal with soils, yields, breeds of cattle, number of eggs per hen and liters of milk per cow, agricultural loans, types of settlement, the economy of diversified farming, comparative costs of colonization in Greece, Australia, California and Palestine, agrarian policy in Prussia, and costs of reclamation. They also deal with the miracle of the rebirth of a people.

Ruppin's frosty exterior was not a pose; it was nevertheless a deception. He might indeed have said to himself and others that he was drawn to Palestine by the prospect of a piece of work to be done. If that had been all, he could have found bigger pieces of work to do in other countries. He believed himself to be, and he was, coldbloodedly practical. Yet, instead of taking service with a great government, which he might easily have done, he was drawn irresistibly to this corner of the Near East.

The unrhetorical manner was a defensive cover for a sensitive imagination. It was Ruppin who persuaded a few Jewish teachers, officials and merchants living in Jaffa, to found the suburb which became Tel Aviv. He bought up the empty grounds almost up to the river Yarkon. There was a great hullabaloo about "Ruppin's folly"— miles and miles of waste, uninhabitable land; it took nearly twenty years to disclose that this incomprehensible fantasy was the most far-sighted step taken in the history of modern Palestine. In the pursuit of purely practical methods, Ruppin became involved in violent theoretical disputes. He was accused of leftist leanings because of his promotion of the collective system of colonization. He answered, in all honesty, that he was always looking for the best human material to work with, took it wherever he found it, and happened to find it in the socialistic *Halutzim*. He had been engaged by the Zionist Organization to direct one of the sections of an emergent homeland. He was not concerned with theory, but with results.

So he was. He looked for maximum results with the

means at his disposal. Nevertheless, his subtle understanding of the psychological power behind the drive
for collectives bespoke something beyond the capacities
which we usually call "practical." So his election of
Palestine as the field of his life's work bespoke something
beyond the search for a field of effectiveness. This is
what makes him one with Joshua Chankin. Had there
been no Jewish Homeland in the making, had there
been only philanthropic enterprises, Chankin would
have remained in Russia and become a revolutionary,
Ruppin in Germany, to become an academician or
administrator.

The movement reached into deep levels of sentimental
association in men, and into concealed or open stores of
temperament. It is impossible to imagine someone like
Shmarya Levin touched off by any other enterprise
than the Return. His incredible persuasive powers, his
brilliant dialectic skill, could not have found elsewhere,
in Jewish life, the unique provocation constituted for
him by the Zionist theme. We cannot, for instance,
imagine Menachem Mendel Ussischkin devoting to any
other social project the monomaniac obstinacy which
he bestowed upon Palestine for fifty years. Henrietta
Szold would have been a noble figure under any circumstances; but what theme other than the Palestinian
would have provided so perfect a setting for her self-
fulfilment? Ahad Ha'am was destined to become a
notable thinker, whatever the period of Jewish history
into which he was born. But, born as he was into the
period of the Return, he would have been condemned
to spiritual futility had he not centered his intellectual
life on the national renaissance. What would Vladimir
Jabotinsky have been to us without Zionism? Or if we

consider the foremost — as many believe him to be — of our contemporaries, Chaim Weizmann, we may be certain that, but for the movement which swallowed him up, he would have been just one of the world's distinguished chemists. And so the list may be lengthened almost indefinitely.

I have called this chapter "Men from Nowhere." The title is not meant to imply that if they had not found the Zionist arena they would have been nobodies. That would not be true either of them or of the "anonymous" ones, the "weavers in secret" as Chaim Nachman Bialik has called them. It is meant to imply that in our time there has not existed any other Jewish enterprise which could have mobilized them in a single aim. They come from "nowhere" in the sense that an Edmond de Rothschild and a Baron de Hirsch would have looked for them in vain to represent the magic element of attractiveness in their well-meant and generously subsidized plans for the improvement of the lot of the Jewish people.

The test of democracy in a nation or movement is the degree of congruence between the fulfilment of distinguished careers and the longings of the common folk. Where the first occurs at the expense of the second, or irrelevantly to them, life goes awry. The last title of greatness must be withheld where the congruence does not exist, even if we are confronted with extraordinary talent; and it must be bestowed in the presence of this congruence even when the talent is less than extraordinary. Many persons not at all in sympathy with the idea of a Jewish Homeland in Palestine have expressed astonishment at its record of achievement; and all the more when they remember the seemingly unpropitious beginnings and the slowness of the initial response. Whether or not it is a subject for astonishment, the phenomenon can be understood only as a demonstration of democracy, and I have attempted here, with what I am afraid is indifferent success, to indicate the elements of this particular manifestation of democracy. Undoubtedly it will read to some like a piece of propaganda; but it is primarily propaganda for democracy rather than for Palestine. In any case the story cannot be told without an accompanying explanation, and this is the only one I can think of.

CHAPTER ELEVEN

The Days of the PICA

◈

THE PICA (Palestine Jewish Colonization Association) was, it will be remembered, the institution to which Baron Edmond de Rothschild transferred the direction of his Palestinian enterprises in 1899. The framework of the institution was Baron de Hirsch's ICA, or rather that little segment of it which was devoted to work in Palestine. Rothschild had begun to take note of the criticisms levelled against his administration. He was still a long way from the fuller understanding of Zionism which came to him in his latter years; but he was already aware of the inadequacy of his privately managed philanthropy. By concentrating the direction in the hands of the PICA, a quasi-public body, he relaxed, to some extent, the pressure of his personality on the administrators and farmers. Incomplete though it was, this voluntary abdication was a remarkable moral achievement; it was, at the same time, a partial though unformulated recognition of the need of the democratic background in the colonization of Palestine.

Practical work in Palestine by the World Zionist Organization as such did not begin until 1907, a full decade after the calling of the First Congress. There was, it is true, a certain activity on the part of the Anglo-Palestine Company, the banking subsidiary of the Jewish Colonial Trust; but it is not unfair to leave that out of the account. It is customary to say that the reason for this long hiatus between declaration and performance lies in the particular twist which Herzl gave to the direction of Zionist affairs in the formative years of the Organization. He was primarily concerned, as we have seen, with the creation of the perfect political setting for the building of the Jewish Homeland. The settlement of a thousand Jews more or less in Palestine did not mean anything to him. Of course it is true that this almost exclusive emphasis on the diplomatic and political had a deterrent effect on the work. Nevertheless it is wrong to saddle it with the major responsibility for the delay. The Russian Zionists, though part of the Congress, had retained a certain degree of autonomy in the Odessa Committee, which was concerned exclusively with practical work. But Russian Jewry was not responding yet; it was not contributing, in funds, more than a fraction of what Rothschild was pouring into the PICA; and in man-power it did not begin to contribute significantly — after the First Wave of 1882 — until 1904. Nor were the contributions of other scattered Palestine societies, in western countries, at all representative of a national movement. Actually Zionism did not get under way until the years preceding the First World War.

Meanwhile the field was occupied, literally and figuratively, by the PICA. The level of its administration was considerably higher than that of the privately owned institution of Baron de Rothschild. Not that Rothschild did not have the final say in the PICA; not that he was not, in the last analysis, the ultimate benefactor and authority. But there had come a change. The officials of the PICA had more method. They saw the problem in larger outline. A long list of settlements stands to the credit of the PICA during the period under review: Mechsah, Yema, Milchamiah, Kineret, Mizpah and others. Errors in judgment at least had educational value. The gradual shift from the policy of quickly-acquired independence for individual farmers meant the abandonment, in part of mono- and money-agriculture. Baron de Rothschild, through the PICA, bore the cost of the uprooting of large areas of vineyards. The land was re-planted. Orange culture was extended; the planting of wheat, barley, sesame, fodder, almonds and peaches was encouraged. There was considerable experimenting, and there were flurries of enthusiasm for this or that particular culture, with consequent over-emphases, which led to failures, each of which, however, left some positive value behind it. The merits of crops were argued, the arguments led to demonstrations, and meanwhile the colonists were learning. One can read in a book that the orange tree yields in three years, the almond in five, the olive in five to twelve years; that olive has the advantage of longevity — it will flourish for a century or more — plus that of needing little attention, while orange has the advantage of larger immediate returns. Olive will give you food, oil, soap; orange will bring money. One can read in a book about the market for rubber and bamboo, for aromatic oils from roses, for raw silk, for which mulberry trees are needed. But between reading in a book and carrying out the experiment there is an enormous difference. For skills and temperaments and even social outlook enter into the actual experiment.

The social outlook of the PICA administration played a great part in the formation of its colonies and the direction of experiments. On the one hand there was the Baron's anxiety to establish an independent Jewish farmer class in the minimum of time. On the other hand there was the slowly growing realization that this emphasis on quick returns was narrowing the prospect of wider settlement. A farmer encouraged to think only in terms of his own economic advancement was by that token discouraged from thinking in terms of a national regeneration. A later pioneer records in his book how, looking for work in one of the older colonies, and pleading less for himself than for the cause generally, he received the answer, from a *Jewish Palestinian* farmer: "But I am not a Zionist! I am a farmer! I have nothing to do with national causes!"

The PICA became aware of this problem and tried to meet it, at least partially, in its own way — very different from the method of the Zionist Organization in later years. It opened a school at Sedjera. But it made the mistake of confirming the new workers in the old outlook. The trained men were given the school land, in small parcels. They were given the necessary capital, to be repaid on easy terms: and so a new group of individualist farmers was created, again under conditions which discouraged the employment of Jewish labor.

The PICA was not able, in those years, to transform itself into a national agency. Whether or not it realized that a Jewish land-working class could be created only by national or nationalized methods, it retained to the end its emphasis on individualism. And yet, as I have said, it learned. It was a remarkable demonstration of nationalist sentiment when Baron de Rothschild founded, at the close of the First World War, the two collectivist colonies of Tel Hai and K'far Gileadi, near the Syrian border. No one would have believed him capable of such an act. But he perceived that, if those points were to be occupied and held, it would be absurd to appeal to self-interest. Only a collective group inspired by the ideal of the Jewish Homeland would answer the call. Joseph Trumpeldor and his comrades went up to Tel Hai to work the soil. He and six companions were killed during a raid by the Halsa tribe; but the soil has remained Jewish to this day.

It is impossible to determine whether the time of the domination of the PICA, namely, the years preceding the First World War, was ripe for a complete nationalist effort. But it is clear that much was lost because of the individualist outlook of Baron de Rothschild. Where the colonists were successful, resistance developed to change. The younger generation was not integrated with the life of Palestine. The women were not workers. A miniature planter aristocracy developed, with Arab workers dominant in the colonies. Snobbery crept in, class consciousness, a provincial hankering after fashionableness. It was not an uncommon thing for the well-to-do colonist to spend two or three months of the year in Europe. In this atmosphere the younger sons, who would not inherit the estate, drifted to the cities, or left the country.

These were the negative elements in the successful colonies. In the unsuccessful colonies a spirit of discouragement prevailed. Arthur Ruppin reported, in 1907, that many of these colonies looked like old people's homes. There was no follow-up. The children saw how their parents had wasted their lives in a futile effort to create a Jewish farmer class, and refused to sacrifice their own lives to the same unattainable ideal. There was no room for them in Palestine, and certainly none for newcomers. In Petah Tikvah 1,200 Arabs were employed at a daily wage of five or six piasters (twenty-five to thirty cents). The Jewish workers, mostly in positions of responsibility, were less than a tenth of that number. The same or similar proportions were to be found in Rehovoth, Rishon le-Zion and elsewhere. The colonies, then, were Jewish in ownership and management, Arab in character. The children of the well-to-do colonists would not become workers on the land; they did not want to. The children of the poor colonists may have wanted to; they could not.

Thus the conditions had been created for the struggle which was to follow with the long-delayed awakening of practical Zionism.

CHAPTER TWELVE

The Religion of Labor

❊

THE Second Wave set in for Palestine toward the close of the year 1904. Its character, and its lasting effect on the structure of Jewish Palestine, can be understood only in the light of its origins.

The Russian pogroms of 1881 had followed a period of comparative tranquillity, and broke upon a Jewry in which the modernized element was weak and formless. The pogroms which began with Kishineff, in 1903, were the climax of a long period of bitter persecution, segregation, discrimination and repression; they broke upon a Jewry in which the modernized elements were strong and had crystallized out clearly. By "modernized" is meant here educated by events and by discussion to meet realities in contemporaneous terms. The programs might differ; they might be mutually exclusive; they might even be hostile; but they spoke the language of the time. They were interpenetrated with current ideologies.

Hatred of Czarism burned deep in Russian Jewry; the reaction to it ranged all the way from the extremes of flight (whether by apostasy or migration) to the extremes of action (whether by revolution or Zionism).

In between were variations of adaptation. The orthodox masses waited for the storm to pass; the Russifying upper economic strata waited for western liberalism to penetrate to Russia. All the discussions round the Jewish problem with which we of the middle twentieth century are familiar were already familiar to Russian Jewry fifty years ago. They will be found set forth completely in Sholom Aleichem's novel, *In the Storm*.

A superficial analysis would classify Zionism with flight rather than with action. That was, and still remains, the argument of revolutionaries and even of liberals. But flight is not just a question of motion. It is a question of "from" or "to." Apostasy was flight *from* Judaism, not *to* Christianity. Migration was *from* Russia, not *to* any particular country. Zionism was motion *toward* a difficult, hazardous and imaginative creative task.

A similar revolutionary ardor characterized those young Jews who elected to fight Czarism on the Russian field, and thus incidentally help solve, as they thought, the Jewish problem, and those who sought, instead, to create a new Jewish life in a Jewish Homeland, free from the social injustices both of Russia and of other countries. Just as the Russo-Japanese war did not create the revolutionary forces which scored their short-lived triumph in 1905, so the pogroms of 1903–1905 did not create the Zionist forces which brought the Second Wave to Palestine. They had been accumulating, in both instances, for generations. Their similarity is attested by the fact that there was a continuous crossing of the lines. Zionists have gone back from Palestine to Russia because they were not satisfied with the progress of Jewish Palestine; revolutionaries (like Manya Sho-

111

chat, in the period now under survey, and Pinchas Ruthenberg, the builder of the Palestine Electrical Works, a decade later) came over into the Zionist movement.

The Second Wave may be looked upon as a resurrection of the *Bilus*. It was proletarian in outlook, middle-class in origin, though chiefly of the lower middle class. Like the *Bilu* movement it despised the mercantile prison house of Jewry, and exalted the religion of labor. But as a movement, this segment of Zionism was more self-conscious, of ampler proportions, and better equipped than the *Bilus*.

It was interpenetrated with the ideal of a cooperative form of society. So, of course, were the *Bilus*. But in the thirty-year interval between the *Bilus* and the Second Wave, an education in the spirit of organization had taken place. The *Bilus* were unable to break through, in part, at least, because they lacked the sense of form; in part, too, because no wider social impulse, from an active Zionist movement, came to their aid. The immigrants of 1904 and 1905 found little help when they landed. But by 1907, the Zionist Organization was in action, weakly enough at first, to be sure, but with gathering strength.

They found, too, what was painfully absent in the *Bilus* — the man who was to become their symbol. His name was Aaron David Gordon (he is always referred to by the Hebrew initials of his given names, Aleph Daled Gordon). He was middle-aged — almost fifty — when he abandoned a position he had held for twenty-seven years as an administrator, a white-collar worker, on one of the estates of Baron Guinzburg, and threw in his lot with Palestine. He, too, was one of the "men from nowhere." He chose to illustrate, in his own life, the process of the occupational restratification which had to accompany the national rebirth in Palestine. Heroically he worked out, on his own aging body, the painful transformation which was demanded of a whole people.

They sometimes call him the Tolstoi of Palestine, and there was something in his patriarchal appearance which recalled the sage of Yasnaya Polyana. But the parallel is unjust to both men. Aleph Daled Gordon was not a great artist like Tolstoi. Tolstoi, on the other hand, had not the natural simplicity of Aleph Daled Gordon. The impressions I have gathered from those who remember Gordon make me think of the strange figure of Anton Karataev, in *War and Peace*. In middle and old age Aleph Daled shared with the workers the hardships of the pioneering time, wielding pickaxe and mattock side by side with the young folk, radiating cheerfulness and delighting in simple work. He was, however, quite unlike Karataev in another way; Gordon was a writer and thinker, deeply concerned with the inner problems of the Jewish people. But he did not write because of an artistic impulse. He wrote as he talked, to explain himself to his fellow-workers.

He believed that no social movement had meaning if it did not change the life of the individual while it sought to change the life of the social organism. Therefore he did not subscribe to the escapist theories which wait for an improvement in the social order to bring about an improvement in the individual. If Zionism did not affect him affirmatively in its application, it could not affect the Jewish people affirmatively in its final success. His own life was an illustration of the

Zionist revitalization of the Jewish people. He had become a worker, and had found it good. Labor, the dedication of one's body to creation, was the proper function of man. Labor is everything. Even culture is, at bottom, the sum of the way we handle things. Give *all* to labor, was his cry. How, he asked, could the Jewish people fulfil its destiny in its own land if it did not literally work that destiny out?

There was an element of exaggeration in this emphasis on physical toil. It led to a somewhat grudging admission of the usefulness of the executive and manager and organizer, as though these were necessary evils. But the exaggeration was an inevitable feature of the revolt against the over-intellectualized, over-mercantilized life of the exile. A people compelled by persecution to live by its wits had forgotten the exaltation of manual labor as it had been known to the sages of old. Here was the reaction.

Thus national necessity and ethical impulse fused in the rush for land and labor. The resistance came from the old colonies. There labor was not considered noble in itself. If anything was a necessary evil, it was labor. The high moral tone which the newcomers took irritated the colonists of the PICA. The newcomers demanded jobs not only because they had to live, but because they represented a regenerative principle in Jewish life — a regenerative principle which, by implication, was beyond the character of the established colonists. They demanded jobs in the name of the national renaissance.

That kind of talk was hard to listen to — especially when Arab labor was at hand, much cheaper, and without any such moral pretensions. The old-timers, the men who had gone through the hard early days of Petah Tikvah and Rishon and Zichron Ya'akov smiled contemptuously at the young enthusiasts. "You talk big!" they said. "*You* are the carriers of the Jewish rebirth! But *we* are the people who left the cities and became farmers. How long will we remain farmers if we open the colonies to you?" And the others answered: "The Baron's money gave you your chance. Now you have become plantation owners the needs of the exile mean nothing to you. Some of you were idealists in the old days of the *Bilu* movement. What has happened to the ideals?"

So the colonists called the workers *Shmendriks*, tatterdemalions, ne'er-do-wells, — also revolutionaries and anarchists; and the workers retorted with *Burzhuks!* and *Boazim!* Boaz, the wealthy farmer of Bethlehem, who married Ruth and became through her one of the forebears of the Messiah, somehow emerged as the symbol of the middle-class colonist! It is a little touching to think that the workers turned to the Bible for the terminology of their economic struggle, though the instance quoted does seem to bear rather hard on Boaz. It is also illustrative of the relationship in which this social antagonism stood to a unifying past. The land and its memories had drawn both elements out of the ghettos, had drawn the middle and the working class with equal strength. The land and its memories had to resolve the struggle.

We must neither blur nor overemphasize the bitterness of the fight. The upbuilding of Palestine has not been a sweet idyll throughout. There was a great bitterness between the old colonists and the workers. There were strikes, demonstrations, picketing; there were arrests by the Arab police; there were riots. On the other hand, the PICA, the inspiration, support and guide of the old colonies, gave a collectivist group its first chance to demonstrate the practicability of its methods.

This was in 1908, four years after the beginning of the Second Wave. Manya Wulbischevitch (afterwards Shochat) was one of the leading spirits of this group, and here we may note an instance of the difference between the idealism of the *Bilus* and that of the 1904 immigrants. Manya Shochat had learned something about organization before she came out to Palestine. She had worked with a collective in Pinsk. She was not then a Zionist. She tells, in her story in *The Plough Woman*, how she came out to Palestine because of a trick played on her by her brother, and how, after she had seen the country, there grew up in her "a deep and passionate love" for it, which has lasted through all her life. But the collective in Pinsk had taught her certain social techniques that the *Bilus* never knew.

Fifteen men and three women made up the collective which received from the PICA management of the farm of Sedjera, the first contract of its kind in the Jewish colonization of the country. The farm had been running at a deficit, in spite of the employment of Arab labor. The collective took over the field and dairy work on the same terms as the Arabs, that is, in return for one-fifth of the harvest. And it worked for a year and a half successfully. Krause, the director of Sedjera, was helpful, sympathetic and cooperative. And the reasons for the comparative success of the collective illuminate the future story of Palestinian colonization.

Instead of attempting to compete with Arab labor on

its low level of subsistence, the collective met its problems by organization. A communal kitchen was set up, so that workers did not have to eat out. The effect was both a saving in money and a lifting of the morale. The work was not handed out, as it had been till then, by the management. It was discussed at a meeting of the workers, and assumed by them. When there was not enough work for all, a member of the collective would not wait around idly. He would take on work outside the collective, and contribute his wages to the common fund.

Through it all ran the constant themes of the "religion of labor" and the redemption of the land. The experiment at Sedjera was watched with intense interest throughout the country, and its continuance for a year and a half was looked upon as a great triumph. It dissolved without a deficit! That was hardly enough to build a future on; but it was a success. It was something the *Bilus* had not been able to achieve.

This was the period when the Zionist Organization was making its first experiments in collective settlements, and we shall deal with them at greater length. But many years were to pass before a balance was established in the country between private initiative and collectivist enterprises. The problem was to be agitated at the Zionist Congresses. New conditions were to emerge in Palestine, and other factors than the immediate economic demands and ideals of the colonists and workers were to come into play: the pressure of numbers from the diaspora, the question of security in the country, the growth of a strong labor party in the Zionist movement, the creation of the city cooperatives, the establishment of a network of economic institutions by organized Jewish labor in Palestine and, above all, the growth of the Jewish National Fund — all these are interwoven with the story of the land collectives. But the tiny beginnings of this entire aspect of the rebuilding of Palestine go back to the first definite crystallization of modern Zionist method and philosophy, and the clearest utterances belong to that early period.

CHAPTER THIRTEEN

Ha-Shomer

🌼

KIBBUSH AVODAH, the conquest of labor, was the slogan of the young men and women of the Second Wave. It had many facets of meaning: the conquest of the labor position, that is, of a place on the labor market; self-conquest in labor, that is, the transformation of the individual and the people; and conquest of the economic problem, that is, of the structure and occupational distribution of the Jewish settlement.

Connected with *Kibbush Avodah*, or we might say an extension of it, was the conquest of the right to self-defense. This surely seems strange to us today; but nothing recalls more vividly the limited vision and inspiration of the old colonists than the obstinate resistance which they presented to the idea of Jewish self-defense. From the beginning they had accustomed themselves to the thought of Arab guards on their property. In part it was a hangover of long exile experience; Jews never having exercised the functions of government, Jewish guards and policemen were oddities. It certainly was not lack of personal courage in the old colonists which moved them to hire Arabs as watchmen. People without personal courage do not go into ill-governed territories with a tradition of banditry. It was part of the general absence of that national inspiration which alone could produce a revolution in habits and outlook.

The problem is as old as statecraft itself: the foreign mercenary or the native militia. Over and over again historians and philosophers point out that a citizenry which must hire its defenders from the outside cannot long endure in freedom. Perhaps the invocation of big historic examples, like ancient Rome and mediaeval Italy will strike the reader as a trifle bombastic in connection with our subject: that of a few Jewish colonists and a handful of Jewish boys from the ghetto. Nevertheless the principle is exactly the same, and those who have difficulty in recognizing a principle before it involves a few hundred thousand individuals will see this one vindicated in the later history of the Jewish Homeland.

The Jewish colonists were, of course, not satisfied with the Arab guards or watchmen. What employers of foreign arms ever are? The guards were, in many places, somewhat more than complacent toward the primitive acquisitive instincts of surrounding villagers or visiting herdsmen. Nowhere were they prepared to risk life and limb in defense of Jewish property. To the regular wages they paid their guards, the colonists added the regular item — which fluctuated with the character of the guards — of inevitable losses by collusion.

The paradox of the situation lay in the following: Jewish colonists would not employ Jewish guards, in part because the Jewish guards were, ideologically and as an economic group, at odds with the colonists; nevertheless, they were perfectly aware that the Jewish guards would be much more reliable and devoted than the Arab guards. The Jewish guards, on the other hand, despised the property psychology of the Jewish colonists, but were eager to demonstrate their superiority as defenders of the property in question.

In justice to the colonists it should be added that though they trusted the intentions of the Jewish guards, they strongly doubted their abilities. It was not in the nature of things that Jewish boys, lately from the ghettos and villages of Europe, should handle guns, manage horses, stand up to a fight and organize a defense. It took a long time to convince the colonists that they were mistaking habit for nature.

The first organization of Jewish guards sprang up in Palestine in 1907, and again we must glance back at the diaspora to trace the movement to its source. The Russian pogroms of 1903 to 1905 had been accompanied by a gradual change in the reaction of the Jewish communities. When they began, they had witnessed a pitiful passivity on the part of the Jews. Half the horror of Kishineff was in the defenselessness of the victims. Toward the end, an organized resistance had developed. Largely futile, because of the attitude of the government and the military, the Jewish self-defense had a salutary effect within the Jewish people itself. At Gomel, in 1904, the Black Hundreds encountered their first resistance, organized by the youth of the *Po'ale Zion*, the Socialist Zionist wing. And from Gomel came the members of first group of *Shomrim* ("Guards") who organized in Palestine.

There were twenty of them in all; and between 1907 and 1909 their number increased only by six. They took themselves with inconceivable seriousness. They had to. Like the *Kibbush Avodah*, the conquest of self-defense was part of a moral revolution; and the fewness of the initiators made a painful contrast with the magniloquence of their program. They dramatized themselves; they surrounded their little organization with a ritual, with a touch of mystery; they adopted a flag, coined a ringing slogan: "In blood and fire Judaea went down, in blood and fire Judaea shall rise again;" and they subjected themselves to a rigid discipline. Their standards were high. They accepted new members only after long training, and after proof of complete reliability. They constituted a sort of order, training applicants in all the skills of their calling: shooting, exercises, horseback riding, military tactics. To join them a man had to have, besides the physical and moral qualifications, their philosophy of the national renaissance. They were not interested in adventurers. A new member could be accepted by a two-thirds vote of the entire body; but punishment, up to and including expulsion, could be imposed by a simple majority vote. A committee of three was in command. A *Shomer* was expected to carry out orders under all circumstances and in the face of any danger.

It is remarkable to note how quickly they managed, by this moral exclusivity, to establish a tradition, and to make it appear — as indeed it was — that to join the *Shomrim* was a privilege extended to few. Their records, reproduced in part in the books *Yizkor* and *Kovetz ha-Shomer*, make up a course in the foundations of history. The stories are short and simple; they are bare recitals of incidents, descriptions of situations, tributes to persons. It is the basic stuff of life.

A young man comes to the *Shomer*, a candidate for admission. He is not quite up to the rigid standard, but they decide to give him a trial. For four years he is trained and watched. Something is still lacking in him — personality, the last touch of courage, complete obedience. In the fifth year he is rejected, and he shoots himself. There is a scandal — but the *Shomer* does not lower its standards.

A Palestinian boy, son of a colonist of Metullah, the northernmost settlement, runs away from home, to join the *Shomrim*. His father wants to bring him up in his own way of life, as an individualist settler. The boy has the new philosophy of *Kibbush Avodah*. The *Shomer* tests him, finds him acceptable, admits him. The protests of the father are ignored.

A young *Shomer* is in love with a girl in one of the colonies. He is only eighteen, and homesick. He receives a letter from the girl; her parents invite him to stay with them for a week. He applies for leave, is refused, and goes AWOL. On his return the council holds a session. It is a time when the need for *Shomrim* is particularly acute. But the boy is suspended for a year. Discipline is more important than the particular tasks in hand.

Despite their self-dramatization, the *Shomrim* had a very sober view of their mission; and the principle of their discipline was nowhere clearer than in the code of relations with the Arabs. Self-defense, not revenge; restraint, patience and intelligence. Whatever could be done by friendliness should not be done by force. Many years afterwards, in the riots of 1936 and succeeding years, when Arab extremists were doing their best to reduce the country to chaos by provoking the Jews to indiscriminate reprisals, the principle of *Havlagah*, of order and self-restraint, became a slogan with the whole *Yishuv*.

Not all the *Shomrim* were children or grandchildren of the ghetto. Two of the most famous in the early records were the brothers Zvi and Yechiel Nissanov. They came to Palestine, together with their mother, from the wild country of Daghestan, where men carried guns as they did in the West here a century ago, and where the feud was the popular form of justice. Zvi and Yechiel were fighters from their boyhood on. The mother seems to have been of the same stuff — a wholly a-typical Jewish mother. Of the father there is no mention.

The three of them settled in the colony of Yavniel. The sons became *Shomrim*, and Zvi was assigned to the nearby settlement of Meschah. One day he returned for his mother, and as they rode back toward Meschah they caught glimpses of armed men skulking behind trees and rocks. Zvi urged his mother to ride ahead, while he stayed behind and covered her flight. She refused. She said, bitterly, "Here the enemy doesn't come out into the open, as they do in our country of the Caucasus." And, when one of the lurking bandits exposed himself, she cried: "Shoot first, and shoot quick. I would rather his mother wept on his grave than I on yours!"

There was no shooting that day. But not long after, when the mother was again in Yavniel, the other son, accompanied by a friend, set out to visit her. Near Yavniel they were suddenly set upon by a large band, and Yechiel was mortally wounded. His friend drove the wagon at a furious pace to the Jewish colony, and

124

when the mother of Yechiel came running out, she beheld the dead body of her son. Her first question was: "Did he kill any of them before he was killed?" Her second: "Shall we not take revenge?" She demanded that the *Shomrim* of Yavniel ride out at once to exact a life for a life. This was forbidden sternly by the discipline of the *Shomrim*. A vendetta once begun continues in an endless cycle. The record says: "We decided against it, and it was hard for the mother to agree, for where she came from it was otherwise."

How had the *Shomrim* come to Meschah in the first place? A quarrel had broken out there between the Jewish employers and the Arab guards, who — like many other guards in the Jewish colonies — were not Palestinians, but foreigners, in this instance Moroccans, *Mughrabis.* Later a guard was found dead, and the rumor went out that he had been killed by one of the colonists. After that it was impossible to hire Arab guards, and the *Shomrim* were called in.

So it was, again, in the colony of Bet Gan. There too a quarrel had broken out, and one of the guards, a Circassian, was dismissed. He returned one day, called his former employer out of the house, shot him down, and escaped. Nothing was left to the colonists but to turn to the *Shomrim*.

The latter always drove a hard bargain; not in the matter of pay, or of conditions of service, but in line with their national program and their social philosophy. They demanded that Jewish workers be given employment in the colonies. They demanded further that their organization be recognized. *Shomrim* did not take service individually, but as a body. Nor was this merely a political point. They acted as a body in their defense of the colonies, taking on the character of a general militia.

This enabled them to make, in spite of their small number, a show of force which obviated the use of it. So, for instance, there was the story of Yehezkiel Chankin and his horse. Yehezkiel was stationed at Ben Shemen, near Lydda, and his mount was the envy of the countryside; for no Arab in the vicinity possessed anything like it. One day the horse was stolen, almost from under Yehezkiel's nose. No one had witnessed the theft, and there were no footprints to show in what direction the thief had gone. But nearby there was a famous Sheikh, who was known to wield great influence over the Arabs. Ten *Shomrim* were rounded up. Armed, mounted, and in full regalia, they came out to the Sheikh on a "visit."

They were received with all the high ceremonial courtesy of Arab hospitality, and bidden to an elaborate feast. They ate and drank, they talked with their hosts of this and that, of the weather, the crops, the goodness of God and the meaning of life. Throughout the feast no mention was made of the stolen animal. But at the end of the meal, the spokesman of the *Shomrim*, having no doubt belched politely, as the custom is among country Arabs, to testify to the fullness of his stomach, remarked quite casually that a horse had strayed from the colony of Ben Shemen. It might conceivably have been stolen, though this was doubtful, since there were no thieves in the neighborhood. However, the horse was easily recognized since it was an exceptionally beautiful and high-spirited creature. Should anyone know of its whereabouts, he was politely requested to bring the animal to Ben Shemen.

Long before the *Shomrim* had taken leave of their hosts, the horse was back at the colony.

There was, again, a little incident at Meschah, after the *Shomrim* had taken over. A donkey had been lost, and was reported to be sojourning with a certain Arab tribe of the neighborhood. Six mounted *Shomrim* went out to investigate. Yes, the donkey was there, and the Arabs did not even claim it as their own. But they had found it, and they wanted a reward. Now a reward of this kind was inadmissible, for it opened the door to abuses. The *Shomrim* did not argue the point, nor did they make any threats. They merely drove off an ox, and offered it in exchange for the donkey. An eye for an eye, an ox for a donkey. The exchange was made amicably, and no one was the worse for the incident.

Point by point the *Shomrim* won the respect of both Arabs and colonists. One of the great early triumphs was the taking over of the protection of the large settlement of Rehovoth. Here conditions had become intolerable. The guards were numerous, lazy, ineffective and dishonest. Poaching on the land of the Jews had become a sort of right with fellaheen and shepherds. The first thing the *Shomrim* did was to halve the number of men needed for the area. Then they set about teaching the local Arabs that a new regime had begun. When an Arab calmly and impudently led his camel into a Jewish orchard, the Jewish guard rode up and warned him off. The Arab looked at him contemptuously, as if to say, "Don't you know the rules here?" The Jew dismounted, to talk it out with the intruder. But the Arab was not to be convinced. He would not talk. He merely tried to push the *Shomer* aside. What followed was a brief but decisive battle, from which the

Arab withdrew probably more grieved than hurt. Great was the astonishment in the surrounding villages when the story got about. Almost as great was the astonishment among the colonists when they discovered that the lawless old days were really gone.

On the evening when the contract was at last signed with the colony of Rehovoth, the *Shomrim* of the locality arranged a great celebration. The program must have consisted mostly of songs and speeches, for besides these there was little to make merry with. Such as it was, even this celebration came to an untimely end; for it had barely got under way when word came that rioting had broken out at Benyamina, up on the Sharon plain. Every man who could be spared was wanted up there. The celebrants scattered, the songs remained unsung, the speeches unspoken. By morning the reinforcements had arrived at Benyamina.

This was the difference between the hit-or-miss system of the old guards, and the organized movement of the *Shomrim*. For the first it was a job, for the second a personal and national ideal. The *Shomrim* looked far ahead, and their dreams were large. They planned to create a center for their order, and in 1913 they founded the colony of Tel Adashim. There the wives of *Shomrim* would live; there the men would return on furlough; and there young *Shomrim* would receive their training. It did not turn out as they dreamed, but neither was the enterprise a loss. It was one of the episodes in the tradition, and Tel Adashim left behind it a body of experience.

Two young men are remembered, Avramson and Fleischer, who went out of Tel Adashim to live among the half wild Turcoman Bedouin tribes in the hills above Merhaviah. To them was assigned the task of learning the ways of the nomads. They lived with the Bedouin for two years; they dressed like them, in *abayah* (cloak) and *kefiah* (headdress), ate their food, studied their ways and came to speak their language. They learned, among other things, the thieving technique of roving shepherds, how to prey on neighboring tribes, and how to graze flocks at night in the fields of others. Avramson was very popular among the Bedouin, and the Sheikh pleaded with him to go over to the Muslim faith. He would receive a beautiful girl and a flock of one hundred and fifty sheep. Avramson replied courteously that if he were minded to turn Muslim he would do so without reward; for the time being he wanted nothing more than to learn the shepherd's trade, and return to his own people.

Very few of those first *Shomrim* are alive today. Some have died natural deaths, many were killed in line of duty. Their names are overlaid by those of more recent heroes, and the entire period of their irruption into Palestinian life now seems to belong to a fabled age. Nevertheless, they are not wholly forgotten. Their memories form a network over the Homeland. There was Yechiel Nissanov, already mentioned, "Yechiel the Mountaineer," who came from Daghestan and fell in Galilee; there was Meyer Chazanovitch, who came from Minsk, and was killed in the fields of Merhaviah; and Samuel Friedman, who came from Lithuania, and was killed near Rehovoth, on the boundary of Zarnoga; David Leviathan, killed near Ramleh; Ben Zion Meshevitch, killed in Hederah; Israel Finkelstein, killed in Ben Shemen; Dov Schweiger, killed on the road between

Tiberias and Mizpah; Mendel Portugali, killed in Bet Gan, in Galilee. There is hardly a corner of Jewish Palestine, hardly a field, where some *Shomer* did not fall in the early days — long before there was talk of Arab riots, and of Arab revolt. If the *Yishuv* of later years knew how to face the threat of mass attack without panic or retreat, the memory of the first *Shomrim* had not a little to do with it.

CHAPTER FOURTEEN

The Zionist Synthesis Begins

◎

THIS has been hitherto the regular cycle of Jewish enterprise in Palestine: big talk; disappointing beginnings; astonishing results. It was in 1907, at the Congress held in The Hague, that the World Zionist Organization adopted Chaim Weizmann's program of the synthesis between political and practical Zionism: not to give up the ultimate objective of a Charter of Jewish right to Palestine, but not to wait with the practical work until the Charter had been obtained. Instead, to press ahead, so that achievement in Palestine would constitute part — perhaps the most convincing part — of the propaganda for the Charter.

In that year the Palestine Department was created, and Arthur Ruppin went out to take charge of the work. The Jewish National Fund, his chief instrument, had collected less than a quarter of a million dollars in the six years of its existence. Originally it had been intended that no land purchases were to be made until the accumulated capital amounted to a million dollars. But Zionist synthesis applied to instruments as well as propaganda. If the Jewish National Fund did something practical with the small means at its disposal, it stood a better chance of attracting funds than if it rested its appeal solely on its ideology, and waited for an impressive beginning. This was, in fact, how it turned out, not only with the Jewish National Fund but with the Jewish Colonial Trust. And again, when Ruppin asked for a Palestine Land Development Company with an initial capital of $250,000, the Congress gave it to him — on paper. Actually he had to start with $25,000.

Let us make a rapid survey of the general state of affairs at this stage. There were, together with the men and women of the Second *Aliyah*, or Wave, over seventy thousand Jews in Palestine. That is to say, the Jewish population had about doubled since the time of the *Bilus* a quarter of a century before. Now, instead of less than two per cent on the soil, there was more than five per cent. In both respects, then, there had been a certain degree of progress; but nothing, as yet — at least as far as quantity was concerned — to reflect a national movement. The community in Palestine was still lacking both in economic soundness and in unity of purpose. Culturally and ideologically it was a heterogeneous mass. As a whole it certainly could not be called Zionist in the modern practical sense. There were Jews from Arabia, Bokhara, Samarkand, Persia, Morocco and the Yemen. There were Sephardic Jews who were Arabized, looked like Arabs, spoke Arabic and often dressed like Arabs. There were the Jews of the old East European religious immigrations. There were the PICA colonists. And there were the proletarian newcomers.

In the cities, the Ashkenazi, or European, Jews were still predominantly pensioners of the *Halukkah*, or else

132

petty traders. To a large extent they were untouched
by the Zionist ideal. So were the old oriental communities, which were not recipients of *Halukkah* charity,
for those collections were made only in Europe and
distributed only to former members of the donor communities. The Sephardi and Ashkenazi Jews were on the
whole as strange to each other's ways as a third generation American Jew to an immigrant from a hasidic
townlet in Poland. A similar gulf, though in respect of
different matters, separated the *Halukkah* Jews from the
more recent European arrivals.

The mass of the city populations, in Jerusalem,
Hebron, Tiberias and Safed, was without a political
physiognomy. Even in Jerusalem, where the Bezalel
School of Arts and Crafts had recently been founded by
Boris Schatz, and where a beginning had been made
toward the setting up of a national library — both
under the new Zionist influence — the old community
had remained unaffected. It constituted a majority
of the general population, it had orphan homes, hospitals and schools, but it played no part in the political
life of the capital. The reason lay in the queer economic
background. Here was a community which depended
for the major part of its livelihood on charitable collections in far-away Europe. Apart from the deadening
effect of such dependence, there was no interlocking of
vital interests with local conditions. The fluctuations in
the economics, the piety and the generosity of European
Jewry were of more concern to the receivers of *Halukkah*
charity than the development of Palestine. The attitude
toward Zionism was on the whole hostile. Zionism was
a disturbance of the *status quo;* it was, as in the days of
the *Bilu,* an interference with *Halukkah* collections; but,

more than that, it was an impiety to those with the Messianic fixation, and a standing reproach to the unproductive. *Halukkah* Jews did not go on the land; they did not hold with those new-fangled notions about the sanctity of labor; and they were violently opposed to the secularization of the Hebrew language as an instrument of the national renaissance.

Jaffa was different. It had never had a considerable Jewish community. The protagonists of the Return, arriving from Europe, did not find, in Jaffa, the discouraging environment of the ancient Palestinian ghettos. So they made Jaffa their center. The 8,000 Jews who constituted the Jaffa community by 1907 were of the new stamp. The city had a large number of artisans and several workshops. It had a *Gymnasium*, or High School, where the language of tuition was Hebrew — a great innovation. It had the beginnings of a Jewish labor movement. Jaffa was the port of arrival, and close to it lay the Judaean colonies where work might be obtained.

There is a fascination in observing how the shape of things in a historic process, once being set, remains long after the original mould has been broken. The era of the *Halukkah* has long since disappeared, and with it the ancient divisions and fragmentations of the Jewish community of Palestine. Other divisions exist, but those which influenced the first creative efforts are almost forgotten. Nevertheless, the center of Jewish urban life in Palestine today is Tel Aviv, the city of two hundred thousand inhabitants, which grew out of the northern suburb of Jaffa founded by Ruppin. Tel Aviv, not Jerusalem, is the capital of Jewish Palestine. It is true that modern industrial development could not have centered on inland Jerusalem, up in the mountains. Factories must be located near ports; moreover, towns spring up in agricultural areas, of which there are few about Jerusalem. But this does not account for the disparity between the development of the two cities. Had the Jerusalem community been more receptive to the newcomers thirty and forty years ago, had workers' groups found an easier foothold there, some of the disadvantage of the location would have been overcome, especially as transportation improved.

But Jaffa got the start, instead, and has kept the lead. Tel Aviv has not been displaced even by Haifa, which, from the industrial point of view, is better placed than Jaffa and agriculturally has behind it the colonies of the Emek and of Galilee. The colonies of the Emek, however, came later than those of Southern Judaea — an additional illustration of the point I am making.

The problem before the midget Palestine Department set up by the Zionist Congress in 1907 was that of breaking the heavy deadlock in the problem of Jewish ruralization. The fresh human material recently received by Palestine was of a high standard. It was young, vigorous, idealistic and intelligent. It had initiative and colorfulness. It contained large numbers of the "men from nowhere." The present-day leaders of labor Palestine — men like David ben Gurion, Berel Katzenelenson, Yitzhak ben Zvi — were of that group. The *Shomrim* were of it. But it had nowhere to go. There were no industries to absorb it, and the land was owned by the PICA colonists, who relied on Arab labor.

What could the Palestine Department do? It controlled, as an agency of the Zionist Organization, three

135

little parcels of land, owned by the Jewish National Fund, at Hulda and at Ben Shemen, in the south, and at Kinereth, where the Jordan leaves the Sea of Galilee, in the north. The land was not settled by Jews as yet. Since, under the provisions of the Turkish law, all land remaining unworked for three years reverted to the state, these areas were leased to Arabs. But this was a dangerous as well as unprofitable situation. In a little while the Arabs would be claiming squatters' rights. On the other hand, what was the Palestine Department to do? With the few thousand francs at its disposal it might perhaps have settled half a dozen families on the soil, that is to say, it could have repeated, on a miniature scale, the efforts of the PICA. What point was there to that?

If the Zionist Organization was to strike the new note of the national purpose, it would have to operate, however microscopically, in a totally different spirit. It could not propose to a few families that they settle on the land and become successful individualist farmers. But it could propose that the limited means at its disposal be utilized as the beginnings of the training and transformation system. The motive was not to be either the financial success of the enterprise or the establishment of another group of independent farmers. It was to be the national purpose — the conversion of city dwellers into land workers.

However, this was not enough. The PICA already had a school at Sedjera. There was also Mikveh Israel. The fundamental difference between the training at Sedjera and Mikveh Israel and the training at Ben Shemen or at Hulda lay in the ultimate outlook. The PICA, having trained a man, was prepared to help him set up as a farmer. That was as far as it went. It was not prepared to help a group of workers with a social ideal in the carrying out of a collective enterprise. But this element of social idealism was an integral part of the national fervor which had brought the young men and women of the Second Wave to Palestine. The ordinary incentives of self-advancement, of "bettering one's condition," of personal success, repelled them. They did not want to enter the competitive struggle which they had left behind them in Russia. They wanted to settle in collective groups on nationally owned land. Many of them were already working in collectives — but for others, not for their own group. One such collective we saw at Sedjera. There was another — the Romni Collective, from the name of the Ukrainian townlet of its origin — at Petah Tikvah. There were scores of individual workers scattered in the Galilean settlements. There did not yet exist a settled collective working its own piece of land. This was the lacuna which the Zionist Organization had to fill.

The first attempt was made in the autumn of 1908. It opened inauspiciously, and it ended in failure. Eight young men of the Romni Collective went up from Petah Tikvah to occupy the plot of land at Kinereth. They went up with the blessings and hopes of all the land-workers of Palestine — the vanguard of the new form of redemption. But they carried a hoodoo with them, the hangover of a violent dispute which had raged about another Zionist enterprise. At Ben Shemen, near Petah Tikvah, on land of the Jewish National Fund, a forest of olive-trees was being planted, as a memorial to Theodore Herzl. The supervisor, a man called Berman, had, in order to make a good showing in the matter of expenses, employed Arabs for the planting — to the boundless resentment of the Jewish workers in the nearby colonies. One day a group of these workers came out to Ben Shemen, uprooted the saplings, and planted them again — all free of charge — as a protest. The scandal was followed by a reconciliation, and when the Romni group went up to Kinereth, Berman accompanied it as supervisor. But up in Galilee the other workers were less forgiving; and though they did not, as was first suggested, boycott the Kinereth settlement, they eyed it with forebodings.

Eight young men, housed in a ruined Arab *khan*, or inn, working from dawn to dusk on insufficient food, guiding the plough with one hand and carrying a revolver in the other, represented for one year the new Zionist dispensation on the land of Palestine. Bedouins burned their threshing floors and malaria burned their bodies. On top of this the supervisor reverted to his old hankering for cheap Arab labor. In 1909 the workers at Kinereth — those of them who were not in the hospital at Zichron Ya'akov — withdrew, temporarily defeated.

A year later six men and one woman took over, on a one-year contract, part of the Kinereth tract, lying on the further or eastern side of the Jordan; and in 1911 ten men and two women of the Romni Collective replaced these — and Daganiah was founded.

Let us note these numbers carefully; eight young people, then seven, then twelve. Those were the beginnings. Young people in a waste land, on the border of Palestine, fronting wild Trans-Jordan; young people without neighbors, thrown perpetually on each other's company, experimenting with a democratic way of life. It looked like another of those Fourierist and Owenite dreams the ruins of which are scattered throughout the Old and New Worlds. "But we are different," these Palestinian pioneers said. The others had not had behind them a tradition of thousands of years to reinforce the modern ideal. The others had not been the vanguards (a dozen made up a vanguard) of a national redemption.

Palestine watched; the diaspora watched. Some of the watchers were hopeful, others merely curious, many cynical. Democracy would not work, especially among Jews, the most individualistic and contentious of peoples. Were not these people of Daganiah the ones who had quarreled with their own Zionist Organization, uprooted the saplings of Ben Shemen, and, at Kinereth, before they themselves retreated, forced the dismissal of Berman? Were not these the talkers, the theorists, the Russian revolutionaries, the boastful youngsters who said: "We want no supervisors and experts to boss us. We want to be instructed, not directed. We'll be our own managers?"

We shall not rehearse the story of the early trials and sufferings of Daganiah. It was, with unimportant variations, the story of the *Bilus*, the story of the founding of Petah Tikvah, the story of the attempt at Kinereth. And it was to be repeated, with variations, a hundred times in the coming years, until the settlements were so many that — except in remote areas — the old loneliness had been overcome, and the old inexperience and uncertainty no longer existed. But this must be borne in mind: the young people of Daganiah were not adventurers, and they were not playing at heroics. They were intelligent and determined men and women who wanted to set up a collective farm. They were eager to learn;

they were interested in the technical problems of agriculture and of social management. In short, for all their youthful enthusiasm, they meant business.

Of the problems which evolved in these collectives, of the lessons which time taught them, more will be told later. At this point we shall only note that Daganiah became the mother of the *kvutzoth*, or collectives. Today she does not stand alone. Nearly three thousand Jews are settled in collectives in that area of the Jordan valley alone. Daganiah itself is in two sections, A and B; the collectives of Bet Zera, Afikim, Melhamia, Kinereth, Tel Or, and others, are its neighbors. Near by are the Ruthenberg Electrical Works, where the Yarmuk falls into the Jordan. The rickety shacks and tattered tents of the first settlers have long ago been replaced by fine stone houses, set in magnificent groves of trees. The children and grandchildren of the settlers work the fields of Daganiah, or attend its schools. Daganiah remains till this day the symbol of the new method.

Kinereth was a failure; Daganiah was a success; Merhaviah was a failure; Ben Shemen was a success. Merhaviah was the most ambitious of the Zionist enterprises in those years. Franz Oppenheimer, the agricultural economist, was its moving spirit. Merhaviah was to be the first of a series of large cooperative or collective units, taking in a thousand workers at a time. The reasons for its failure need not detain us; they are no longer relevant to Palestinian problems. But none of the failures were complete losses. In all of them something was learned, from all of them issued better trained men and women.

The value of the work done in those years by the Zionists is not reflected by the number of points they settled, or the population of the settlements. In both respects they were still far behind the PICA. When the First World War came, there were forty-three Jewish colonies, of which only fourteen stood to the credit of the Zionist Organization. But hundreds of workers had been trained at Ben Shemen and Hulda and the girls' training farm erected on the site of the first failure — Kinereth. A wind of freshness swept over the old colonies where the new workers were admitted. Ruppin, in his report to the Eleventh Zionist Congress (Vienna, 1913), tells this moving little story:

"About a year ago we purchased some two thousand dunam of land in the twenty-year-old colony of Kastinieh, and sold it in parcels to a number of buyers. As the new buyers did not come quickly enough, and the soil had to be worked, we sent up eight of our workers from Hulda and Ben Shemen for that purpose to Kastinieh. About half a year later the buyers came, and we wanted to withdraw our workers from the colony. Thereupon the entire council of Kastinieh appeared before me and implored me not to do it, but to leave the workers in Kastinieh. Ever since the workers had appeared an entirely different life reigned in the colony: it was from these workers that they had learned, for the first time, what work really was, and they had perceived that all their previous work had been nothing but a joke. These are their own words. They had become 'exhausted,' and had forgotten the work; now they had begun again to go into the fields. Being a small colony composed entirely of old people, they had trembled at the thought of their neighbors, and had hardly found the courage to do any sowing; since the arrival of the workers it was the neighbors who trembled."

Hulda and Ben Shemen were, then, something more than training farms. They were centers of revitalization for the Jewish colonies. They were also innovators. Ben Shemen led the way in the introduction of rational dairy farming, and neighboring colonies followed suit; until that time not a liter of milk had come from a Jewish colony into the townlet of Tel Aviv! And this though Petah Tikvah and Rehovoth were near at hand. Hulda and Ben Shemen, again, trained the first Jewish workers in the planting of olive and almond trees. But above all, the Palestine Department taught the workers how to overcome, by organization, the handicap of the cheapness of Arab labor.

Here we see again necessity and idealism in creative interplay. Because they were predisposed by their philosophy to cooperative enterprise, the workers of the Second Wave successfully met a situation which would have defeated the toughest individualists. A communal kitchen, a common fund, common quarters, are possible only where a strong community spirit, interpenetrated with a common ideal, converts the surrender of individual ambition into a cheerful affirmation. Men cannot be forced into cooperation; even the direst need produces only a temporary and unstable alliance where the cooperative spirit is lacking. Had this spirit not appeared among the Jewish workers in Palestine they could not have established themselves in the old colonies, and they could not have laid the foundations of the cooperative systems on the land and in the cities. They would have been forced out of the country.

Many were; and not workers alone. David ben

Gurion, the labor leader, who came to Palestine as a boy in 1904, and is today the Palestine chairman of the Jewish Agency Executive, has made the statement that only a fraction of those who constituted the Second Wave stayed on. The Second Wave carried with it large numbers of Jews who had no Zionist inclinations. Palestine was for them a country like any other. They had not the stomach for the gruelling uphill struggle, so they left as soon as the opportunity presented itself. Even among those who believed themselves to be Zionists there were some who could not stand the test. But those that did remain were the strongest, the most devoted and the most adaptable. They had, besides their passionate vision of a renewed Jewish civilization, the qualities of ingenuity and endurance. The handicaps of Palestine were selective agents of incalculable importance.

CHAPTER FIFTEEN

The Revival of Hebrew

◎

How far had the Jewish awakening to the Return developed on the eve of the First World War? And what evidence was there by way of achievement in Palestine that this awakening did not find the Jewish people lacking in the qualifications which distinguish a creative sentiment from a futile sentimentality?

This is not an academic question. It is as practical as it is fascinating, for it covers the political realities of that time, and reaches down into the mysteries of a national life force. For two thousand years the Jewish people had nurtured the dream of the Restoration, but it had never made a serious attempt to convert the dream into reality. Granting that no opportunity had ever been presented before, and that the Jews had therefore done well to take refuge in Messianism, rehearsing meanwhile the cultural and sociological gestures of a rural Palestinian life, was it not possible, and even probable, that the dream had become a substitute for action? Was it not possible that will had long since dissolved in reverie, and that the faculties needed for independent state-building or state-maintenance had atrophied with disuse?

Suppose that, in 1914, the Jewish position in Palestine had been what it was about half a century before. Suppose that, in 1914, there had been in the country thirty-odd thousand Jews instead of nearly one hundred thousand; suppose that the percentage on the soil had been less than two per cent instead of nearly ten; suppose that the vast majority of the Jews had been mendicants, pious enough, scholarly enough, but strangers alike to labor and to political reality. Or suppose, even, that the work of Baron de Rothschild and the PICA had already made its mark and that the country contained a considerable number of successful Jewish planters and colonists, but that they employed Arab labor almost exclusively, while there was no sign of a Jewish proletariat on the land or in the cities. Suppose, finally, that there had been no Zionist movement, or that the Zionist movement had exhausted itself in petition and propaganda for a Charter, but had done nothing to demonstrate a practical intent and capacity. Would a Balfour Declaration have been possible? Or, having been issued, would such a declaration, followed by the Mandate for a Jewish Homeland, have led to anything if the Jews had had to begin, after the First World War, from the point they occupied in 1882, or even in 1897; that is to say, if everything so far recorded in this narrative, except the PICA work — namely the *Bilu*, the *Shomrim*, the conquest of labor, the creation of the authority of the Zionist Congresses and of its instruments, the Jewish National Fund, the Palestine Land Development Company and the Anglo-Palestine Bank — still had lain in the future?

How did it come about, then, that the historic opportunity which was presented with the dissolution of the

Turkish Empire, found the Jews sufficiently advanced, by anticipatory preparation and effort, to make the offer of a Jewish Homeland reasonable? It would be mysticism, pure and simple, to talk of a prophetic instinct in the Jewish masses, a premonition of the now-or-never moment, which set in motion the *Hibbat Zion* and prepared the stage for Herzl. We shall have to fall back on the last refuge of rationalism and call it coincidence.

But the most remarkable element in the coincidence still remains to be described, and that is the revival of the Hebrew language as symbol and instrument of the unification of the Jewish community in Palestine. We have already had a glimpse of the political formlessness and social fragmentation of the pre-Zionist settlement. This was a condition rooted in the diversity of the old immigrant groups, and in the moral effects of the *Halukkah*. It was, however, exacerbated by the intrusion of external factors. Palestine had become, toward the second half of the nineteenth century, the battleground of contending European influences. The Powers were waiting for the demise of the Turkish Empire and sharpening their claws for the dismemberment of the carcass. Russia, Germany and France were jockeying for control of the area. England was interested, though to a lesser degree. Germany already had formulated her Berlin to Bagdad policy; Russia had always been interested in the fate of Turkey, the controller of the Dardanelles; France had always looked upon the Levant as her peculiar domain. England's concern centered on the Suez Canal and the route to India. Each of the Powers was ready to use whatever material came to hand for the assertion of its influence in the locality. They built hospices and hospitals and monasteries; they watched jealously their rights under the system of capitulations (rights of extraterritoriality) — and they were not averse to making use of the Jews. Even the Russian government joined in this game. At home it exploited the Jews by making them the safety valve for its policy of social repression; in Palestine it "protected" them in order to assert its rights in the Near East. The manner in which Jews have been exploited for political purposes is one of the supreme demonstrations of human ingenuity. At home their talents are encouraged for the development of a country and their unpopularity is used to deflect popular resentment against tyranny; and when they migrate they are still exploited (as by the Czarist government in the case here mentioned) for the extension of foreign influence, or (as by the Nazi government two decades later) for the propagation of a divisive anti-Semitic sentiment in foreign countries. Seldom has a people been blessed with such sacrificial versatility.

One of the methods employed in the strategic maneuvers about Palestine was infiltration of cultural influence via the Jews. The *Alliance Israélite*, having its headquarters in Paris, made French the language of tuition in the system of schools which it maintained in Palestine. This is not to say that Adolphe Crémieux, founder of the *Alliance*, intended this organization to be an instrument of French imperialism. He merely happened to be a patriotic Frenchman. The Evelyna de Rothschild School in Jerusalem used English as the language of tuition. The money happened to come from England. The *Hilfsverein der Deutschen Juden*, main-

147

taining another system of schools and kindergartens in Palestine, favored German. The Russian Jews, with their loathing of Czarism, resisted the use of Russian. The *heders* and schools of the old Russian-Jewish settlements turned from Russian. They used mostly Yiddish.

It was only with the coming of the Zionist immigrants that Hebrew began the fight for unification. The urchins attending the various school systems used, during school hours, the language of their "patron" countries. When they met on the street they had no medium of communication until the spread of Hebrew came to their rescue. So it was French, German, English or Yiddish at school — and Hebrew in the street.

By 1913 Hebrew had made considerable progress. There were already several schools in the colonies where it was the language of instruction. Notably, the Jaffa *Gymnasium* — the first Jewish High School in Palestine — set a powerful example. But the struggle was long, bitter and involved. Hebrew could not have made headway among the children if it had not become the language of the home; and we have seen that the old, pietist communities resented the secularization of the immemorial sanctities, among which Hebrew, the language of prayer, was supreme. When Eliezer ben Yehudah came to Palestine, sixty years ago, and made Hebrew the language of his home, refusing to permit the use of any other, he was denounced throughout the community as an atheist. Ittamar ben Avi, his son, who died recently, told me many curious stories of the persecution which the family had to endure because of the "impious" insistence of the father on Hebrew as the language of ordinary converse. Neighbors were outraged when they heard the mother say, in the language of Isaiah and Amos, "Little Ittamar, blow your nose," or, "Tell the grocer I won't pay more than half a piaster for a herring even if he stands on his head" (the grocer, presumably. M. S.). Ittamar's father naturally went to synagogue services like every other Jew; indeed, he was specially pious for a time; but in the eyes of his fellow-worshippers his prayers were unacceptable, because he had debased the sacred tongue, dedicated to communion with the Most High, by adapting it to gross daily purposes. This attitude may seem absurd in the eyes of, let us say, English-speaking Jews, for whom the majesty of the King James Version of the Bible is in no wise diminished by their natural use of English in the home and office and factory. Still, a little touch of sympathy and understanding came to me on my first visit to Palestine, when I sat down in a restaurant in Jerusalem and looked at the posters on the wall. I had been reading Isaiah that morning, and I was still aglow with the tremendous denunciation of the hypocritical bringers of sacrifices, a denunciation which reaches its climax in the thundering phrase: *Dirshu mishpat!* "Seek justice!" And on a poster in front of me, in letters a foot tall, was an advertisement, *Dirshu glidah!* "Seek ice-cream!" I could not but feel an inward grimace of discomfort.

For me, too, in spite of my sympathy with the revival of the language, Hebrew had been mostly the vehicle of great religious, ethical and spiritual communications. How queer it was, for a time, to buy a round-trip bus ticket from Tel Aviv to Jerusalem in Hebrew, or to discuss with the tailor, in Hebrew, the alterations I wanted made in a pair of trousers. Even after a number of years of habituation to the new situation, the old fixation would haunt me, and send up twinges of astonishment into my concious mind at odd moments. It still startled me, as late as eight or nine years ago, when, standing at the corner of the Allenby and Nachlat Benyamin Streets in Tel Aviv, I heard the traffic policeman bawl out, in excellent popular Hebrew, a careless driver. Though by then Hebrew was definitely the dominant language of the Palestinian Jews, and all its rivals had been pushed from the field.

It was a long, arduous process; for not only was the language a sanctity, reserved for prayer and study (it should be noted, however, that when, in the old days, Palestinian youngsters studied Bible and Talmud in *heder* or *yeshivah*, they translated the Hebrew and Aramaic into Yiddish); and not only were the masses foreign to it; there was also lacking a modern terminology for the school, the workshop, the office and the laboratory. No wonder my astronomer friend was so delighted when he found an old geography book in Hebrew prepared a hundred years before. Probably there were other, similar anticipations, and probably quadratic equations were being solved in the biblical tongue before modern Hebrew schools were established in Palestine. For the renaissance of Hebrew began — and here again we have an instance of the national preparation in advance of the national opportunity — in Europe, and there were Hebrew periodicals of high merit and considerable circulation in Russia in the eighties and nineties of the last century. There was a great efflorescence of Hebrew literature. Ahad Ha'am and Reuben Brainin and Michah Joseph Berdischevski were Europeanizing the stylistic qualities of the language; Chaim Nachman

Bialik, Saul Tchernichovsky, Jacob Cohen, Zalman Shneur were writing modern Hebrew poetry which stood comparison with the best that was appearing in English, French or German. But it was a far cry from these distinguished cultural reversions to Hebrew to the folk revival of the language. Bialik, the greatest of the modern Hebrew poets — and one of the great poets of all time, of any language — was particularly concerned with the problem of the masses. He did not want to be the poet of an educated clique, of a coterie of intellectual snobs. He wanted his language to become that of schoolchildren, peasants and factory hands.

A well-known story tells how, one day, soon after he had settled in Palestine — this was in the late nineteen twenties — Bialik was taking a stroll with Ahad Ha'am. They were discussing the question which is the subject matter of this chapter — the popular, national revival of Hebrew; and they agreed that until Jewish children in Palestine played and shouted spontaneously in Hebrew, the problem would not have been solved. A little boy happened to pass them as they conversed. Ahad Ha'am called the youngster over courteously, then suddenly reached down and tweaked his ear. The boy let out a yell of pain, ran across the street, turned round, and squeaked furiously: *Hamor zaken!* — which is good Hebrew for "You old donkey!" Thereupon the aged philosopher turned beamingly to Bialik, and said: "Now *that's* what we need!"

It could not have happened without the disciplined collaboration of the parents. And here we come across a peculiarly interesting circumstance. The leaders in the propagation and discipline of Hebrew were the proletarians! This is not to deny the considerable role which was played by scholars, intellectuals and the middle class. But it must be stressed again that the resistance to the secularization and revival of the language came from the old settlers, particularly in the cities. In the PICA colonies, which were inhabited mostly by *Hibbat Zion* groups, Hebrew had taken root. However, one usually associates a cultural program with a middle class, not with workers. Nor was the Hebrew discipline complete in the middle-class settlements. The workers, the *Shomrim* and the members of the collectives, whose life was hard enough without the additional burden of a "new" language, turned from Yiddish to Hebrew, and added to their other torments the seemingly unnecessary one of self-conversion into Hebraists.

This was a process which had to be sustained for many years. I remember visiting the workers' colonies in the years following the First World War, and wondering at the self-mastery of the young men and women who were determined to make Hebrew the language of their new Homeland. It was a painful thing to see them, when they gathered in the evening, exhausted by the day's labor in field and swamp, refusing to relax into Yiddish, or Russian, or German, or Polish, the languages to which they were accustomed — and, instead, breaking their teeth on Hebrew. The conversation was Hebrew; the discussions were in Hebrew; the periodicals they read were Hebrew; other languages were forbidden, by common agreement. Their Hebrew was as yet fragmentary; they had to grope for words and expressions. It would have been so natural for them to relapse into their mother tongues, so natural and so restful. They would not do it! On top of their other trials, unavoidable once they had come to the country, there was this seemingly gratuitous linguistic torture.

If they had not displayed this obstinacy, Hebrew would not have established itself as the unifying language of the Homeland any more than Gaelic (in spite of much exhortation and effort) established itself as the language of liberated Ireland. There the tongue of the conqueror has prevailed. The discussions of the Dail are in English. The poetry of Yeats, the plays of Synge, were written and are acted in English. It is not so in the Dail of Jewish Palestine — the *Asefath ha-Nivharim* — or with the poetry of Bialik and Shimonovitch and Uri Zvi Greenberg and Rachel. The triumph of Hebrew was completed only after the First World War; but by 1914 it had entrenched itself so firmly that the English administration had to recognize it as an official language side by side with English and Arabic.

That a unifying single language was needed for the *Kibbutz Galuyyoth*, the ingathered fragments of different exilic countries, if they were to be fused into a coherent and forceful community, is obvious on the face of it. It was by no means obvious, to many Jews, that that language had to be Hebrew. The superficial solution was Yiddish, spoken by most of the Jews of Palestine and by practically all of the newcomers from eastern and central Europe in the early days of immigration. Yet the majority of Yiddish-speaking Zionists and, indeed, all the Yiddish-speaking Zionists of note, opted for Hebrew! They did it in spite of the acute discomfort, to put it at its mildest, which the decision often entailed for them. It must not be thought, however, that only the "simple" folk, the workers and pioneers, found the transition to Hebrew a strain. Fantastically enough, the masters of the written Hebrew word were much more at home, as far as the *spoken* language was concerned, in Yiddish! They were likewise, in many instances, lovers and adepts of Yiddish prose and poetry. Chaim Nachman Bialik, the supreme figure in modern Hebrew poetry, wrote magnificently in Yiddish too, and preferred Yiddish to Hebrew for purposes of conversation. Reuben Brainin, the leading Hebrew essayist, spoke Hebrew with difficulty, but wrote and spoke an excellent Yiddish. Shmarya Levin who (as I shall soon tell) played a great role in the language battle in Palestine, on the *Hebrew* side, was the greatest *Yiddish* orator of his time.

They spoke Hebrew at all public gatherings in Palestine; they spoke Hebrew for show, out of a sense of duty, out of a feeling of rightness, and in their love of the language. But most of the older people never achieved ease of conversation in Hebrew, however naturally the pen between their fingers turned to Hebrew. Shmarya Levin was once asked: "Doctor, how does it feel to speak Hebrew for two hours, and then to revert to good old homey Yiddish?" Dr. Levin thought awhile and said: "It's the same wonderful relief as riding bareback on a donkey for two solid hours, and then getting off and walking on one's own legs."

There were, in those days, some seven million Yiddish-speaking Jews in the world; there were only two or three hundred thousand (a fraction of that number was in Palestine) who knew Hebrew, far fewer who spoke it naturally. No wonder it seemed to many nothing short of insane to insist on the revival of Hebrew — this apart from the religious opposition; and an outsider, visiting

154

Palestine and witnessing the bitter struggle which went on in the early days between Yiddish and Hebrew, was completely bewildered to observe that the most distinguished and most obstinate protagonists of Hebrew were men who were deeply attached to Yiddish, who enjoyed its literature and even added something to it, men whose tenderest childhood associations had a Yiddish background

Why Hebrew, then, rather than Yiddish? The answer takes us deep into the character of the revolt against diaspora life which gave Zionism its strength. Yiddish, for all its sweetness and intimacy, in spite of its Mendeles and Sholom Aleichems, was the language of exile, and bore upon it the imprint of exilic humiliations. The return to freedom meant the return to the language of the ancient freedom of the Jews. It was a necessary gesture of spiritual self-liberation. It was also an affirmation of the glorious past. To Zionists brooding on the great memories of the Kings, the Prophets and the Maccabees, it was unthinkable that the resumption of the national theme on the national soil should witness the perpetuation of Yiddish as the language of use and the confirmation of Hebrew in its exile role of a sacred memorial of an irretrievable past. Granted that for the parents Hebrew would always be difficult, granted that they would always hanker after Yiddish; for the children Hebrew would be natural.

For the children it would be natural in a profound sense. The land into which they would be born had acquired its imperishable name through Hebrew-speaking men and women. The language was one with the land, if we think of that land not merely as a random territory but as the theater of the unique utterances of the Bible. Hebrew *could* not be a secondary language to the new generation, if the bond between it and the land was to be enduring. And it turned out as the Zionists had planned. The associations which to me, for instance, are a cultural acquisition are to the children of the Emek, the Valley of Jezreel, an immediate experience. I have seen little tots come out of the kindergartens of Nahalal and Ain Harod and Beth Alpha to play in the morning sun, and they have looked up at Mount Gilboa, or at the Carmel range, or at the hills of Southern Galilee; and I have heard them clamor, as children do everywhere, for a story. What better stories could their teacher tell them than the one about King Saul and Jonathan and David and the wars against the Philistines (and there was Gilboa right before them); and the one about Elijah and the prophets of Baal and the wicked King Ahab (there was Mount Carmel, on the other side); and the one about the Prophet Jeremiah, trailing through this very valley after the Jewish prisoners being carried into the Babylonian captivity (there were the hills they must have climbed); and all of it told in the language of the record, in Hebrew. The triple cord of people, land and language was woven into their minds, and a triple cord shall not easily be broken. To these children the Bible is not only sacred; it is the source of their first awareness of their childhood surroundings.

I have dwelt at length on the reinstatement of Hebrew as the living language of Palestine in part because of the intrinsic interest of the incident, for nothing like it has been witnessed elsewhere; but in part also because it is the answer to the question propounded at the head of this chapter: "What evidence was there by way of achievement in Palestine that the national awakening did not find the Jewish people lacking in the qualifications which distinguish a creative sentiment from a futile sentimentality?" The forty odd colonies, the working class on the soil, the little factories in Jaffa were important evidence. But more important was the progress already made before the First World War in the unification of the Jewish community by way of the Hebrew language and the strengthening of the national spirit through the conversion of the powerful past into the present.

The struggle was by no means over. In years to come the Hebrew-Yiddish dispute flared up fiercely. There were extremists on both sides, Yiddishists who flaunted Yiddish in public places, Hebraists who scowled at the sound of the exile language. There were fist fights and small riots. There were insults and repressions. But the most important engagement in this campaign for Hebrew took place on the eve of the First World War, and its issue was of decisive importance.

Wolf Kalonymos Wissotzky, the rich tea merchant of Russia who was Ahad Ha'am's employer and Maecenas (he has already been mentioned in this narrative) donated the sum of one hundred thousand roubles for the creation of a technical school — afterwards known as the *Technikum* — at Haifa. The negotiations with the Turkish government for the right to purchase the land, and for permission to open the institution, were conducted by the German Jewish philanthropic organization called the *Hilfsverein der Deutschen Juden*. The *Hilfsverein* was assimilationist and anti-Zionist; its interest in Palestine was purely philanthropic. The heads of the

Hilfsverein were patriotic German Jews; and since it was their government which had taken the new *Technikum* under its wing (we must remember that those were the days of the capitulations in Turkey, and foreign governments had certain extraterritorial rights) they demanded that the language of instruction in the *Technikum* should be German. Wissotzky was, as we have seen, an ardent Hebraist. In Jewish matters Ahad Ha'am was his right-hand man. But neither Wissotzky nor Ahad Ha'am could stand up to the pressure of the *Hilfsverein*, which of course had the backing of the German government — and the German government, interested like the others in extending its influence in the Near East, was anxious to gain this additional foothold of a German-speaking educational institution.

When the decision of the *Hilfsverein* became known, the Zionist world in Palestine and in the diaspora was rocked to its foundations. The first Jewish scientific center in Palestine was to conduct its courses not in Hebrew, but in German! Protest meetings were called in every Jewish community. Shmarya Levin toured Germany and bitterly attacked the jingoistic *Hilfsverein* in a series of famous addresses. It was all in vain. The *Hilfsverein*, secretly pledged to the German government, stood its ground. On the day when the *Technikum* was to open in Haifa, the teachers who had been engaged and the pupils who had enrolled went out on strike. "No Hebrew, no *Technikum!*" The *Hilfsverein* withdrew its support not only from the *Technikum*, but from the other schools which it maintained in Palestine. Shmarya Levin, who was in Palestine when the strike occurred, left at once for America (he is remembered here by thousands of Jews) to raise funds for the taking over by

158

the Zionists of this section of the Jewish educational system of Palestine. He was in the United States on this mission when the First World War broke out.

Thus began the Zionist administration of the schools, and the fusion of the divergent linguistic influences into a single Hebrew system. Here again it was only a beginning; the point of the incident lies in the spirit which it revealed. Zionism was at last finding itself — and, as we shall see, just about in time.

CHAPTER SIXTEEN

In the First World War

◎

THERE is an old Jewish saying: "God prepares the cure before He sends the disease," which some interpret as a eulogy on the foresight of Providence and others as a reflection on the Divine Economy. Even a pietist could not assert that the sufferings visited upon the Jews of eastern Europe in the First World War were compensated for by the opportunities which emerged from it for the rebuilding of the Jewish Homeland. It is true that the horrors of Nazism, with its insane program of extermination of the Jewish people, have eclipsed the memory of what the Jews of Poland, Russia, Galicia and Roumania endured between 1914 and 1918 while the opposing armies of Russia and the Austro-German Alliance trampled back and forth across their communities. Yet, even in those days, Sholom Aleichem was able to say bitterly: "Yes, this is a Jewish war — a war for the extermination of the Jews." On the other hand, even a cynic must stand at gaze before the coincidence which we discussed in the last chapter. On the eve of the First World War, Zionism was strong enough to challenge successfully the attempt of a powerful assimilationist group to pervert the rebuilding of Palestine to dishonest ends. The role which Palestine has played subsequently in alleviating part of the agony of Jewry in the post-war years (or, we should say, the between-war years) must be traced to the stage of development attained in the pre-war years. Two decades would have made a fatal difference.

The First World War did not raise the Jewish problem in the acute ideological form it has taken on since. But that a Jewish problem existed was evident to anyone who was not blinded by doctrinaire prejudices; and that an integral part of its solution was the rebuilding of a Jewish Homeland in Palestine seemed a reasonable assumption to nearly all the leading statesmen in the Allied countries. But that assumption might not have seemed so reasonable if there had not been a certain body of achievement in Palestine, and if there had not existed an organized Jewish sentiment able to press its claims on the world.

A detailed account of the steps which led to the Balfour Declaration cannot be given here; but a summary must be included, for the history of the development of Jewish Palestine is intimately connected with the history of the legal and moral status of the idea. Two countries led in advocating the creation of a Jewish Homeland in Palestine: England and America. A British Prime Minister, Lloyd George, and an American President, Woodrow Wilson, lent it the weight of their authority. With them were ranged a galaxy of the most distinguished men of the time: Arthur James Balfour, Jan Smuts, Lord Milner, Henry Cabot Lodge, Lord Robert Cecil and a host of others. But it must not be imagined that the adoption of the policy of a Jewish Homeland, later incorporated in the mandatory system of the League of Nations, proceeded of itself. It was, in fact, bitterly fought — chiefly by Jews, and particularly in England. It is true that the anti-Zionists represented no considerable body of opinion. But they were influential, and they were, in some instances, moved by convictions which verged on the fanatical. While Chaim Weizmann in England and Justice Louis D. Brandeis in America were urging the Zionist case, Claude Montefiore (a great-nephew of Sir Moses Montefiore), Lucien Wolf, David Alexander and Edwin Montagu (later Secretary of State for India), leading English Jews, moved heaven and earth to prevent the issuance of a favorable declaration by the British government. The matter was settled on November 2nd, 1917, when Arthur James Balfour, Secretary of State for Foreign Affairs, addressed to Lord Rothschild, for transmission to the Zionist Organization, the following Declaration:

> His Majesty's Government view with favor the establishment in Palestine of a National Home for the Jewish People, and will use their best endeavours to facilitate the achievement of this object, it being clearly understood that nothing shall be done which may prejudice the civil and religious rights of existing non-Jewish communities in Palestine, or the rights and political status enjoyed by Jews in any other country.

The Balfour Declaration has been the subject of endless debate; it has been examined and re-examined for every conceivable interpretation. Much has been made of "*a* Jewish Homeland . . .," and of "the rights and political status enjoyed by Jews in any other country." The latter phrase has been tortured into meaning that the existence of a Jewish Homeland in Palestine would, without such a proviso, implicate Jews everywhere in a sort of Palestinian citizenship; the former phrase has been tortured as violently into meaning any size of Jewish Homeland, as long as it had a certain measure of local autonomy. Indeed, it has been asserted (as we shall see) that the Jewish Homeland intended by the Balfour Declaration already exists, and that, the obligation to the Jewish people having been discharged, further Jewish immigration into Palestine shall cease as of the year 1944.

What the framers of the Balfour Declaration had in mind has, however, been made quite clear in a series of statements which Lloyd George has reproduced in his memoirs.

Of Arthur James Balfour, the most Zionistic of England's statesmen, he writes:

"As to the meaning of the words 'National Home' to which the Zionists attach so much importance, he (Balfour) understood it to mean some form of British, American, or other protectorate, under which full facilities would be given to the Jews to work out their own salvation and to build up, by means of education, agriculture, and industry, a real centre of national culture and focus of national life. It did not necessarily involve the early establishment of an independent Jewish State, which was a matter of gradual development in accordance with the ordinary laws of political evolution."

The following was President Wilson's view:

"I am persuaded that the Allied nations, with the full concurrence of our Government and our people, are agreed that in Palestine shall be laid the foundations of a Jewish Commonwealth."

Lloyd George himself saw it thus:

"There has been a good deal of discussion as to the meaning of the words 'Jewish National Home' and whether it involved the setting up of a Jewish National State in Palestine. I have already quoted the words actually used by Mr. Balfour when he submitted the Declaration to the (Imperial War) Cabinet for its approval. They were not challenged at the time by any member present, and there can be no doubt as to what the Cabinet then had in their minds. It was not their idea that a Jewish State should be set up immediately by the Peace Treaty without reference to the wishes of the majority of the inhabitants. On the other hand, it was contemplated that when the time arrived for according representative institutions to Palestine, if the Jews had meanwhile responded to the opportunity afforded them and had become a definite majority of the inhabitants, then Palestine would thus become a Jewish Commonwealth. The notion that Jewish immigration would have to be artificially restricted in order that the Jews should be a permanent minority never entered the heads of anyone engaged in framing the policy. That would have been regarded as unjust and as a fraud on the people to whom we were appealing."

If these were the impressions of the statesmen who were responsible, after long deliberation and many consultations with associated governments, for the issuance of the Balfour Declaration, it is not be be wondered at that the Jewish world received it as an unequivocal recognition of the Jewish claim to Palestine, and as an act of complete restitution. Immense demonstrations were held in England, America, Russia, South Africa, Canada — indeed, in every country on the Allied side which had any considerable Jewish community. It was universally felt that no incident of comparable importance had occurred in Jewish history since the Emperor Hadrian had destroyed the Jewish Homeland and founded Aelia Capitolina on the ruins of Jerusalem.

How was Palestine faring in the meantime, and what was happening to the colonies and city settlements which by the decision of the Allied Powers had become the official foundation of a Jewish Homeland? The condition of the country was wretched in the extreme. The Arabs of Palestine hated their Turkish rulers, but they had not the spirit or organization to rise. The "Revolt in the Desert," which T. E. Lawrence led, had no repercussions west of the Jordan, and very little east of it, for that matter. But there was disaffection, and the Turkish authority was as feeble and undecided in war as it had been incompetent and corrupt in peace. Djemal Pasha, the military commander for Syria and Palestine, was a rabid Turkish nationalist. His program was the suppression of all minority cultures and groups. If the Arabs represented a passive hatred of Turkey, the Jews represented an active and creative national group. Djemal's hand was therefore heaviest on the Jews. A series of brutal expulsions began in December, 1914, but they led, not to mass transfer of populations, as was intended, but to chaos, for there was little transportation, and that little was requisitioned by the army. The colonies were raided repeatedly; in particular the Turks were anxious to get at the *Shomrim*, or Jewish guardsmen, and remove all arms from the hands of the Jews.

The Jews themselves were divided on the issue of the

war. They had as little reason to be grateful to Turkey as had the Arabs. The prevalent sympathy was pro-British and later, when America joined the war, pro-American. But the issue was confused at first by the fact that Czaristic Russia, the outstanding country of reaction and anti-Semitism, was one of the Allies. It was a confusion which extended to the whole Jewish world — and to the whole liberal world as well. Yet, even before the Kerensky revolution had removed the Czar and his clique from power, it was clear to many Palestinian Jews that the Allied side represented the progressive force of the world. When Vladimir Jabotinsky, then a brilliant young Russian journalist, turned up in Cairo, to agitate for a Jewish legion, hundreds of young men from the Palestinian colonies and towns stole through the Turkish lines to join him, and the Zion Mule Corps, which served with great distinction in the Gallipoli campaign, was formed. Later the Jewish Legion fought for the liberation of Palestine on Palestinian soil. The destruction of the Turkish Empire owed nothing to the Arabs of Palestine, little to the Arabs of Syria, or of Iraq. The Jewish contribution, small though it was in the sum total of the Allied effort, was disproportionately large for the Jewish population of Palestine. This curious circumstance, this contrast between the Jewish volunteer contribution to the liberation of the whole Arabian world of Asia Minor, and the comparative supineness of the Arabs themselves, was to recur, in even sharper form, twenty-five years later in World War number two.

One calamity after another descended on the Jewish settlement. First came the expulsions, the arrests, the seizures, the torturing and the hangings. Then came a

166

plague of locust. That was followed, two years later, by the division of the country, when the British advanced upward from Egypt, and Galilee was cut off, for some twelve months, from Judaea. The Jewish population of Palestine shrank, through deaths, flight and expulsions, from close to 100,000 to about 55,000. Had it not been for the intervention of American Jewry on the one hand, and the resourcefulness of the young people in Palestine on the other hand, the Jewish settlement might have been completely destroyed.

In America, Louis D. Brandeis headed the Provisional Committee for Zionist Affairs. Large sums of money were raised and forwarded, with the assistance of the Joint Distribution Committee. Henry Morgenthau, American Ambassador to Turkey, used his considerable influence in Constantinople to ease the pressure against the Zionists and Jews generally in Palestine, and was particularly helpful to Arthur Ruppin, the head of the Palestine Department. The moral effect of the intervention of American Jewry at this point in the history of Zionist work, when the World Zionist Organization had been torn asunder by the World War, was not less significant for the Jews of Palestine than the material results.

The shifts to which the colonists and workers were reduced in those years of confusion and hunger, the obstinacy with which they clung to the country, the steadfastness with which they nurtured, in the midst of chaos, the hope of a Jewish Homeland, make up an epic within an epic. But it is one which can be told only at great length, or hardly at all. For it consists o˙ a thousand individual stories of courage and endurance in undramatic things; one concerns a collective of shepherds in the hills of Galilee; another a collective of vegetable growers, founded in haste, maintained for a year or two, just to live through the war (many such collectives were formed in that period); a third the hiding of *Shomrim*; a fourth the three men who gave themselves up voluntarily to the Turkish authorities, in place of their comrades, believing that their Austrian citizenship would save them — but who paid the penalty with their lives. Through those ghastly years, 1914 to 1918, the continuity of the Jewish settlement was somehow maintained, so that the ending of the war did not find the work of thirty years a complete ruin.

It was more than maintained, for in a moral sense it was greatly furthered. One of the most astonishing incidents in Zionist and Jewish history — an incident which should some day find its place among the episodes familiar to all mankind — belongs to that time. The Balfour Declaration was issued in November, 1917. In the spring of 1918, Dr. Weizmann came out to Palestine at the head of a Zionist Commission, authorized by the British government to initiate the work of the rebuilding of the Jewish Homeland. General Allenby had by that time conquered the southern half of the country, up to and somewhat beyond Jerusalem; the northern half was still in the hands of the Turks and Germans. On July 24th, 1918, General Allenby and his staff were invited to attend a strange ceremony: the laying of the foundation stone of the Hebrew University.

The group of British officers stood in the midst of a Jewish crowd assembled on the summit of Mount Scopus. Southward lay the conquered area, and eastward, beyond the Judaean Wilderness, lay the Dead

Sea. From the north the mutter of artillery maintained a background to the brief addresses. The summit of Scopus was almost bare; the country round about desolate; the city of Jerusalem, glittering in the sunlight, lay dreaming behind its ancient walls. There was hunger in the land; the danger of war was heavy in the air. But here, on the hill from which the Romans had directed the destruction of the Jewish Temple nearly twenty centuries before, the cornerstone of a modern temple was being laid, and among the languages used in the dedication and prayers was the one which the ancient priesthood would have claimed as its own. It is a pity that no record seems to exist of what was in the minds of the British officers.

CHAPTER SEVENTEEN

Quality or Quantity?

❀

IT ALL sounded so simple on paper. The victorious Allied Powers had said to the Jewish people: "Go, all of you who so desire, and rebuild your Homeland in Palestine." What remained then, for those Jews who found life intolerable in the diaspora — and there were millions of them — but to pack up and go? Those that had means would sell out and go forthwith; those that had none would get help from their better situated coreligionists. In a few years the Jewish State would be reconstituted, and the ancient dream of the Jewish people, or at any rate of the greater part of it, would be fulfilled: everything exactly as Theodore Herzl had foreseen it.

But between this exhilarating *simpliste* program and the realities of life lay an immense gulf, or rather series of gulfs, a whole labyrinth of them. There was, to begin with, the occupational problem. Palestine needed: first, workers on the land; second, workers in the cities; third, professionals and merchants. European Jewry, under historic compulsions, had developed occupationally in exactly the opposite direction: first, merchants and professionals; second, city workers; third (a long way behind), workers on the land. A tremendous mass inversion had to take place if Palestine was to be built on solid foundations.

Could that be done in a few years? Could hundreds of thousands of individuals be retrained, and the habits and traditions of centuries overcome, by fiat? An individual can make the transition from city to land, from office or shop to field, if he is exceptionally gifted in physique and character. A mass can do it only if it is caught up in a historic process, and process means not only deep-going forces; it means also time. The great colonizing project of Baron de Hirsch in the Argentine failed because it did not call up, in the masses, the support of a historic association. Palestine had the associative element in sufficient measure; but could it remake a people overnight?

The first problem, the occupational, was bound up with a second, the psychological. The Jews were, to a large extent, a sophisticated and literate urban element. Tens of thousands of them might talk yearningly of a simple life on the soil; more, they were prepared to endure a great deal in order to realize that ideal. But they were quite incapable of giving up their intellectual standards, either for themselves or their children. We have just seen that almost before they had started the purchase of land for the great expected immigration, the Zionist leaders laid the foundation stone of a University! It will therefore hardly come as a surprise to learn that between the years 1918 and 1921 the Jews spent, in Palestine, over two million dollars on education, and less than $600,000 on colonization! Both the University project and the emphasis on the schools were denounced by many Zionists. This was all nonsense, they said. Schools could wait; social planning could wait; selection of the human material was out of place. Every penny should be spent on bringing Jews in, bringing them in anyhow, bringing them in with or without preparation. Let half a million Jews be thrown into Palestine in one year (this was the so-called "Max Nordau Plan," named after its sponsor. A more fitting title would be the "Pell-Mell Plan," or the "Planless Plan"). Suppose two hundred thousand of them migrated, or died, there would be three hundred thousand left. Repeat the process a second year, a third, a fourth — and the back of the problem would be broken. But this extraordinary business of schools and collectives and cultural enterprises would get the Homeland nowhere. Especially as money was not coming in as fast as had been hoped (gulf number three between hope and reality), since the richest Jews, with a few notable exceptions, stood aloof from the Zionist effort; and as the Administration of Palestine did not show itself as cooperative as the Jews had anticipated (gulf number four); and as Russian Jewry, the most creative Jewish center up till that time, was cut off from participation by Russian government decree (gulf number five); and as Jewish leftists everywhere were fighting the Zionist movement (gulf number six); and as various territorial projects for Jewish resettlement were diverting attention and effort from Palestine without settling Jews anywhere (gulf number seven) — to go no further.

We need not go into the merits of the pell-mell plan. It is sufficient to note that the great majority of Zionists were opposed to it; and whether or not the disparity between the money spent on colonies and the money spent on schools was too great even with the special psychological make-up of the Jews taken into account, the fact remains that it represented roughly the will of the Zionists. In the years immediately following the war, the Zionist leadership was afraid of a planless and indiscriminate migration. It was afraid of a recoil. A great dispute then arose round the question of quality versus quantity; one side said that given quantity, quality would emerge afterwards; the other side said, given quality, quantity would follow. One side said: "If you niggle over quality, you will lose the historic opportunity;" the other side said: "If you neglect quality you will have a fiasco." It was therefore not a dispute as to the ends, but as to the means.

If there had been a limitless supply of money, the qualitative view might have been combined to some extent with the quantitative. But the funds at the disposal of the Zionists were never more than a fraction of what they could have used. Ussischkin, in 1920, asked for an annual budget of four million pounds for Palestine. He got less than a quarter of that sum. Yet it was not just a question of money. One hundred million pounds could not have hastened beyond its natural tempo the conversion of the human material; the strongest will is limited by the operation of social and historic laws.

As to the quality of the human material and the strength of will among those who, in the years 1919, 1920, 1921, were determined to get into Palestine, even against the intentions of the Zionist leadership, there can be only one opinion: they were of the highest. Even so, it was permissible to temper admiration with caution; it hurt, but it could not be helped. In those now far-off years, wandering throughout Europe, I met in the wretched Baluta of Lodz, in the equally wretched Franciskaner of Warsaw, in the Dragoner and Grenadier streets of Berlin, in the rue des Petits Blancs Manteaux of Paris, as well as in the middle-class districts, the young vanguard of the Third Wave — the *Halutzim*, or pioneers, who wrote into the history of the Homeland a chapter as distinctive and fascinating as those of the *Bilus* and the *Shomrim*. The word *Halutz* applies just as properly to the preceding pioneers; but somehow it came to be attached to this group of the Third Wave, and the time of the *Halutzim* is always understood to cover the years following the First World War. These prospective pioneers, as one encountered them in Europe, were at once a thrilling and disturbing phenomenon.

Their enthusiasm and devotion made one think of some great religious movement in the purity of its inception. Their probable usefulness in the task they were approaching was, even to the most benevolent observer, a matter of conjecture. Children and grandchildren of the ghetto, they suggested anything but horny-handed sons of the soil. They were, for the most part, a nervous, high-strung lot; their physique was second-rate as compared with that of the solid, muscular agricultural and laboring immigrants who had once poured out of Norway and Sweden and Poland and Italy into America. The shadows of two thousand years of insecurity haunted their eyes. They talked passionately of a normal life on the land, of a stable, healthy national existence in Palestine. They talked too passionately on the subject; they were slightly insane in the pursuit of sanity, abnormally determined to be normal.

The *Hachsharah,* or training farms of the *He-Halutz* organization, which was later to play a great part in the transitional period, were not yet in existence. Group preparation was hardly known. Singly or in couples, the young men cut loose from their moorings and sought a way to preparation and to Palestine. Penniless, unworldly, unskilled in any trade, they took to the road, planning to pick up a trade as they worked their way to a port, while they saved enough money for the last lap of the journey, across the sea from Trieste or Constanza to Palestine. And through a thousand odysseys they reached their goal, or died on the way.

I encountered them by the score. In Bordeaux, in the spring of 1919, two boys came to me in the Military Intelligence Office where I was working — two ragged, feverish-looking Polish boys. A certain Palestinian, who was studying medicine at the local University (he is now a physician in Jerusalem) and supporting himself by teaching me Hebrew and carrying parcels for grocers, had given them my name. Their parents, who were in Poland, had sent them to France shortly before the outbreak of the war, to study at the University of Montpellier. When the war came, and they were stranded without funds, they tried to join the Foreign Legion, and were rejected. They had worked, since then, at every conceivable occupation, barely keeping themselves alive. Now they were again in touch with their parents, who had lost everything and wanted their sons to return. But they were not going. Their eyes were fixed on Palestine. What did they want of me? Not money, but any sort of job which would enable them to save the fare for the sea-journey. And I, looking at them, thought: "Good God! Is this the stuff of a

175

pioneering generation? Are these our peasants-to-be?"
I do not remember what help, if any, I was able to
extend to them. I remember only my concern for them
and for the future of a Jewish Homeland which would
have to depend on such builders.

In the fall of 1920, I was living in Hallensee, Berlin,
and made the acquaintance of another Polish boy who
was apprenticed to a Bavarian shoemaker who had his
store at the corner of Joachim-Friedrichstrasse and the
Kurfürstendamm. "Apprenticed" is hardly the word,
since there was no contract and the Bavarian acted
more out of charity than in the belief that his "appren-
tice" would ever learn the trade. Myself the son of a
shoemaker, I have some feeling in the matter, and I
was distressed to see the Polish youngster holding his
awl as if it were a pen, and examining a pair of shoes
with the dreamy intentness of a Talmudist. His story
was long and depressing. He had left Warsaw the year
before, with Palestine as his ultimate destination, shoemaking as the profession which would fit him for a
creative role in the country. Why shoemaking? He
answered that he had so often gone barefoot that he
had conceived a passion for the making and mending of
shoes. He left Kovno and walked for two weeks till he
reached Warsaw, where he could not find employment.
From Warsaw he walked to Breslau. There he lived
chiefly by selling one-half of his ration cards in order to
have money with which to buy something with the
other half. Breslau brought him no nearer to fulfilment,
so he moved on to Vienna, where, having for a time
cleaned spittoons in the Krystal Café and the Simpli-
ciccimus Cabaret, he took service with a Jewish shoemaker on the Judengasse. He learned little there, this

Jewish shoemaker never having finished his own apprenticeship, and being a *shuster* only in the derogatory Yiddish sense of the word, that is, a botcher. Such as he was, however, the shoemaker did not last long. He died before the *Halutz* had cut his first pair of soles. From Vienna the determined youngster retreated a distance from Palestine, and came to Berlin. It was, however, as Lenin would have said, *reculer pour mieux sauter*. In Berlin he fell sick, and lay two months in the Charlottenburg *Krankenhaus*. One would have thought that by then he was ready to go home to Kovno. Nothing of the sort. He managed somehow to ingratiate himself with the Bavarian shoemaker at the corner of our street, where I found him. He was quite certain that before long he would be in Palestine, making and mending shoes.

In the winter of 1920 to 1921, I was living in Vienna, and in the nearby village of Huttelsdorf I encountered, among a group of roadworkers, a frail Jewish boy, ill-clad, ill-fed, who was breaking stones in freezing weather and making barely enough to keep him alive. But of that "barely enough" he spent only one-half on food, and he passed his nights rent-free in an unwarmed, rat-infested cellar. The rest he was saving for the fare.

These and others occur in my notes or my memory. Who could have foreseen what Palestine would do for them? For I met many of them again, in Ain Harod and Bet Zera and Bet Alpha and Nahalal, and they were hardly to be recognized. Bronzed by the sun, healed by the attainment of their purpose, the shadows gone from their eyes, the premature wrinkles from their faces, they typified the Jewish transformation in its extremest sense. Not that Palestine had been easier for

them than the lands of the intermediary ordeals. Very
rarely did a *Halutz* find a place on a colony waiting for
him when he at last set foot in Palestine. Land for new
settlements was just being bought, the preparation was
just being started. Our roadbuilder of Huttelsdorf probably found his first employment breaking stones, along
with hundreds of other young Jews and Jewesses, for
the network of roads then being laid down between
cities and villages. It was just as hard to break stones
under the semi-tropical sun of Palestine as under the
winter skies of Austria. Nor did he eat much better
than in the old days. But he knew that at the end of
the road he was building now — quite literally at the
end of it — there would be home. Our shoemaker of
Hallensee did not have to clean spittoons as he had
done in the Krystal Café. But it is not likely that he
stayed at shoemaking. The chances are that he joined
the drainers of the swamps of Bet Alpha and Merhavia;
and a swamp is, so to speak, a sort of natural spittoon.
But he knew that when *this* spittoon had been cleaned
it would never be soiled again. The foul, stagnant area
would be converted into fruitful land, for himself and
for his comrades.

Years passed before the young men and women of
the Third Wave were definitely settled on the land or in
the city. By then the men and women of the First Wave
were old, and those of the Second Wave middle-aged.
The newcomers sustained the tradition, and set at rest
the fears of those who doubted, not their willingness or
faithfulness, but their sheer physical adaptability. The
protagonists of "qualitative" colonization had not quite
known how superb was the material at the disposal of

the ideal. I have said that without the work done by the men and women of the Second Wave, there would probably have been no Balfour Declaration, in spite of the colonies of the PICA. In the spring of 1914 Baron de Rothschild visited Palestine, and publicly declared to the Zionists: "What you Zionists have done is perhaps not much, but without you my work would have been dead." It is equally true that without the men and women of the Third Wave, the first post-war period of growth would have been impossible; the Fourth and Fifth Waves would never have followed; the Jewish Homeland would have remained a documentary curiosity, a tribute to British and American statesmanship and a memorial to the departed creative spirit of the Jewish people.

CHAPTER EIGHTEEN

The Third Wave

❀

I HAVE used the word Wave (of immigration) as a substitute for the Hebrew *Aliyah*, which means, literally, a "going up," a phrase with a double meaning implicit in the original. An *Aliyah* meant, for instance, a going up to Jerusalem, as on a pilgrimage; just as, in the synagogue, an *Aliyah* is the mounting of the pulpit, to read from the Torah. It also means an ascent or sublimation, as applied to a mystic in communion with God. The overtone is therefore that of a going-up to liberty, to high experience, and the overtone is present in the use of the word to indicate the successive Waves of immigration.

Each Wave had its own character and its special place in the history of the new Palestine. The first was the opening demonstration of the will to the Return, from 1882 on; the second was the beginning of the practical crystallization, from 1904 on; the third, from 1919 to 1924, was the laying and extension of the foundations for the great subsequent expansion. Between 1919 and 1924 great affirmative changes were affected in the corporate nature of the emergent Homeland. The first instrument of Jewish self-government was created, the *Asefath ha-Nivharim*, or Assembly of Deputies, representing the *K'neseth Israel*, the Jewish community; though it was only in 1928 that it became a legal personality, with certain very limited legislative powers. The fragmented labor movement fused into the *Histadruth*, the Hebrew Federation of Labor, which dominates the social structure of Jewish Palestine. The political and national complexion of Jewish Palestine took on the outlines which remain till this day, and will probably remain into the remote future.

It need hardly be said that in the time of the Third Wave, too, there were violent disputes among the Zionists as to the general planning — this apart from the major question of "quality versus quantity," already mentioned. The differences in outlook were made sharper by the decisive circumstance that now the building of the Homeland was proceeding under international guarantee, with the sanction of the fifty-one members of the League of Nations and the special and separate approval of the government of the United States, by the unanimous resolution of both Houses of Congress (June, 1922). It was felt on all sides that this was the crucial period, and now the big showing had to be made. Were the Jews serious, or were they not, in their demand for a Jewish Homeland? To put it bluntly, did they have the goods, or didn't they?

The major divergence of opinion, the one which led to a disastrous split in American Zionism in 1921 (there were other contributory causes which are not relevant to this narrative), hinged on the question of "business methods." One party believed that the colonization of Palestine could best be furthered by the application of, or at least emphasis on, the principle of self-liquidation. Public funds, donations, money contributed without expectation of return, should play a secondary and perhaps minimal role, such as they play in the general economy of all countries. Investment was to be the keynote of the new phase of development in Palestine; the country must be made attractive to capital, otherwise there could be no considerable development. The other party denied the validity of this premise. It pointed to the fact that all the colonization companies which had been founded in the sixteenth century to help in the development of America had been financial failures — and in America the pioneers had not had to pay exorbitant prices for every inch of land they occupied. It held the view that capital would be attracted to Palestine only when, by the sinking of public funds, by the preliminary sacrifices of idealistic groups, the country had developed to the point where an average businessman or manufacturer would consider it a fair risk to transfer his savings and his enterprise to the country.

One element in the first group went so far as to say that the time had come to dissolve the Zionist Organization, which had existed only for the purpose of obtaining the Charter (now the Mandate). The job before the Jews was purely technical, and should be entrusted to technicians. The men who had led the movement until then should retire in favor of the new type, better fitted for the new phase. And against this it was argued vehemently that the propaganda work, within the Jewish people and outside of it, was by no means done. It would be a long, long time before donated funds would cease to play a major role in the upbuilding, and before

Jews who were not deeply Zionistic, and who had money to invest, would turn to Palestine. It would be just as long, also, before the propagandizing of the non-Jewish world could be given up as superfluous.

The second group remained in control of the movement. It would be futile to attempt, at this date, to determine the rights and wrongs of the discussion; we need only note that the outcome was the result of a democratic test, and the decision supported by a large majority. The general consensus was, that the building of the Jewish Homeland had not yet, and would not for a long time, become a purely technical proposition, to be turned over to industrialists, financiers and experts generally. Not that the cooperation of such men was not eagerly sought. And not that business method was undesirable. But the character of the Return was as yet idealistic.

Whether the second group was wholly in the right, or whether (as their opponents averred) their policy was the determining factor, the following figures indicate the financial background of the rebuilding up till 1924. From 1917 to 1924 the general Zionist funds (at first the Palestine Restoration Fund, and then the *Keren Hayesod*, or Palestine Foundation Fund), together with the special Jewish National Fund, brought $15,000,000 into the country. (We have seen that $20,000,000 *a year* had been the expectation of the Zionist leadership!). The PICA spent another $1,000,000 a year. The Joint Distribution Committee spent more than $3,000,000 in Palestine during the entire period. Business investment, or private capital, amounted to something more than $3,000,000. The proportion of private investment to public donation was as one to eight.

183

With some fifty-five thousand Jews in Palestine at the end of the war, it was generally accepted by the Zionist leadership that, given the adequate public funds, the country could absorb twenty thousand immigrants a year. Actually, between 1919 and 1924, the Jewish population grew to about 100,000; that is to say, it rather more than recovered the loss occasioned by the war: which might seem disappointing, and indeed was, though not in the measure that many Zionists believed it to be. There were some who pointed, at the end of that period, to the populational transfers between Greece and Turkey, in which nearly three million Greeks and Turks changed places in less than three years. But the cases were not parallel in any way. Three million Greek and Turkish peasants, accustomed to a hard and penurious life on the soil, occupied each others' territory. The resettlement costs were extremely low. Moreover, Greece provided a populational background of five million, Turkey one of thirteen million, to absorb the repatriates. The Jewish populational background was, as we have seen, 55,000. The Arab populational background did not count, for the Arabs were, in respect of the Jewish economy, not consumers. Nor were Greeks and Turks concerned with social ideals. No improvement either in the standard of living or in social organization, no maintenance of a high level of education, was contemplated by the managers of the transfer. If, in view of these considerations, Jewish Palestine increased its population by about eighty per cent in the five years under review, it was a respectable achievement.

But it was more than that when the character of the reconstruction is taken into account. The men and women of the Third Wave had, in even larger measure, the idealism of those who, after 1904, had come to Palestine to carry out the "conquest of labor." The socialist and romantic movements of Europe had imparted a special tinge to their Zionism. In Germany the *Wandervogel*, youthful rebels against the stodginess of middle-class life, its narrowness and egotism, its self-sufficiencies and timidities, and above all its citified psychology, had influenced large numbers of young Jews, who applied the general philosophy to the Jewish position and created the Zionist *Blau-Weiss*. And it cannot be denied that Jewish middle-class life, already on the economic downgrade before the First World War, had become a pitiable spectacle after it, and was obviously in a state of rapid deterioration. The economic function of central and east European Jewry (we exclude the special case of Russia) was dying out, while proletarianization ran up against external resistance and internal psychological habits. Those who travelled through Poland after the First World War, and saw the bulk of its "middle class" clinging desperately, almost insanely, to its status, to its terminology and outlook, were appalled by the picture. A man whose stock-in-trade consisted of a barrel of herrings, obtained on credit, called himself a merchant. The Nalevkys of Warsaw and the Baluta of Lodz were crowded with these peddlers. If a tiny upper level of this bourgeoisie still existed, it served to emphasize, in sensitive minds, the wretchedness of the submerged ninety-five per cent. A dread of everything that could be called "middle-class" haunted the youngsters of the Third Wave. They were determined that, as far as lay in their power, the phenomenon would not be repeated in Palestine; and this determination set the tone for the constructive period of 1919 to 1924, and left its permanent mark on the country.

Within Palestine the war years had witnessed a general extension of the cooperative method. By the end of 1918 there were twenty-nine collectives at work. The newcomers therefore did not have to create these forms, as the immigrants of 1904 had had to do. The question now was: could the forms be expanded, and were they adaptable to new conditions? Could building and road-laying contracts be taken over by collectivist groups? Could the small collectivist colonies grow from tens to hundreds of settlers, and yet retain their character?

The *Histadruth* (Labor Federation), to be described in more detail further on, was the chief instrument in the evolution of the new forms or the adaptation of old ones to the new conditions. Only one instance will be mentioned here. *Solel Boneh* was a contracting office of the *Histadruth*, for house-building and road-laying. It competed for government and private jobs, and it carried them out as a workers' cooperative enterprise. *Solel Boneh* lost money, and was a subject of much dispute at the Zionist Congresses and among contributors to the Zionist funds. It could not have continued without the subsidies of the Palestine Foundation Fund. But it performed two services which were entirely outside the field of private capital. It trained thousands of workers; and it gave them the only form of social organization into which they would pour their enthusiasm. We have seen this picture before in the first work of the Jewish National Fund, in 1908.

It was again the Jewish National Fund which created the possibility for the cooperative method of which the

Histadruth was the central exponent. It may definitely be said that without the Jewish National Fund the new post-war colonization could not have been carried out. In 1921 the Jewish National Fund acquired, in the Valley of Jezreel, a block of land (Nuris), 29,000 dunams, 16,000 of which was swamp. It took over two years to drain the swamp. In the first years the incidence of malaria among the workers was 35%; in the second year, 22%; in the third, 14%. (By 1928 malaria had disappeared in this region, on which were settled 1,500 souls, in five collectives and one individualist colony.) In Nahalal, another section of the Jezreel Valley, the National Fund bought 21,000 dunams of land. In the first year 65% of the reclamation workers suffered from malaria, in the second year 40%. (By 1928 malaria was unknown in Nahalal.) The men and women who did the work, and who in part settled the reclaimed areas, were largely those of the Third Wave. Without them the project could not have been undertaken; and they could not have been harnessed effectively except in the social form which was their interpretation of Zionism.

It should be said that, in spite of the controversies which raged in those days about the subject of the collectives, the Jewish world was filled with admiration for the *Halutzim*, and in Zionist circles the word *Halutz* came to have a special meaning. It represented — and still represents — a type, a Jewish type, symbolizing a period and a moral achievement. It is a specific word, like *knight*, or *cowboy*, the epitome of a historic phase and experience, and it has passed, with its emotional coloration, into the general Jewish vocabulary.

Despite the help which came from abroad, in largest measure from America, the struggle of the *Halutzim* was a hard one. There was never enough money, never enough food, never enough medical service. In 1920, Hadassah, the American Women's Zionist Organization (founded in 1912 by Henrietta Szold) sent out a Medical Unit of thirty-odd doctors, nurses and assistants. It did magnificent work in combatting trachoma (the traditional eye disease of the Near East), teaching hygiene, setting up clinics, and conducting research, for the benefit of Arabs as well as of Jews. But the country could have used ten and twenty times that number. Even if Palestine had not been, as it was, a country which had to be reclaimed and cleansed from the effect of centuries of neglect, and even if funds had been forthcoming in generous measure, the *Halutzim* would have faced a task of extraordinary difficulty. They passed from the city to the soil; from a temperate to a subtropical climate; from a middle-class to a proletarian milieu; from centers of civilization to the rim of the wilderness; from books, movements, theaters, music to primitive isolation. For these things they were prepared. They did not know, however, that often they would have to go short of food in order that the cattle might not, that they would have to build stables before they built houses. But they learned to do that too, and to summon up a wry humor. "We'll manage on less," one of them said to me. "After all, we're Zionists. But our cows are not."

One is tempted to think of them as fierce, single-minded fanatics, untroubled by doubts and therefore never tempted to defection. The picture would be wrong, and would do them less than justice. They were tormented by personal and social questionings. They went down to root problems, and wrestled with fundamental decisions. They asked themselves: had they the right to withdraw themselves from the liberal and proletarian struggle in Europe, and go off to build a Jewish Homeland? Was not this a kind of political desertion? And they answered that they had not abandoned the proletarian struggle; they were carrying it on in their own peculiar way, not through battle and protest, but by the attempt to create a social commonwealth. They had chosen Palestine as the scene of their contribution to the all-human cause. Zionism was for them the special instrument set aside by history for the Jewish interpretation of democracy. They were sensitive to the accusation that they might be looked upon as the tools of British imperialism. But were they to give up Palestine, the *K'vutzah* form of life, and the flight from the middle class, for that reason?

These were in a sense theoretical discussions. Others had a more practical bearing. When at last the opportunity was given them to settle on the land, doubts assailed them as to the practicality of the enterprise. Was this particular place, this outpost in the Valley of Jezreel or in the wastes of Upper Galilee, suitable for colonization? Would this emptiness in time be filled with life, work, cheerfulness and song? Had the soil been properly examined? Had they chosen the right crops?

They scrutinized, too, the implications of their social organization. Would they get along with one another? They were cast away from the world, and the murmur of the big events in which they had once participated came through to them like ghostly rumors. They were like the first men on the moon, all alone here, sustaining an ideal born to them in the cities of Europe, while Europe had forgotten them. They had talked of justice, equality, the eight-hour day — but in a new colony, though there might be justice and equality, there was no eight-hour day. Nature takes no cognizance of theories; sowing and harvest times have their own harsh laws. You must sweat from morning till after nightfall. Weaklings were a burden. How did that jibe with their original dreams?

This was not all. In Tel Aviv, Haifa, Jerusalem, a new city life was springing up. Sometimes a woman of the colony went to one of the cities on a visit. She saw there the old way of life. She met on the streets former friends of hers, girls who had once believed in the communal system, but who had married and had slipped back into the individualist psychology. Up there, in the commune, children were taken care of in groups, by specially delegated comrades. In the evening the parents were allowed to spend an hour or two with the little one; during the day, the nursery was the common home of the children. A painful uncertainty awoke in the visitor's mind, and she brought it back with her to the colony. Was her child getting the emotional environment it needed? Was her little Uri, or Simhah, or Moshe, storing up the affection and joy which were needed to make a balanced man or woman? Or was she, the mother, raising this question only in egotistic selfishness, prompted less by a regard for the true needs of the child than by the deceptive impulse to self-indulgence?

They debated the problem fiercely, always alert to the possibility that they were thinking too much of

190

themselves, too little of the growing generation; always alert, likewise, to the possibility that in their anxiety to discount their own bias, they were undervaluing certain important considerations. (Not for nothing were they the descendants of Talmudists.) Yes, the nursery in the colony was bright and cheerful; it was intelligently conducted; there was none of the sloppiness of the individualist home, none of the impatience, the emotional squalls, the suppressions . . . None of the proprietary egotism of parents . . . But — but — suppose the cheerfulness and intelligence of the nursery were bound up with a certain coolness, an absence of deep emotional experience? Was it not possible that quarrels and reconciliations, strains and the loving resolution of strains, had a more creative effect on the personality than the scientifically balanced psychological neatness of the nursery? Or was this again the special pleading of the frustrated, so-called mother instinct?

The question of egotism in relation to persons carried over into egotism in relation to things. The collectives, especially in those early days, gave no encouragement to privacy of possession or even of retreat. A tent or shack housed a group. The luxury of "a room of one's own" was beyond the reach of the colonists. A young married couple got no more than a corner with a curtain drawn diagonally across it. There were some collectives where the discouragement of personal property was carried to queer extremes. A man literally could not call his shirt his own. When the one he wore went to the laundry, he could not be sure he would get it back; he was given, and accepted, any shirt that fitted him more or less. And there were long talks as to whether this should be so or not; whether it should be

191

exalted as a principle and made permanent, or regarded as part of the discipline of the transition.

There were long talks, also, as to whether the *K'vutzah*, or collectivist colony, was capable of binding a man to the soil. The land was held in common, and as no member of the *K'vutzah* had a room of his own, so he had not a patch of soil he could call his own. But they had heard that the primal instinct of the landworker, the peasant, was for some particular plot with which he identified himself, which he learned to love and understand, so that every clod and furrow had a peculiar appeal to him. Would it not be better, then, to try another form of colonization? Not, God forbid, the purely individualist, with every colonist thinking only of his self-advancement, but the intermediary form of the *Moshav Ovdim*, also on National Fund land, but not as extreme as the *K'vutzah*. On the *Moshav Ovdim* (literally, Settlement of Workers) each man had his piece of land, his plot. He was forbidden, by the statutes of the National Fund, to exploit anyone's labor. But he was not forbidden to profit individually by his superior ability, by his frugality, by his devotion to his work. Was it not permissible for a man, or for a couple, to retain so much of an area for personal initiative? After all, the National Fund sanctioned those enterprises too. There were five *Moshave Ovdim* at the end of the war. Should the *K'vuzah-ites* convert their *K'vutzah* into a *Moshav Ovdim*? Or would that be a concession to anti-social impulses?

No doubt there is, in retrospect, a suggestion of the unreal, perhaps even of the comical, in the deadly earnestness of those groups. But if they had not considered their problems under the aspect of the fundamental and eternal, they would not have held out. They saw themselves as the representatives of a people in rebirth. They were concerned with the ethical implications of their mission. They had not come to Palestine only to restore fruitfulness to barren places; they were restoring to the Jewish people the original moral creativity which had made the soil of Palestine so singular in the history of humanity.

On Friday evenings, when the week's labor was done, they put on fresh clothes and rejoiced in the Sabbath. The world was quiet about them. They forgot the material worries of the weekdays and gave themselves up to the spirit of the tradition. They gathered in the largest tent or shack, or, if that was too small, they sat under the stars, singing, talking, meditating. In those, the best moments, everything seemed worth while. A strange exaltation would often take hold of them — and not only on the Sabbath eve. Moods of mystical fulfilment, akin to the religious rhapsodies of cabalistic adepts, were common among those pioneers of the Emek and of Galilee. The *Hora,* a community dance which drew all the colonists into a single swaying, rhythmic circle, was an echo of the ecstatic dances of their hasidic forefathers. The dancers supplied the vocal music for the *Hora,* letting their voices ring out across the surrounding desolation; and often, when the seizure came on them, they would swing into a *Hora* even on a weekday, after ten or twelve hours of work, dancing and singing until there was no more breath in their lungs, no more strength in their muscles, and they dropped out one by one. Something stronger than their conscious will was in them; they were dancing away their sufferings, their sex repressions, their doubts, their ascetic denial of worldly comfort and worldly ideals; they were dancing out their sense of a youth lost and sacrificed, but also of a reversion to the soil and to the history of their people.

But the most astonishing element in the picture was this: in the midst of their exaltations, their discussions, their theorizings, the *Halutzim* were serious, practical, and even hard-headed. They were learning their various crafts, rapidly and efficiently. They took full advantage of the information furnished them by the agricultural institute which the Zionist Organization set up with headquarters in Tel Aviv, and of the discoveries of the experimental stations at Ben Shemen in the south and Daganiah in the north. They studied soil chemistry, crossbreeding of fowl and of cattle, irrigation, fertilization, management of plant nurseries; and they picked up the trick of being general handymen. Toward the close of the period now being described — the period followed by the Fourth Wave — I toured the country, and marked the solid achievements of the *Halutzim*. I was in Daganiah. In the old days Daganiah and Kinereth had been connected across the Jordan only by ferry. Now there was a sturdy wooden bridge thrown across the river. I asked Joseph Baratz, the leader who had taken the place of Joseph Bussel: "Who built this bridge?"

"The *Halutzim*," he answered.

"Who built those houses?"

"*Halutzim*."

"Who laid that road?" (from Daganiah to Tiberias).

"*Halutzim*."

"Who taught them?"

"I don't know."

It was true. He did not know, and nobody else knew. They had picked it up, here, there, by experiment, by repeated failure. I went up from Daganiah to Rosh Pinah. There, as in many other individualist colonies, the passing tobacco fever had taken hold. (This was 1924.) Everywhere it was grapes and tobacco, figs and tobacco, grain and tobacco, anything and tobacco. (The tobacco experiment was not a success. It could not compete with the Egyptian and Turkish crops.) A tobacco grower said to me, regarding the two hundred *Halutzim* who had come up for the season: "Their work is first-class. You can't get the same service from Arabs. They haven't the dexterity; they won't string up the tobacco leaf as swiftly and as accurately and as patiently as our boys and girls do." Rosh Pinah had come a long way in forty years. With its six or seven hundred inhabitants, with its stores, streets, school, teachers, it had all but forgotten those bitter days of the eighteen-eighties. But north of Rosh Pinah, in a tremendous theater of mountains and valleys, Tel Hai and K'far Gileadi clung to the perilous and sullen slopes. They were re-enacting the story of Rosh Pinah, from its harsh beginnings. Forlorn outposts of the northern wastes, they had paid in blood for their right to be. I was shown the spot where Joseph Trumpeldor was shot down by the Arab who climbed the enclosing wall and offered the one-armed veteran of the Russo-Japanese War the alternative of death or of treacherous surrender. I was shown the loft where two girls were killed in the same foray, and in K'far Gileadi the little circular garden, set apart, where the victims were first buried. I was tempted to ask: "Why did you come out here? Why do you endure and hunger? What drives you and sustains you?" But I knew the answer in advance. It was *"Binyan ha-aretz"* — the building of the land.

The *Ganei Yeladim* and the *Batei ha-K'vuroth*, the nursery and the cemetery, were the two certain possessions of each colony: the future and the past, both equally binding. The parents tasted meat perhaps once a week; they labored from morning to night; they dressed in rags; they forgot the temptations of the city. But no want came near their children. Their children would remember only happiness — and that would bind them to the soil. It was the thought of the coming generation which knew, across the warp of their dreams, the threads of practicality.

Down in the south, in Rehovoth and Petah Tikvah, there was prosperity: green masses of leaves, red roofs and white walls, solid houses, orchards of vine and almond and orange; and beyond the circle of the settlement the hungry, blazing yellow sands from which Rehovoth and Petah Tikvah had been created. The *Halutzim* of the north knew well, and sometimes only too well, the self-satisfaction of the old colonists of the south. They had sought work there, and been rejected. They had competed with cheap Arab labor, sometimes with success, sometimes to be defeated. They were going to create the same centers of comfortable life up in Galilee, but on completely different foundations. The PICA colonists had had a forty-year start; the *Halutzim* would catch up with them in ten. The boast was not easy to believe in 1924. Those that uttered it, however, had, within their idealistic natures, a core of shrewdness and practicality. They kept their word.

Joseph Baratz told the truth when he said he did not know where the *Halutzim* picked up their skills. But by that time a change had come into the operations of the Zionist Organization. Many of the later *Halutzim* could tell you very definitely where they had been trained: on some farm in Poland, Roumania, Czecho-Slovakia, Germany, in some communal workshop, started and maintained by *He-Halutz*, the organization for *Hachsharah*, or preparation. The chaos of the immediate post-war years was replaced by a certain order. Aspirants for Palestine no longer had to seek out their training haphazard, like our stone-breaker and shoemaker. The Return was taking on a pattern.

The pattern was to be shattered and remade several times under the pressure of external forces. The year 1924 marked off one of the periods. The country had formed its cadres for the reception of newcomers. This was true not only in the colonies, but in the cities. Tel Aviv had grown from a village of fifteen hundred in 1914, to a bustling townlet of twenty-five thousand. Industry lagged far behind agricultural development; but there were notable beginnings, such as the silicate factory of Tel Aviv, the cement factory, the oil and flour mills of Haifa, and a score of smaller enterprises, weaving, knitting, watchmaking, candle-making, beds, furniture, cardboard, mineral waters. In the spring of 1924 Tel Aviv held its first industrial exhibit, a very minor affair compared with the imposing Levant Fairs of later years. But it was a start.

The figures which follow do not make interesting reading. They are necessary as markers, and for comparisons. By 1924 Jewish land-holdings totalled some 750,000 dunams (less than 200,000 acres, or 300 square miles); of this the National Fund held somewhat more than one-tenth. There were 120 schools in the country, under the management of the Zionist Organization, with 500 teachers and 12,000 pupils. The *Technikum* had just been opened in Haifa, the Hebrew University was about to be launched, with departments in micro-biology, biochemistry and Jewish and Oriental studies. The Library had some 80,000 volumes. In Jerusalem the new suburbs of Talpioth, Rehaviah and Beth ha-Kerem were springing up, paralleled by Hadar ha-Carmel, Nevei Shaanan and Bath Galim in Haifa and Kiriath Shemuel in Tiberias.

It was a time of ferment and of great hopes. The Emek and Galilee bespoke the rebirth of the land, Tel Aviv bespoke the rebirth of the cities. For all its brashness, tumult and rawness, Tel Aviv was as impressive in its way as the strange new colonies of the north. It was the center of the labor movement as well as of the new industrialization. Under its unappealing exterior of planless streets and tasteless buildings — the first fruits of large scale urban pioneering — there was a spirit of social and cultural enterprise. Tel Aviv was metropolitan in the European and American sense, while it had all the aspects of a frontier boom town. There was not an evening on which a dozen meetings were not in progress, for the discussion of general and specific problems. The town early became the center of the Hebrew publishing trade, and it was amazing to note how a handful of readers — it must be remembered that not all Palestinians used Hebrew — sustained a considerable press and called for dozens of books, originals and translations, every year. To live in Tel Aviv was to be in the swim, intellectually, with the modern currents of thought and theory.

On Saturday evenings, when the "hicks" came in by bus from Rishon and Rehovoth and Petah Tikvah, and other nearby colonies, the Allenby Street leading down to the Casino, and the famous seafront along the Mediterranean, were filled with young people swinging along arm in arm, laughing, talking, singing — with Hebrew already predominating. A traveller who had just left Europe, where the great decline of Jewish life was already perceptible, and where the shadows of the fiercest anti-Semitic epoch in all history had already fallen upon the communities, could not but experience a lifting of the heart in the presence of this manifestation of freedom and of released creative energy; the more so if here, as in the wilds of Samaria and Galilee, he recognized the transformed personalities of the ghetto prisoners he had encountered in the darkening west. There wasn't much yet to Palestine, only a hundred thousand Jews in all, and some of them useless for the renaissance. But it was the one place in the world where Jewish life was not on the defensive — not even when, as we shall have to tell, it was subject to physical attack. For it was not a *holding* defensive; it was a defensive in the midst of expansion. Everywhere else, the best that could be expected was, that no more ground should be lost. Here there was no thought of standing still. And it was this awareness that imparted such an infectious liveliness and hopefulness to the Tel Avivian crowds and the settlements of Jezreel.

THE Fourth Wave came in 1925. It was a tidal wave; it shattered the pattern of the work, upset all calculations and brushed away all plans. Immigration had maintained, since 1919, an annual average of less than 10,000. It was 7,400 in 1924. In 1925, 34,000 Jews entered the country. They came from Poland (17,000), from Russia and the Ukraine (6,700), from Roumania (3,000), from Lithuania (1,750), and from Germany (963), with a sprinkling from the United States and other remote points. The country was not prepared for them. The instruments of the Zionist Organization were inadequate, either on the land or in the cities. There had been no expectation of such a flood, and neither the leadership nor the country knew how to cope with it.

There were two classes of immigrants: the "capitalists" (those with $2,500 or more) and the workers. The former made up a large proportion of the Fourth Wave — nearly 12,000 out of the 24,000; but among them the largest proportion had very little more than the minimum. What was worse, however, than the low financial standard of "capitalist" classification was the absence of a considerable element of *creative* capitalists: artisans, small industrialists, men with ideas and initiative. Some there were, of course; but they came to a land in which business and working conditions were very different indeed from those that they had been accustomed to; and they did not find the guidance they needed. But it is questionable whether guidance could have helped much. The creation of an industry is bound up with the creation of an environment. There must exist both a local supply of skilled labor and a local market. In the absence of the latter, the only hope is export. But an export trade takes time to develop. A country must establish connections and a reputation. All these things came in time; they could not come as the immigrants poured in.

However, it was only to be expected that a large and uncontrolled Jewish immigration would bring to the country a duplication of the occupational picture of the diaspora. Most of the "capitalist" immigrants were middlemen. There had been a time when, in Poland or Roumania, a merchant with the equivalent of $2,500 or $5,000 could make a modest living. That time was passing, was almost gone. And in Palestine, though that capital was sufficient to open a grocery or dry goods store with, there simply was not room enough for thousands of merchants.

First came the great boom, while the money was being spent. Tel Aviv mushroomed out at a fantastic rate. The population almost doubled in a year: it was 25,000 at the end of 1924, 48,000 at the end of 1925. Buildings shot up in vacant lots; streets galloped across the sandy wastes toward the Yarkon River, a fever of speculation took hold of the city. Prices rose correspondingly. Milk, for instance, cost twice as much in Tel Aviv as in London, three times as much as in Berlin, five times as much as in Paris. Rents were comparable with those in a big American city. The German colonists of Sarona (next to Tel Aviv) and the Arabs of nearby villages made enormous profits.

Then came the collapse. Its first signs were perceptible in the latter part of 1925. Many of the Polish immigrants had left some of their possessions behind, to be liquidated gradually. But there was a financial crisis in Poland, and the expected funds never came. The little tailor shops, groceries, pharmacies, shoe stores, entered into frantic competition with each other. They had been too numerous even in the boom time. Now the market was shrinking. The merchants were reduced to pitiful shifts. They fought to the end, holding on to each customer, bringing down their standards of living. They reached a point at which a single customer made the difference between survival and extinction. On seven families they could make a living; on six it was impossible. At almost every corner of Tel Aviv a little stand was opened, reminiscent of the peddlers of the Nalevkys of Warsaw. They sold soda water and cigarettes. The *gazoz*-stand became the wry symbol of the economic collapse, and of the original economic unhealthiness of the Fourth Wave.

The collapse was, of course, implicit in the boom, which had not been caused by the creation of values but by the influx of unemployable money — unemployable, that is, under the circumstances. And as always when this kind of infection takes hold of a population, there was an unreasoning optimism which was impervious to facts. A story was told in those days of a building contractor who undertook to erect a house for three hundred pounds, on which he made a profit of thirty pounds, which covered only a part of his living costs for the period in question. He came out of the deal with a debt of twenty pounds. But he immediately got another contract for a house at four hundred pounds, on which he made a profit of fifty pounds. He paid off the old debt, and wound up with a new one of thirty pounds. Thereupon he got a contract to build a house for six hundred pounds . . . . A friend asked him: "How long do you think you can keep this up?" The answer was: "Good God, how long do you expect a Jew to live?"

The story may be apocryphal; but it was true to the spirit. As always during a false boom, warning voices were lifted in vain. Bitter protests came from the workers, who saw their dreams of an orderly, progressive development under the sign of a cooperative movement suddenly dissipating. The spectacle of a few men growing rich overnight on land speculation added to the resentment. When the boom began to peter out, the little merchants and artisans pressed the Zionist institutions for funds "to tide them over." Always at the end of a boom there is the phenomenon of futile last-minute efforts to reach the prosperity which is "round the corner." The Zionist institutions were not geared to city and industrial development. They had concentrated mostly on the land. The dispute between the *Halutzim* and the leftists on the one hand, the floundering middle class on the other, was exacerbated. The *Halutzim* were called "Bolsheviks;" the middle class, the *bourganim*, were called the "Nalevkyites," those who had brought into the Jewish homeland the shiftless, uncreative, helter-skelter money scramble of the western small bourgeoisie.

In the early part of 1925 there was practically no unemployment in Palestine. By the summer of 1926 there were 6,000 unemployed; the average number for 1927 was 7,000 — nearly a quarter of the whole working class. The Zionist institutions became relief organizations instead of builders. Soup kitchens had to be opened in the cities. A dread word became familiar in Palestine in those days — *Siyyuah*, the dole. In 1926 immigration had fallen to 7,000, with one thousand emigrants, leaving a gain of 6,000. Worse was to follow. In 1927 there were only 2,000 immigrants, and 5,000 emigrants — a *loss* of 3,000. The old struggle for *Kibbush Avodah*, the conquest of the labor position, flared up anew on the land. There were strikes in Petah Tikvah and Zichron Ya'akov, and British Tommies were called in by the colonists to "restore order." There were strikes in the cities, notably at the match factory which had been opened in Acre, attended by violence. It was a hard time for Palestine; it was a harder time for the whole idea of the Jewish Homeland. For now the oppositional groups had their chance, and all the old arguments were brought out with new force in the Jewish communities throughout the world: "There is no room in Palestine for more Jews. Jews are unable to get along among themselves. Jews are city dwellers, not agriculturalists."

The years 1925–1928 were a crisis in Palestine and a crisis in the Zionist movement. Not that the Zionists wavered in their beliefs; but it was hard to explain why, when the rest of the world was booming (the famous pre-1929 period) the Jewish Homeland should offer such a discouraging spectacle of want and strife. Looking back, we realize now that the crisis was not inherent in the plan as a whole. It resulted from an attempt to rush the process beyond a certain natural tempo. The Jewish Palestine of 1924, with its slightly more than 100,000 inhabitants, was not able to absorb, organically, a sudden increase of thirty-odd thousand population. The composition of the population was far healthier than at any time in the past. There were 20,000 souls on the land — not quite a large enough proportion — but we must remember that in 1882 there was less than 2% on the land. Factories and workshops gave a livelihood to 10,000; there were 10,000 in the class of small artisans: tailors, shoemakers, carpenters, locksmiths, etc. There were 3,000 in the class of unskilled laborers, 12,000 in that of officials and professionals (much too high), 15,000 in commerce and transportation (again much too high), and 30,000 without a genuine occupation — which meant, mostly, the surviving *Halukkah*. Had the entire Jewish population been productively engaged, with the right proportions in the various occupations, it could have absorbed 15,000 to 20,000 newcomers in one year. As it was, 34,000 precipitated a three-year crisis.

But when the crisis came to an end, in 1928, it could be seen that, in effect, the country had room for newcomers if they came at a given rate. There was a stampede into Palestine, but none from it. The gain had been made in a costly, disorganized fashion; it would have been larger if it had proceeded gradually; but it was unmistakably there. In 1924 there had been a little over 100,000 Jews in Palestine; in 1928 there were 162,000. The ratio of the Jewish to the Arab population had risen from 13% to nearly 20%. By the end of 1928 unemployment had fallen to 1,400, and the dole had been abolished. By the spring of 1929 unemployment had practically disappeared.

The orange industry was booming; the Jewish National Fund had at last acquired the lead over the PICA in the acquisition of land. Swamps were still being drained, settlements extended. New factories and farms were absorbing labor, new methods of agriculture and dairy farming were increasing the yield. The Fourth Wave had at last levelled out. Many of the "capitalists," having lost their money, became workers — an indirect approach to *Halutziuth*, perhaps not less painful than that of the original *Halutzim*. After the shock and trial, the Homeland emerged stronger than ever, strong enough, indeed, to face the great test of 1929.

The institutional life of the *Yishuv* had been growing steadily in the midst of seeming chaos. The Hebrew University was officially dedicated and declared open in April, 1925. The original research program was extended, and classes were opened for undergraduates. The Hadassah medical system was spreading through the country. Besides the hospitals at Jerusalem, Tel Aviv, Tiberias and Safed, it maintained a training center for nurses, offices for infant welfare, and bacteriological and chemical laboratories. The *Kuppath Holim* (Sick Fund) of the *Histadruth* now had 15,000 members, and two sanatoriums in the country: at Motzah, near Jerusalem, and on Mount Carmel, above Haifa. The Ruthenberg Electrical Works had been started at the confluence of the Yarmuk and the Jordan. One of the oddities of that period was Palestine's paying off of its share of the Ottoman Debt. That queer phenomenon of the 19th and early 20th centuries, on which Herzl had based his diplomatic manipulations, survived the First World War; and the liberated sections of the Turkish Empire, which had never benefitted from the borrowings of Constantinople, were called on to pay in part for the follies and inefficiencies of the vanished regime. Palestine's share was $4,000,000 (the other Turkish provinces never met the "obligation"), of which it paid off the last $3,000,000 in 1928; and it is fair to say that though the Jews then constituted less than 20% of the population, they contributed, in taxes, half of the repayment, and made a good deal of the second half possible for the rest of the population. Palestine, under the spur of the Jewish Homeland, had become the most progressive country in the Near East. The time was approaching for the fulfilment of the larger hopes which the Fourth Wave had tried to anticipate. But in between lay a period of storm which, briefer and more violent, seemed to carry a greater threat to the enterprise than the crisis of 1925 to 1928.

CHAPTER TWENTY

The Watershed of 1929

❀

EVERY person with a modicum of sophistication knows that the easiest way to win a reputation for "intellectual integrity" is to refuse to take sides in a controversy, even when there does happen to be a right and a wrong in it. One repeats vague generalizations, like "Oh, it's undoubtedly six of one and half a dozen of the other," or, "The other man has a case, too," and thus one caters to the mental laziness of those who will not bother to investigate but who nevertheless want to feel that they know something about the matter. It is always tempting to put on this honest front with a dishonest purpose. The hard way is to stick to the truth as one sees it, and to run the risk, or rather face the certainty, of being called biased. I have chosen the hard way in this book, and therefore feel at least entitled to the foregoing interpolation. In particular I shall be called biased when I come to the subject of the Arab riots in Palestine, and the general attitude of the British colonial administration to the growth of the Jewish Homeland. But only those have a right to speak of bias, in these or other matters, who have taken the trouble to investigate.

The year 1929 may be described as a watershed in the history of modern Palestine in two respects: 1) It witnessed the first organized attempt to intimidate the Jews, by physical force, from continuing with the Return; the attempt was a total failure, and so, from that point on, the physical courage and determination of the enterprise, if one may so put it, was permanently placed beyond dispute. 2) The year 1929 is a watershed in the relations between Arabs and Jews. Those relations have never been the same since, and never can be the same. The establishment of an understanding has become a task which must follow new lines. For the riots of 1929 were engineered (I use that word with the utmost deliberateness) in order to create a situation which was supposed to have caused them; and the move was a partial success.

Between 1921 and 1929 Palestine was at peace. When, in 1924, I traversed the country in every direction, much of the time on horseback, sometimes only with an Arab guide, there was no question of security. The marauding spirit which had infested certain areas during the Turkish regime had disappeared under British rule. I went from the Valley of Jezreel up through Galilee as far as Metullah with one companion — a Jew like myself — and never, among the lonely hills and passes, did we have a sense of danger. During those eight years Arabs and Jews mingled in Tel Aviv and Jaffa, in Jerusalem and Safed and Tiberias and Hebron, as French and British mingle in Montreal, Boer and Englishman in Johannesburg. To talk of a political consciousness among the Arab masses, of an accumulating resentment, throughout that period which saw a threefold increase in the Jewish population, is to ignore the record. Arabs were glad to do business with Jews; Arab peddlers in the Jewish colonies and urban settlements, Arab fishermen in the streets of Tel Aviv, were part of the everyday picture. Arab landowners freely sold land to Jews, or collected rents from them. Arab visitors in the Jewish movie-houses and cafés attracted not the slightest attention.

The peacefulness of Palestine, especially by contrast with the unrest in Syria and in North Africa, was a subject of frequent comment. This must be borne clearly in mind if we are to understand the nature of the riots of 1929. It is on the face of it absurd to speak of a "gathering storm" when the skies remained clear for eight years. One would have to be able to point to sporadic outbreaks, occasional clashes, flickers of lightning, as it were, in order to sustain such a thesis. But they are not to be found; and this extraordinary circumstance calls for an explanation.

A land cannot be built up, consistently and systematically, as the Jews were building in Palestine for eight years, in the face of a deep-seated, organic resentment on the part of the majority of the population, without frequent explosions and the use of repressive force. The Arabs outnumbered the Jews ten to one in 1921, five to one in 1929. Between those years the Jews were visibly laying the foundations of their Homeland, creating colonies, extending cities and suburbs. If it is suggested that British bayonets kept the Arabs from manifesting their resentment, three striking facts remain to be explained away. First, the British maintained only a token force in Palestine, and the land was at peace, whereas in Syria, where the French maintained thousands of troops, the land was in a turmoil. Second, Arab rioting in 1936 and later took place when there were considerable British forces in the country. Third, bayonets might *repress* or *prevent* rebellion; they cannot *encourage* cooperation, and the progress which has been described in the previous chapters would have been impossible without a readiness on the part of the Arabs to accept the benefits of cooperation with the Jews.

The Arab nationalist movement was the preoccupation of a small, privileged urban and landlord class. It did not have beneath it the groundswell of a people's emotional participation. A top layer of five per cent of merchants, professionals, moneylenders, landowners and muftis (priests) thought in terms of an independent Palestine which they would rule and continue to exploit, but more effectively than in the old Turkish times, when they had been only the secondary exploiters. The villagers who worked in the Jewish colonies, and who sold their fruit, vegetables and fish in the streets of Tel Aviv, only knew that for the first time in their memory, or in the memory of their fathers, they were making a decent living.

For eight years the efforts of the Arab nationalist leaders to arouse general resentment against the Jews on political and economic grounds ran up against the resistance of simple fact. The masses who were remote from the Jews were more concerned with the grinding cruelty of the Arab usurers and effendis than with nationalist theory; those who were in contact with the Jews were prospering. There remained only one hope for the "nationalists" — and that was to unloose a religious frenzy among the Arabs.

The riots of 1929 were specifically of a religious character. That is to say, they were precipitated by a skilful and unscrupulous campaign of propaganda designed to prove that the Jews were planning to seize and destroy the Moslem holy places and to proscribe the Mohammedan religion. Thus, shortly before the riots, the Young Moslem Association of Haifa published the following proclamation to their coreligionists in Palestine:

"Some people have applied to us with the request to give them the details regarding the latest events and the Jewish attacks on Moslems and their holy places: the Jews have ancient aspirations regarding our Mosque el Akzah (the Mosque of Omar) in Jerusalem . . ."

Agitators in Jenin, Beisan and villages in the Valley of Jezreel reported variously that the Jews had killed hundreds of Arabs in Jerusalem, cursed Mohammed, insulted the Mohammedan religion, thrown bombs into the Mosque of Omar, or totally destroyed it. The Arab Executive, justifying the subsequent riots, proclaimed: "The Jews, whose aggressions have surpassed political aims to religious ones, whose provocations have latterly become insupportable, as admitted by the government, were responsible for the present troubles." When the agitation had done its worst, and the riots had died down, the British authorities put pressure on the Arab Executive to deny that the Mosque of Omar had been attacked by the Jews. The President of the Arab Executive issued the provocative statement: "The Mosque is with God's help intact, and will forever remain intact in Moslem hands."

The new move on the part of the Arab leaders, the

switching from political to religious propaganda, did not have immediate results, but that it was dangerously effective was obvious to everyone in Palestine. In spite of frantic appeals from the Jewish leaders to the British administration, no effort was made to check the flood of inflaming rumors carried to the country by the press and by word of mouth. It was not until three weeks *after* the riots that the government made the spreading of false statements of this kind a criminal offense. But affirmative action, while there was yet time, would have made negative action unnecessary. Nothing would have been simpler, for instance — the suggestion was made in vain a few days before the riots broke out — than to bring to Jerusalem, at government expense, a few score Arabs from various points in the country, to show them the Mosque of Omar, intact and unscarred. A show of force, too, would have obviated the use of force. British troops and naval ratings were on call in Egypt, a day's journey distant, and at Malta, two days' journey distant. They were brought in fast enough when it was too late, when the damage had been done, not merely in the destruction of lives and property, but in the poisoning of the relations between Jews and Arabs. The second was more disastrous than the first; it was the major objective of the Arab leadership; and a calm survey of the records shows that, whatever it felt about the riots themselves, the Palestine administration was *not concerned* with keeping the atmosphere clean.

The details of the riots are of interest today because they serve to illuminate the forces at play in Palestine, and continue to point a lesson. One hundred and thirty-two Jews were killed, several hundred wounded. The

213

number of Arabs killed and wounded was never established — for a significant reason. The Jews had nothing to hide, for they acted in self-defense; the Arabs were the attackers, and when, as at Huldah and Beth Alpha and other points, they came up against resistance, first on the part of the Jews, later on the part of the police and military, they carried off their dead whenever they could, and the wounded did not seek hospital aid, lest their villages be implicated in the assault. It was strange to read the government bulletins, as they were being issued those days, and to note the dishonest "fairness" (precisely what I have spoken of at the beginning of this chapter) of their tone. For they labored to create the impression that Jews and Arabs had flown at each others' throats and that the government was trying to separate them. Nothing could have been more false, or better calculated to reassure the Arab assailants. I shall give some fantastic instances of this official hypocrisy. But first I shall quote an interview issued by the Grand Mufti of Jerusalem — Haj Amin el Husseini — shortly after the outbreak of the riots.

Said the Grand Mufti to a representative of the Reuter News Agency: "Jewish ambition and greed are responsible for provoking the Arab attack, *in order to gain the support of the whole world* . . ." The religious leader of the Palestine Moslems *did* assert that the Arabs were the attackers; he only added that the Jews had deliberately behaved in such a way as to goad the Arabs into an attack, in order that they, the Arabs, should be placed at a moral disadvantage *vis-à-vis* world public opinion. It must strike the reader at once that there is, in this statement of the Grand Mufti's, a touch of that stupefying impudence which we have learned to associate with Nazi anti-Semitism, and with Nazi propaganda generally ("the bigger and more fantastic the lie, the more difficult to resist it"). The reader will not be mistaken. This is the same Grand Mufti who, in the Second World War, made common cause with Hitler; who before that had been willing to accept Mussolini as the Protector of Islam; who, with a band of devoted followers, obstructed the United Nations in Asia Minor, and was ready to sell out his people as long as he could retain his position of power. (A recent report has it that he is out of favor with the Nazis, and has been arrested in Berlin for failing to deliver the goods.) It is not an accident that the moving spirits in the Arab riots against the Jews thus fitted into the pattern of the totalitarian conspiracy. But of this, more later. Here we are concerned with the historic details of the Palestine riots of 1929.

While the Grand Mufti spoke of an attack on the Jews, the government created and clung to its pattern of "mutual hostilities," of "clashes." The government was a "neutral" in a collision between two unruly forces. There was, so to speak, a civil war in Palestine, and "in all fairness," "as a matter of intellectual integrity," one should not place the blame on either side. The government's first bulletin (August 24th, 1929) read:

"*Disturbances have broken out* in Jerusalem and other parts of Palestine during the last twenty-four hours, resulting in the destruction of life and property. Government are taking the necessary measures to restore order and are carrying out their duty of protecting the lives and property of *all* the inhabitants of Palestine *without distinction*, and will continue to do so until order is completely restored. It is the duty of *all* sections of the population to desist from acts of violence and of all persons to return peacefully to their normal occupations."*

In the Arab city of Beisan (or Beth Shan) between thirty and forty Jewish families lived in the midst of some two thousand Arabs. On August 24th the Jews were attacked; the government issued the following report:

"Yesterday morning *a clash occurred* between Arabs and Jews resident in Beisan. Two Jews were severely wounded and eight slightly wounded. Order was rapidly restored."*

The attempt to create the impression of equal guilt is peculiarly inept in this instance, where the Jews, outnumbered ten to one, would have been insane to provoke trouble and *where the government itself could not report even one Arab slightly wounded.*

Even worse, if one can speak of degrees in this connection, was the case of Hebron. Like Safed, Hebron was a center of the old, pre-Zionist type of Jewish settlement. A *Yeshivah* (talmudical college) gave the tone to the Jewish community, which took little part in the new political and economic activity. Here, on the morning of the Sabbath (August 24th, 1929) one of the beastliest pogroms in the long history of Jewish pogroms took place. Sixty-five Jews — men, women and children — unarmed, defenseless, were slaughtered in less than two hours. *Not one Arab was hurt until belated action was taken by a British officer.* So flagrant was this instance of one-sided assault that it was impossible to deny it altogether; but a curious twist was given to the facts by the government report, which ran thus:

* Italics mine: M. S.

216

"A serious attack on the Jewish quarter of Hebron yesterday morning resulted in heavy loss of life. It is reported that more than forty-five Jews and eight Moslems were killed, and more than fifty-nine Jews and ten Moslems wounded." The impression to be gathered from such a report is that Moslems attacked, Jews defended themselves, and there were casualties on both sides. The impression is false, and it was intended that it should be so. The Jews of Hebron were not of the fighting kind. This was not attack and defense; it was outright massacre. The Arabs were killed or wounded *after* the pogroms, by the British police.

For a week this strange game of covering up the Arab rioters and murderers went on — until the High Commissioner, Sir John Chancellor, who was absent in England, returned. He issued the first statement which could be regarded as a just representation of the facts:

"I have returned from the United Kingdom to find to my distress the country in a state of disorder and a prey to unlawful violence.

"I have learned with horror of the atrocious acts committed by bodies of ruthless and bloodthirsty evil-doers, of savage murders perpetrated upon defenceless members of the Jewish community, regardless of age or sex, accompanied, as at Hebron, by acts of unspeakable savagery, of the burning of farms and houses in town and country, and of the looting and destruction of property.

"These crimes have brought upon their authors the execration of all civilized peoples throughout the world...

"In accordance with an undertaking which I have given to the Committee of the Arab Executive before I left Palestine in June, I initiated discussions with the

217

Secretary of State when in England on the subject of constitutional changes in Palestine. In view of recent events I shall suspend these discussions with His Majesty's Government."

It was as though a fresh wind had blown across the country, driving before it the miasma of misrepresentation and innuendo which — strange as it may sound — caused more heart-burning among the Jews than the physical horrors of the riots. For the Jews did not lose their heads. They knew very well what was at stake: their reputation, their permanent relations with the Arabs, the standing of the Jewish National Home in the eyes of the world, the entire course of future developments. Their indignation was directed more against the subtle hostility of the greater part of the Palestine Administration than against the Arab leaders, whose measure they had taken, or against the mobs which had been goaded into the attack. In the Memorandum of the Jewish National Institutions, addressed to the High Commissioner on September 2nd, the case was summed up thus:

"In the midst of the quiet work of peace and reconstruction, a work which oppressed no individual and no community, inflamed mobs were sent against us; they shed the blood of hundreds of people, subjected many to unspeakable tortures, butchered children, raped women, desecrated synagogues, burned holy books, and destroyed considerable property, the fruit of the great labors of the Jewish people throughout the diaspora. For ten days the Jewish community found itself exposed to murder and destruction, and it is still within the shadow of that danger. Although the picture of the events was so clear and obvious, the Government has

218

attempted in its official communications, published during the very days of bloodshed, to depict the events as a strife between two races, in which it is not clear who was the attacker and who the attacked. In this attempt to distort the truth concerning these events, we see not only an attempt against our lives and welfare, but an attack on our dignity, and an intention to present to the world a distorted picture of the character of our community, which from its founding here has cherished the ideal of peaceful and honorable relations with all religions and races . . ."

In the contrast between Sir John Chancellor's proclamation, and the conspiracy of confusion conducted by most of the Palestine Administration before and *after* the proclamation, we have a mirror of the dual British attitude toward the building of the Jewish National Home. It is inaccurate to say that England, or the British Government, was consistently opposed to the Jewish National Home; it is equally inaccurate to say that it has been consistently helpful, or has lived up to the spirit of the Balfour Declaration and its implementation in the Mandate over Palestine. Of this equivocal situation which, at the present time of writing, has developed into a phase of official opposition, more will be said in the sequel. But I have dwelt at length on the riots of 1929 because they crystallized with unmistakable clarity the fatal consequences of the internal struggle of the Palestine Administration, in which the opponents of the Jewish Homeland had the advantage. What such opponents were doing in Palestine, how they came to be entrusted with a task which was so obviously repugnant to them, belongs to the exposition in Chapter XXII.

So far I have dwelt on the negative features of the events of 1929. There were, in the midst of disaster, positive features. The "uprising," as the Arab leaders called the riots, was in itself a failure. What those leaders had hoped for, immediately, was the unleashing of such a frenzy of mob passions, that the Jewish Homeland would be shaken to its foundations. What happened was bad enough; but it was not commensurate either with the hopes of the Arab leaders, or with the objective possibilities *if the Arab masses of Palestine had really been filled with resentment against the Jews.* The time was well chosen. The High Commissioner was out of the country. The Jewish leaders, too, had left, to attend the founding of the Greater Jewish Agency in Zurich. There was not a quarter of a regiment of English police and soldiers between Metullah in the north and the Egyptian frontier in the south. A real "uprising" would have resulted, as the Arab leaders planned that it should, in the slaughter of thousands of Jews.

Particularly instructive is the fact that of the 132 Jews killed, nearly 100 belonged *not* to the settlements against which the Arabs were supposed to harbor the greatest resentment, i. e., the "newcomers," the builders of the National Home, but to the old settlements, like Hebron and Safed, where there actually lingered a dislike of Zionism! This was due in part to the fact that the "newcomers" could not be attacked with impunity; but what it revealed, unintentionally, was that the attack, such as it was, did not have a national character, did *not* represent a spontaneous outburst against the builders of the Jewish National Home. Certainly there were attacks on the colonies, as on the outskirts of Tel Aviv. But in the large majority of cases it was proved that the attackers were not those Arab neighbors who, according to the Arab Executive, were infuriated by the presence of strangers. The attackers came from a distance; their motives were a mixture of inflamed religious sensitivity and the hope of loot. Nor were there wanting numerous instances — which the Jews were quick to acknowledge and emphasize — of generous and courageous neighborly cooperation in that time of provocation and lawlessness. At Gaza, at Ben Shemen, at Artuf, at Hebron and at Tiberias, Arabs, at the risk of their lives, intervened, openly or furtively, against the mobs. And again: the supineness and hostility of the majority of the Administration found an offset in the behavior of individual officials, and, particularly, in the action of a group of Oxford students who happened to be on pilgrimage in Jerusalem, and who took up arms in defense of the Jews. The riots established beyond all doubt that there were still foundations of peace on which a future could be erected. It would be harder now; blood had been shed; hatreds had been artificially fostered and nourished; the old, simple course of side by side development of the two communities had been interrupted. But there was no thought among the Jews of retreating, or of suspending their constructive work.

This is the most important point to be made here. The Jewish spirit was not broken. If the Arab leaders had hoped for a sudden Jewish exodus from Palestine, they were bitterly disappointed. If, like them, certain British officials had expected that the situation would be so bedevilled that Jews would stop coming to Palestine, they too were soon disillusioned. The greatest period of Jewish development in Palestine followed close on 1929.

A few days after the riots, I made a new tour of the country, and visited, together with Colonel Frederick Kisch (he was then the Chairman of the Jewish Agency in Palestine; in 1943 he was killed in action on the North African Front, where, as a Brigadier, he was General Montgomery's Chief of Engineers), the outpost colonies which I had not seen since 1924. Beth Alpha, nestling at the foot of Gilboa, had suffered five attacks on Sunday, September 25th. Arabs of the tribe of Sagar, others from Fakua and from Tubas, had assembled at the entrance to the Valley of Jezreel, where Beth Alpha had been strategically placed to cover the interior settlements. The attackers had to overwhelm Beth Alpha before they could launch an assault on the other colonies; but they never got past the entrance. After the fifth attack they retreated, taking their dead with them. We found Beth Alpha quietly at work again, at its dairy farming, its poultry- and bee-keeping, its corn and vine growing. The swamps I had seen there years before were gone; the tents were replaced by stone buildings. The school and the library were untouched. Only the children were absent, having been sent inland, to Geva; but they returned soon after, and life resumed its normal course.

We went up to K'far Gileadi, clinging to its hillside near the northern frontier, almost under the shadow of Mount Hermon. K'far Gileadi had not been attacked. Perhaps the Halsa tribe remembered too well the heroic defense put up nine years before by Trumpeldor and his companions. When I had last seen K'far Gileadi there had been three stone buildings and many wooden shacks. Now there were two rows of neat stone houses, a plantation, a little eucalyptus grove — and thirty-two children. There was a kindergarten and a school. There was a brightness and spiritual alertness about the place and about the people, which made one feel that this was not a frontier colony, but a center of civilization — which it was.

On the way back we paused at Daganiah, prosperous among its groves and fields, at Ain Harod, the largest of the Emek settlements, and at Afule. We went to the Ruthenberg Electrification Works, on the Yarmuk, a startling apparition of modernistic buildings in the howling wilderness. At every point we listened anxiously — we who came from the outside — for the reaction to the "uprising." It was as simple as it was unanimous, and it can be summed up in a paraphrase of a famous American battle cry: "Why, we haven't even begun to build."

CHAPTER TWENTY-ONE

The Fifth Wave

◎

A NEW note must now be sounded in our narrative. We are leaving behind us the time when the handful made history. The statistical begins to overshadow the episodic. Once, when ten men went up to Gederah, in 1884, or when seven went up to Daganiah, in 1908, they were the substance of history as well as its symbol. Now we are entering a time which deals in tens of thousands. In a single year more colonies will be founded than in a whole generation before the First World War, more Jews will enter Palestine than in two generations. The individual episode becomes only an illustration.

The year 1929 was designated as the watershed in certain aspects of the rebuilding of Palestine. For the aspect now under consideration, that of the shift from the early heroic to the later practical, we cannot point to a single year. Certainly the old atmosphere of spiritual romance had begun to die out with the Fourth Wave — that of 1924. The singing, dancing *Halutz*, the pioneer who gave up his life to a dream, was receding into a phase of the story. Other types, harder-headed, more soberly realistic, were displacing him. There was even a period when a grave injustice was done to the *Halutz*, and in the enthusiasm of the great numerical and material upswing, it was forgotten that, but for him and for the character which he imparted to the beginnings of the structure, the sternly practical men would never have got their chance. In the years immediately following the riots of 1929 Palestine was getting set for the fulfilment — at long last — of the mass Return. And in 1933, 1934, 1935, the miracle was being accepted as a commonplace.

They were right, in one sense, those men and women who said, in 1929, "We haven't even begun to build." They were wrong in another: the idealists, the representatives of the inmost spirit of the Jewish people, had already put up the framework. The years 1929, 1930, 1931, 1932 proceeded at a jog-trot pace; 4,000 came in the first of those years, somewhat less than 10,000 in the last. Then the Fifth Wave began to roll eastward: 30,000 in 1933, 42,000 in 1934, 60,000 in 1935. By the end of 1933 Palestine had 245,000 Jews; by the end of 1934, 300,000; by the end of 1935, 375,000. The large mass still came from Poland, but there was a steadily growing contingent from Germany: 7,000 in 1933, nearly 10,000 in 1934, a somewhat smaller *recorded* number in 1935. I emphasize, *recorded*. For, as the pressure increased in Europe, the rate of immigration set by the government became totally inadequate to the need. It was inadequate, too, in respect of the unfolding economy of Palestine. There were two kinds of immigration, *Aleph* and *Beth*; *Aleph* was conducted officially, with government sanction; *Beth* consisted of those Jews who saved their lives "illegally," who stole their way into the Jewish Homeland, fleeing the wrath to come in Europe.

It was a time of dominant labor scarcity in Palestine. The Jewish Agency kept pressing the government for entry permits, or certificates. The government yielded reluctantly, always behind the demand, and docking from the certificates granted an arbitrary number to cover the "illegal" immigrants. For April to September 1934, the Jewish Agency asked for 20,000 labor certificates; it received less than 7,000. For April 1935 to April 1936 it asked for 30,000. It received 11,205. *But during those years thousands of Arabs from Transjordan, the Hauran, Syria and even Egypt entered Palestine, all of them illegally, to fill the gap in the labor market.* In 1934 there were 1,500 Haurani employed in the Jewish orange groves of Petah Tikvah alone; in 1935 there were 3,000 of them employed in the four leading Jewish villages, in addition to 3,000 local Arabs. Only in September, 1935, was there a slight setback, when unemployment among the Jews rose to 5,000, but disappeared almost immediately. What had happened? The lightning had flickered; the big crack had appeared in the structure of civilization. Italy had invaded Abyssinia. The repercussions were felt in the whole Mediterranean world. They subsided temporarily, to return in more violent form later. For the time being Palestine continued at its tremendous task.

It is not the purpose of this book to supply the statistics of the growth of Palestine. These are obtainable in the official records of the Jewish Agency and of the government of Palestine. I am concerned more with tendencies and character. But there are tendencies and characteristics inherent in the figures themselves. If, in 1924, an influx of 30,000 Jews disturbed the economy of the country for three years, while in 1935 twice that number were absorbed with comparative ease, the contrast becomes qualitative as well as quantitative. Jewish Palestine was coming into its own. The long preparatory, experimental era, the era of uncertainty, was at an end. The Jewish Homeland was emerging perceptibly, year by year.

Tel Aviv was, at the end of 1935, a city of 135,000 inhabitants. It had been a suburb, a cluster of houses north of Jaffa, a quarter of a century before. Haifa, with its splendid new suburbs, had a population of 100,000, of which one-half was Jewish — almost twice the number that all Palestine had when the *Bilus* set sail from Constantinople. There were 71,000 Jews in Jerusalem. Only Tiberias and Hebron and Safed, the cities of the old time, had stood still. The Ruthenberg Electrical Station, which I had seen them building only a few years before, was working full blast; the consumption of electrical power had risen from 5.3 million kilowatt-hours in 1930 to 50.4 million.

There were 160 colonies, with a population of 70,000, and of these nearly one-half were the creations of the Palestine Foundation Fund and the Jewish National Fund. The institution which had started operations under Ruppin in 1908 with a few thousand francs, now had assets of $21,000,000. Jewish citrus groves covered 160,000 dunams, and produced $7,000,000 worth of fruits per annum. Dozens of colonies were self-supporting; some were already paying back their loans to the Palestine Foundation Fund; dozens of new ones were being founded.

The Palestine Electric Corporation showed a profit of $300,000 in 1933, of $500,000 in 1934. Factories were rising in Tel Aviv, Haifa, Ramath Gan, Petah Tikvah — metal works, glass works, silk dyeing and finishing works — factories for essential oils, cotton spinning, wire, stationery, woodwork, automobile bodies, buckets, carbon paper, shoes. Once, in the early days, they had asked: "But what on earth can Jews produce in Palestine?" — and the answer had been given in the form of the old Yiddish jest: "Everything that begins with an *a*: a bed, a table, a book, a shirt." Now it was no longer a jest. The tide of private initiative was rising. It will be recalled that between 1919 and 1924 the public funds (donations) poured into the country by the Zionist foundations had exceeded private investment in the ratio of eight to one. Now private investment, encouraged by the priming pump of national institutions, was catching up. Twenty, thirty, forty million dollars a year came into Palestine; and, in contrast to the picture in 1925 (the Fourth Wave), this was employable money. It was set to work immediately.

In those crescendo years little Palestine recalled the 19th century epoch of American expansion, with one crucial difference: In Palestine there was a vivid consciousness of the need for healthy social development; there was a fear of the unchecked scramble system, of individualism running wild. The consciousness was not universal; the checks were imperfect; still, much was done in that direction. But here I am seeking, primarily, to convey something of the exhilarating tone of that time, and the statistics thrown into the text are less for specific information than for the purpose of recalling the swift rhythm of growth. The Haifa harbor was being built at last, to replace the primitive port of Jaffa. The latter was as old as Jonah's time at least (it was Joppa then), and had remained unimproved for over two thousand years, without a jetty, without docking facilities. In 1935 and 1936 Jews were already talking of *Kibbush ha-Yam*, conquest of the resources of the sea, as they had talked before of *Kibbush ha-Aretz*, conquest of the resources of the land. The Palestine Maritime League was founded shortly after, and by 1938 there were 1,500 Jewish fishermen. Later the Atid Navigation Company was founded, maintaining a coastal service between Egypt, Palestine, Cyprus and Turkey.

Meanwhile the Dead Sea works were producing tens of thousands of tons of potash annually, and providing 75% of Great Britain's bromine supplies. The University was opening new departments, the agricultural station at Rehovoth was making new discoveries. The Daniel Sieff Research Institute, headed by Dr. Weizmann (scientist, statesman, industrial chemist, cultural Zionist in the old tradition — he has been all things to the movement), was opened in 1934 and soon became the finest laboratory of its kind between Europe and Japan, employing a group of distinguished scientists from German and other European universities. Hadassah had turned over its hospital system to the municipalities and the *Kuppat Holim* (Sick Benefit Fund) of the *Histadruth*, and was concentrating on the University hospital of Jerusalem and preventive medical work. Before long it was to initiate the magnificent Youth *Aliyah* enterprise. There were fifty thousand children in the Jewish school system, exclusive of teachers' institutes and other higher academies.

In Tel Aviv the first Industrial Fair was held in 1929—
a modest, small-town affair, with three hundred local
firms participating. In 1932 the Levant Fair was opened,
an ambitious and genuinely imposing exposition on the
lines of the "world fairs" which are familiar in the western world. It was, to be sure, somewhat smaller than
the New York World Fair of 1939; but it had all the
features, good and bad, which are by now the tradition
of that sort of thing: the *papier mâché* buildings, the fa-
çades, the garishness, the pride, the ballyhoo, the usefulness, the boosting of *Totzeret ha-Aretz* (home goods),
the amusement park, and the happy evidences of productivity. Thirteen hundred firms participated, the
governments of Syria, Egypt, Cyprus, Poland, Roumania, Turkey, Bulgaria, the U. S. S. R., Italy and
other countries were represented. A great Maccabee
Sports Festival, with three thousand contestants and
contingents from Great Britain, the United States,
Austria, Czechoslovakia, Poland, etc., was held in a
specially built stadium. An American promoter would
have been in his element in Tel Aviv — and many were.

Everywhere — work, planning, projects, expectations.
The Huleh marshes were being drained; they would
nourish thousands of Jewish — and Arab — families.
The Women's International Zionist Organization, the
PICA, the American Palestine Corporation were active
on the land and in the cities. The theater flourished,
books and periodicals poured from the presses, a Musical
Conservatory was founded in Jerusalem, the Palestine
Symphony Orchestra was being organized by Bronislaw
Hubermann, and gave its first performance in 1936. And,
finally, the Palestine government showed a mounting
surplus, which reached $20,000,000 in 1934. I am afraid

this last touch is rather an anti-climax, for in the western world the governments were showing deficits of *billions*. Palestine consoled itself with the fact that *its* trivial figures were on the credit, not on the debit, side of the ledger.

The Jews still had their differences with the government. There was the matter of the restricted immigration, already touched on. There were other matters. Though the Jews contributed well over half of the government revenue (they were less than one-third of the population), they benefitted in much smaller proportion than their numbers — we will not say their tax contributions — warranted. There was now an expanding Arab school system, with 66,000 pupils (1934). It received from five to ten times the subsidy granted to the Jewish schools, though the latter had 50,000 pupils. Far too few Jews were employed on government projects, like the Haifa harbor works. But the Palestine Administration was in those years under the direction of the most imaginative and sympathetic High Commissioner it has ever had — Sir Arthur Wauchope. He was hampered by that dualism of attitude, in London and among his own subordinates, of which I have spoken and will speak again. In the circumstances he did well by the country, and in later years, out of office, he showed by his utterances in London how deeply impressed he had been by the Jewish and general significance of the emerging Homeland.

And so, with all the difficulties and obstacles taken into account, it may be said that ten more such years as we have just reviewed, ten years of peace and reconstruction, would have seen the Jewish Homeland completely established and this part of the Jewish problem solved. Those ten years were not granted to the Jews; they were not granted to the world generally. Long before the Second World War broke out officially, in 1939, its "unofficial" preparations were beginning to paralyze the creative will of the nations. Various dates may be set for the opening moves, the preliminary skirmishes of the great onset; Japan in Manchukuo in 1931, Hitler's advent to power in 1933, Italy's invasion of Abyssinia in 1935, Italian and German intervention in Spain in 1936. At whatever point we place the first portents, it is certain that by 1936 Palestine had become one of the advance battlegrounds, and this in many senses which will yet have to be explained.

Meanwhile we have still to cast a glance at what was, humanly, the characteristic feature of the Fifth Wave: the absorption of tens of thousands of German Jews into the Jewish Homeland.

Two misconceptions must be removed at the outset. First, the Fifth Wave was not predominantly German-Jewish. Jews escaping from Nazism were outnumbered two and three to one by Jews escaping from Polish anti-Semitism and economic decline. Second, it is quite wrong to assert that, until the rise of Hitler, German Jews had not participated in the upbuilding of the Jewish Homeland.

The distinguishing German-Jewish touch in the Fifth Wave is not related to the volume of immigration, but to the peculiar and poignant human side of the story. In the universal cataclysm which has overwhelmed the European and other peoples, the dolorous pre-eminence of the Jews in the tragedy has been obliterated. Similarly, the distinctions in suffering (there are certain

232

grades, varieties and nuances of pain on this side of the grave, and on this side only) between Jewish communities has been wiped out. The volume and intensity of pain endured by Polish Jewry was almost forgotten in the dramatic reversal of fortunes which came upon German Jewry. One was accustomed to the wretchedness of the former; the sudden comedown of the latter touched new chords of compassion. And so, from 1933 on, the cry of German Jewry rang louder in our ears than the all-too-familiar plaint of the Polish millions; whence it came about that the saving of German Jews through Palestine made a livelier appeal to the imagination than the saving of Polish Jews.

Moreover, as we had long been familiar with the sufferings of Polish Jewry, and perhaps less responsive to it, we assumed that in Polish Jewry, too, this long familiarity had bred a certain resignation. We were wrong; but we were blundering round a certain truth. In Polish Jewry a stronger attachment to ancient Jewish values made resistance easier, up to a point. The great majority of Polish Jews spoke Yiddish, had some Hebrew education. The German Jews knew nothing of the first, little of the second. The German Jews had, for by far the most part, accepted it as an article of faith that they were forever, unchangeably and unchallengeably, Germans. There was, of course, a fine German Zionist movement, marked by great intelligence and devotion; the youth was organized in the *Blau-Weiss* and the *Kartel Jüdischer Verbindungen* (University Fraternities). But in no other country had the ideal of assimilation become so affirmative, dogmatic and impenetrable as in Germany. For that matter, nowhere else had the opportunities offered by the Emancipation of the nineteenth

233

century been used to such brilliant effect as among the German Jews. To the superficial observer the long list of Jewish artists, philosophers, scientists, musicians, industrialists, poets and novelists vindicated, in Germany more strikingly than anywhere else, the theory of complete equalization of opportunity. On the whole, then, the atmosphere was peculiarly hostile to Zionism; from the time when the leaders of the Jewish community of Munich called on the municipality to prevent Herzl from holding the first Zionist Congress in that city, to the rise of Hitler and even beyond, anti-Zionism was almost an obsession with German Jews. The arguments which are heard in America today against the moral and spiritual validity of Zionism as a Jewish philosophy were imported from Germany. When the disaster came, the German Jews were much remoter from the thought of Palestine than even the most assimilated Polish Jews. The process of adaptation was correspondingly harder.

Here was a challenge to the Jewish Homeland. There was a definite fear in Palestine, especially among the "old-timers," of the German Jews. Suppose, they asked, the Homeland attempts to absorb a large body of Jews who are not simply non-Zionists, but who have a well thought-out ideological objection to a Jewish State, to Jewish nationalism, to the whole tradition of the Return; suppose these men and women look upon Palestine as they would upon any other country in the world — a place to settle in, not as Jews, but as Palestinians of the Jewish Faith (just as they were once Germans of the Jewish Faith), a place with no significance for them in terms of a specific Jewish civilization; what will happen then to the morale of our Homeland? What help shall we get from them in our task of the Jewish rebuilding?

Will they support us in our demands on the government, or will they form a nucleus of opposition within the Jewish community, with its objective the dissolution of the Zionist program?

These were not academic questions. They were immediate and practical. On the other hand, there was no thought of Jews in Palestine instituting an ideological *numerus clausus* against Jews seeking admission. Was it not in part for just such a contingency that the Homeland was projected, as an answer to the homelessness of the Jewish people? It was one thing to regulate immigration on technical and occupational grounds; the Jewish Agency had been trying to do that for years. It was quite another to put up, or attempt to put up, ideological barriers. For that matter, occupational selection had never worked too well; it was the country which had redistributed the immigrants after their entry. And now, with the floods of persecution rising in Germany, how was it possible even to suggest discrimination?

The problem touched on the very essence of Zionist philosophy. Palestine represented a homecoming not only in the physical, but also in the spiritual sense. The question was, then, would the Jewish Homeland awaken in the assimilated Jew a sense of affinity on Jewish grounds? Would those who had rejected everything but a diffused ritualistic and ethical concept of Judaism come, in time, to feel that in this Jewish Homeland they were wholly, without reservations and interpretations, Jewish?

The questions were debated with peculiar Jewish vehemence. Also, be it said, with peculiar Jewish humor. For there were some wits who said: "There is no problem at all. These Jews are the most practiced assimilators in history. They will assimilate into Judaism before you know it."

There may have been something in the sly dig. There was much more in the faith which most Palestinians had in the healing and unifying influence of the Home-land. Thousands of German Jews came who had never dreamed that their lot would be cast in with *Ost-Juden*, eastern Jews, whose benefactors they had been, whose beneficiaries they were now to become. There came quite a number of baptized Jews, some of whom had been baptized in infancy, others of whom had sought this way to "freedom" of their own accord. And it would be dishonest to pretend that there were not many tragedies of maladaptation. In innumerable Jewish homes of Berlin, Dresden, even Frankfort — the center of German Jewish orthodoxy — it had long been the custom to observe Christmas almost after the Christian fashion, even when there had been no official apostasy. The Christmas tree was a tender childhood memory to thousands of German Jews; and some of them, coming to Palestine, missed the ritual, and could not quite under-stand why other Jews shrank from the disharmony of such a gesture particularly in the new Jewish Homeland. It is odd to recall that German Gentile women who had married Jews, and came with them to Palestine, were often more understanding than their husbands. But however that may have been, there were Jewish homes in Palestine, in those days, in which, on Christmas eve, a tree was put up, with candles and presents, behind shuttered windows.

It was hardly a question of right or wrong. Tact is a better word. The gesture was not religious; it was not associated with faith; it was part of the tribute Jews

236

had sought to pay to a dominant culture, part of the price of admission. Of course it had become a habit, with emotional overtones. It is mentioned here only to indicate how hard was the road of the homecoming.

They traversed it. If there was a percentage of German Jews who regretted that they had not been able to obtain admission to another country than Palestine, there was a percentage of Polish Jews (for instance) who had also looked on Palestine as a way-station, who had entered, found it not to their liking, and left. Certainly many German Jews waited at first "for the storm to blow over," believing in the teeth of all the evidence that Nazism was only temporarily anti-Semitic to such a degree. That phase is gone. It went even before the Second World War broke out. Gone with it is the inner uncertainty of the German Jews, and the concern of the "old-timers" about the role of German Jews in Palestine. Gone are the old jests and jibes. They no longer ask: *Kommen Sie aus Deutschland oder aus Ueberzeugung?* "Did you come from conviction or from Germany?" No one is afraid now that the assimilated German Jews, instead of becoming Judaized, think it their mission to "westernize" Palestine.

The cleavages between German-Jewish, Polish-Jewish, Russian-Jewish are disappearing. The process which welded diverse elements together in the past still continues. Certainly divisions exist in Palestinian Jewry. There are leftists and rightists, orthodox and free-thinkers, capitalists and socialists, extreme nationalists, internationalists, pacifists. A small minority group is opposed to the idea of a Jewish State. But these divisions are not connected with the question of the countries of origin of the immigrants. The German Jews — if

237

they can be designated by that name today — are distributed through all parties and points of view. They have taken their place naturally in the Homeland.

The economic adaptation of the German Jews to Palestine was in essence not different from that of other groups; but it had its own touch. As human material, the German Jews had a special value. If they lacked the fantasy and reckless idealism of the early immigrants, they brought with them other assets. They were better trained, more methodical and reliable. A minority among them started a flurry in the wrong direction. They had been part of the luxury trade in Germany, and it was natural for them to make a start in their own line. The immediate effect was noticeable in a sudden blossoming of shops and restaurants which reminded one of the Kurfürstendamm in Berlin. But the standard of living which this implied was beyond the means — and away from the purpose — of Palestine. For a year or two there was talk of the "Kurfürstendamm psychology," as there had been talk of the "Nalevky psychology" after 1924, the time of the Fourth Wave. The attempt faded away. The great majority showed themselves much more adaptable, and often highly ingenious. Professors became chicken farmers: a whole colony of poultry breeders, Ramoth ha-Shavim, was created near Tel Aviv, of former German doctors, lawyers, dentists and academicians. A city window-cleaning service was set up by others. They turned to chauffeuring, and even shoe-shining. Numbers of them became peddlers. For a certain period, while the Hitler government was testing out how far it could go in persecution of the Jews without over-shocking world opinion, and before it discovered that it could go as far as it liked, Jews leaving

Germany were able to take certain possessions with them. The *Ha'avarah* or transfer system was instituted. Jews in Germany used their money to obtain certain goods, which were exported to Palestine; or else it was their own property which was released. It should be noted that no money was sent into Germany from Palestine. Nevertheless, the appearance of German-made goods in Palestinian shops, or among Palestinian peddlers, when Jews everywhere in the world were leading in the boycott against Germany, set off much unthinking criticism. It was forgotten that the purpose of the boycott was to cut down Germany's receipts of foreign currency; that to construe this policy so as to prevent German Jews from bringing out of Germany, while they could, the remnants of their life's savings, was to invert its purpose, and to aim at the victim the blow intended for the oppressor. However, this phase, too, passed and must be remembered only as one of the unnecessary and unjustified handicaps imposed on the German Jews coming to Palestine. What remained was a strong net addition to the human resources of the country—new factories, new industries, and, above all, an advance in scientific management.

It was possible to watch, almost as in a social laboratory, the therapy wrought on a given element by the character of the Homeland. It may be called a lesson in the infection of health. The most striking aspect of the German-Jewish adaptation was that of the children, from whom the affirmative changes spread to the parents; that is, when the parents were also in Palestine, which was sometimes not the case. For there were fathers and mothers who sent the young ones on in

advance, hoping to follow, and others who shipped them
to the Jewish Homeland without prospect of ever seeing
them again — parents who said: *Mit uns ist es aus*. "We,
the old people, are done for. You at least can save
yourselves." But those that came to Palestine were, as
we have seen, for the most part alien to the problems
of the country, without psychological and spiritual preparation for this special environment. Many of them
understood, of course, that the old patterns were gone
forever. Their children would not follow in the economic and social footsteps of nineteenth- and early
twentieth-century German Jewry. They would have to
"come down" in the world, join the ranks of the workers.
Some, however, did not understand even this much.
Even fewer apprehended in advance that the status of
the *Po'el*, the worker, in Palestine, was not quite the
same as anywhere else. To this was added another
barrier: there were so many parents who did not know
how to say to their children: "To be at home in the
Jewish Homeland, you must be Jewish through and
through." They had nothing to say it with.

The resolution of these contradictions came about in
a manner which imparts to the long evolution of the
Jewish Homeland a touch of the mystically prescient.
It was as if just this case had been foreseen and provided
for by the obstinate idealism of the founders.

In the spring of 1933, I visited on several occasions
the children's farm-school of Ben Shemen, not far from
Lydda. A contingent of the German youth had just
arrived, the first, I think, of its kind. Attractive, clean-
cut youngsters, well brought up, bright, eager — and
still a little bewildered. They came, predominantly,
of professional and mercantile families. They had been

taught to look upon a middle-class life, a high school and university education, as their natural heritage. They were too young — the oldest were not yet sixteen— to understand the personal implications of the calamity which had overtaken Jewry. They formed their own clique at first, for they were among "strangers." I drew some of them into conversation, in German, of course, and would wind up by asking them what they planned to become. Invariably the answer would be, "A doctor, like papa," "An architect, like Uncle Rudolph," "A lawyer, like Uncle Richard." It was not that they looked down on the laborer. It just did not occur to them that they could be otherwise than of their own tradition.

In the Ben Shemen school the educational system was pointed toward preparation for Palestinian life. Half the day the children attended classes, as they might have done elsewhere. Part of the remaining half was devoted to work and training, to the management of the farm, the sewing and planting, the milking of cows, the cooking, laundry, repairs, carpentry and the like. There was a council of the youngsters, there was a court for the trial of offenders against the discipline of the school. Work, productivity, was the keynote of the system. The place of the worker in the upbuilding of the country, the honorable status of labor, were the implicit themes of the theory behind the system. Not new themes, certainly; but here they were given more than lip service. A graduate of the Ben Shemen school was supposed to pass into his adult role, in field or factory, not only equipped — at least in part — for an actual trade, but wholly equipped for affirmative participation in the destiny of the working class; not imbued with the belief that the best thing to be done with the working class is to rise above it, but happy in the status of the Palestinian worker, who is dedicated to the intellectual, spiritual and economic advancement of the country.

I left Palestine that spring, and did not return till the fall, and then I was once again a frequent visitor at Ben Shemen. The youngsters were still there — but they were not the same. The clique was dissolved. They had, of course, picked up the language. Not this was the essence of the change. It was the complete and joyous sublimation into the spirit of the school. I spoke to them again of their hopes and ambitions. "What do *you* want to be, and *you*, and *you*?" A *nagar*, said one — a carpenter; a *ro'eh*, said another — a shepherd; a *halutz*, said a third — a pioneer. There was no more talk of the professions. There was talk of education, but not of its connection with career and class.

It sometimes happened that this transformation in the youngsters ran counter to the hopes and ambitions of parents who thought that their children merited "something better" than a workingman's life. And sometimes parents in Germany wrote to children in Palestine imploring them to go out and try to earn something as soon as possible, so that the family could be reunited. These were exceptions rather than the rule. In most cases the parents, especially if they were in Palestine, felt that a frightful burden had been taken off their minds; for they had dreaded precisely this question of adapting their children to a new way of life, to lower economic standards, to the "downward" social revision.

The first contingents of the German Jewish youth were followed by many others, not only from Germany. The story of the Youth *Aliyah* remains to be told in its fulness; so far only its outlines have been given out, and its more dramatic aspects. Much deeper, and of far wider bearings, are the details of the total reconstruction of these lives, and of the repercussions on the older generation. It is a facet of the general enterprise, reflecting with peculiar clarity the fusion of Jewishness and of social idealism which was implicit in the far-off beginnings of the movement. No other land in the world, however liberal, friendly and understanding, could have done for the young wanderers what Palestine did to make them dignified, creative Jews.

CHAPTER TWENTY-TWO

A Complex of Problems

🌼

WE LEARN in elementary mathematics that half the solution of a problem lies in the right formulation of it; get your known and unknown factors rightly stated, and the answer often suggests itself. This is a truth which applies to most human problems, too — social, political and psychological.

Half the confusion in popular discussion of what is called the "Arab-Jewish problem in Palestine" arises from faulty formulation, from inaccurate juxtaposition of factors, or from omission of relevant factors. Unfortunately, human problems are not, like mathematical problems, static; they have a history. You cannot, after having failed in the first attempt, say, "Let's start all over again," for the error has been incorporated in the problem as a new factor, and the history of the problem has become part of the problem.

Let us see how the Arab-Jewish problem presented itself at the beginning of the new era in Palestinian history. The Allied and Associated Powers had agreed that there should be established in Palestine "a National Home for the Jewish People." They had agreed further that "nothing shall be done which may prejudice the civil and religious rights of existing non-Jewish communities in Palestine." This policy was incorporated five years later (1922) in the Mandate for Palestine granted by the League of Nations to Great Britain.

Now let us clarify the content of these first factors. What was meant by the words "a National Home"? Did the statesmen who used those words intend to convey the idea of a sort of Andorra Republic, a miniature enclave of a small number of Jews surrounded by an eternal majority of Arabs on the soil of Palestine? If so, why all the fuss, why all the international negotiations, why the appeal to history, Jewish need, the Bible, historic restitution, and the rest of it? Why should the Mandate, in its preamble, have contained this statement: "Whereas recognition has been given to the historical connection of the Jewish people with Palestine and the grounds for reconstituting their national home in that country . . ."? This is altogether disproportionate to a plan for settling a few hundred thousand Jews in Palestine, with minority rights such as were being granted to the Jews of Poland, Lithuania and Roumania.

But the utterances of the heads of the two English-speaking Powers, of President Wilson and Prime Minister Lloyd George, are even more specific, and I quote them once again:

In 1918 President Wilson said: "I am persuaded that the Allied Nations, with the fullest concurrence of our government and our people, are agreed that in Palestine shall be laid the foundations of a Jewish Commonwealth." And Lloyd George, in his memoirs, wrote: "It was not their [the British Cabinet's] intention that a Jewish State should be set up *immediately* by the Peace Treaty without reference to the wishes of the majority of the inhabitants.* On the other hand it was contemplated that when the time arrived for according representative institutions to Palestine, if the Jews had meanwhile responded to the opportunity afforded them by the idea of a National Home and had become a definite majority of the inhabitants, then Palestine would thus become a Jewish Commonwealth. The notion that Jewish immigration would have to be artificially restricted in order to ensure that the Jews should be a permanent minority never entered into the head of anyone engaged in framing the policy. That would have been regarded as unjust and as a fraud on the people to whom we were appealing."

How does this jibe with the qualifying clause of the Balfour Declaration: "Nothing shall be done which may prejudice the civil and religious rights of existing non-Jewish communities in Palestine"? Are we faced here with an irreconcilable contradiction? In other words, do "the civil and religious rights of existing non-Jewish communities in Palestine" include the right to vote away the Balfour Declaration? If that is so, the Balfour Declaration is, in the words of Lloyd George, "a fraud on the people to whom we were appealing," i. e., the Jewish people. But that is not all. If the Declaration is thus made meaningless, it is made so in all its parts, and the guarantee of civil and religious rights to the non-Jewish communities disappears together with the project of the Jewish Homeland. For the guarantee derives its purpose and significance from the very fact that a Jewish Commonwealth is contemplated.

* Italics mine: M. S.

So much for the letter and spirit of the Balfour Declaration and the Mandate which was unanimously ratified by the League of Nations and the government of the United States. If we extend the area of inquiry into the world significance of the new policy, we are confronted by the following picture:

A Jewish problem exists and calls for solution. It affects, on the one hand, at least several million Jews who are homeless in the sense that they are not permitted to regard themselves as a natural, integral part of the local population in the countries of their residence, and in the sense that a longing exists among many of them to resume a Jewish national life, in Jewish surroundings, on the Jewish ancestral soil. It affects, on the other hand, the world at large, which is perpetually exposed to the dangerous effects of the Jewish problem — an ancient problem immemorially exploited by destructive forces. The reconstitution of the Jewish Homeland is at the very least, then, an integral contribution to the regularization of the Jewish position and the mitigation of the evils of anti-Semitism. All of this is indicated in the preamble to the Mandate for Palestine: "Whereas recognition has hereby been given to the . . . grounds for reconstituting their [the Jewish] national home in that country [Palestine]."

Against this Jewish problem, which is the concern of the entire civilized world, is posed, as if it were a counter-weight and more, the "Arab problem." But what is the Arab problem? Is it that of the Arab world, or at any rate of the 11,000,000 Arabs of Asia Minor? Is the building of the Jewish National Home, a recognized prerequisite for the stabilization of the world, an injustice to the Arab people — so much so, in fact, that

247

for the removal of one evil a second, and a greater, is proposed? On this point it is enough to quote the words of the Chairman of the Mandates Commission of the League of Nations, Mr. Orts: ' Was not consent to the establishment of a Jewish National Home in Palestine the price — and a relatively small one — which the Arabs had paid for the liberation of lands extending from the Red Sea to the borders of Cilicia on the one hand, Iran and the Mediterranean on the other, for the independence they were now winning or had already won, none of which they would ever have gained by their own efforts, and for all of which they had to thank the Allied Powers and particularly the British forces in the Near East?"

Is the Arab world pent up in a tiny area in which it is suffocating for want of room? By no means. A whole subcontinent waits for development and for increased population! Subtracting from Asia Minor its deserts and mountains, there is room, in Syria, Iraq, Saudi Arabia, the Hadramauth, etc., for a hundred million inhabitants. Arabia suffers from under-population, among other things. Therefore to talk of an Arab problem in this sense, as created by a Jewish Homeland in Palestine, is to talk gibberish.

If the "Arab problem" is restricted to Palestine, its Arabs, and the Jewish people, we have before us the question of millions of Jews threatened with extermination, or at least with the continuation of the torments of their long exile, in western lands, and *their* desperate need, as contrasted with the question of half a million Arabs (as they were when the Balfour Declaration was issued) or a million (as they are today) to whom, as we shall see, the Jewish Homeland has brought a degree of prosperity unknown in any other Arab country? What sort of juxtaposition of problems is this?

Certainly there are many Arabs in Palestine who say: "We just do not want to become a minority in our own country." Passing over the propriety of the words "our own country" — words which the civilized world has refused to accept in this application — we must ask ourselves whether, in a world so complex and intertwined, racially and nationally as this is, we can unscramble minorities, and whether we should even try. *Minorities are forever a part of the world's populational pattern.* Our task is to protect them. That an Arab minority would have to be created in Palestine as the price of the solution of the major part of the Jewish problem was universally foreseen. Would that all minorities could derive from the majority such advantages as the Arabs of Palestine have derived from the Jews! Would that the lot of Jewish minorities in a score of countries that come at once to the mind had resembled that of the Arab putative minority in Palestine!

The right statement of the Arab-Jewish problem as thus far considered is approximately this: given a world policy which calls for a Jewish Commonwealth in Palestine, on the threefold basis of an acknowledged Jewish historical claim, present Jewish need, and general world need, has the Arab world outside of Palestine a valid counter-claim to that piece of territory, to the exclusion of a Jewish Commonwealth? And have the Arabs of Palestine a valid counter-claim to permanent majority status, again to the exclusion of a Jewish Commonwealth? A formulation which omits any of these factors, or places them in any other relation, must lead to a fallacious answer.

249

This is by no means all of the problem. It may even be asked why, in a narrative devoted to the growth of Palestine, I have adverted to so many extraneous factors. The answer is, in part, that these have been injected into the Palestinian scene; more important, however, is the fact that the above formulation explains the state of mind which induced practically all of the early Jewish settlers, and a great part of the later settlers, to undertake the desperate task of the reconstruction. If we think back to the *Halutzim* of the Third Wave, to the heroic and passionate road-builders, drainers of swamps, founders of colonies, we recall that nothing but the prospect of a Jewish Homeland could have inspired them to endure their trials. The offer of a Jewish *settlement* in Palestine, of ordinary immigrational facilities, would have drawn, of course, quite a number of Jews; it would not have drawn those that actually came, and the history of Palestine would have been quite another than it is.

And now, confining ourselves as far as we can to the Palestinian picture itself, we must ask: "If we take as our premise the Balfour Declaration and the Mandate, and the creation of a Jewish Commonwealth, what are the factors of the Arab-Jewish problem?" I say, as far as we can, for here too external forces intrude. The problem has at least *three* terms, for we shall have to include the British Administration; and it is for this reason that I have chosen to consider British policy in Palestine in the total setting of the Arab-Jewish-British complex.

We begin with the first simplification which is generally offered in this connection: "The Jewish attitude toward the Arabs should have been such that the Arabs would have been won over to the idea of a Jewish Commonwealth in Palestine." The moment we ask, "which Arabs?" the question falls apart, because it is an instance of false formulation. Are we talking about the fellaheen, the landworkers and sharecroppers, who make up, together with the minority in the cities, the great majority of the Palestinian Arab population? Or are we talking about the landowners, moneylenders, priests and professionals? As to the former, they have no say, and have never had any, in the direction of Arab policy. They have received nothing but benefits from the development of Palestine by the Jews. As to the latter, it is nonsense to talk about winning them over to the idea of a Jewish Commonwealth in Palestine, when their ruling passion is — to rule. What can they have in common with a modernizing and democratizing force like the Jewish National Fund, or the *Histadruth*, the dominating elements in the Jewish reconstruction? The landowners, too, have benefitted financially from the development of the country. They have never ceased, even in the midst of their agitation against the Jewish Homeland, to sell land to the Jews, at enormous profits. But the prospect of their displacement from power is perpetually at war with their acquisitive instincts. They would like it both ways: to profit by the presence of the Jews, to retain the position of power.

In 1937 the most thoroughgoing commission of investigation which England ever sent to Palestine, that headed by Lord Peel, reported: "It is difficult to detect any deterioration in the economic position of the Arab upper class. Landowners have sold substantial pieces of land at a figure far above the price it would have fetched before the war . . . In recent transactions mainly Palestinian Arabs have been concerned, and these transactions have been considerable . . . Partly, no doubt, as the result of land sales the *effendi* class has been able to make substantial investments of capital . . . At least six times more Arab-owned land is now planted with citrus than in 1920 . . . some of the capital has been directed to building houses for lease or sale to industrial enterprise . . . In the light of these facts we have no doubt that many Arab landowners have bene-fitted financially from Jewish immigration . . . A member of the Higher Arab Committee admitted to us that 'nowhere in the world were such uneconomic land-prices paid as by Jews in Palestine.' "

Undoubtedly it is a great pity that so much money should have flowed into the pockets of men who had no interest in the welfare of the mass of their own people, of men who were ready to sell out their country to Mussolini and Hitler so that they might, as they hoped, become its rulers even if under foreign dominion. But the land — great stretches of it — belonged to these old families. The government was not prepared to ex-propriate them, or even force them to sell at reasonable prices, for the benefit of either Jew or Arab. It should be borne in mind, further, that while the landowners were leading the "rebellion" against the Jewish Home-land *they continued to sell land to the Jews.*

But what of the Arab masses? Was it reasonable to expect that an Asiatic peasantry, exploited to the limit of human endurance, could be organized in a decade or two by newcomers into a self-conscious, self-reliant national movement capable of throwing off the yoke of the leading families? Concerning the manner in which the Arab peasants fared under the Mandate, the Peel Report says:

"The general beneficent effect of Jewish immigration on Arab welfare is illustrated by the fact that the increase in Arab population is most marked in urban areas affected by Jewish development . . . We are also of the opinion that up till now the Arab cultivator has benefitted on the whole from the work of the British administration and from the presence of the Jews in the country. Wages have gone up; the standard of living has improved . . ."

And again: "Jewish example has done much to improve Arab cultivation, especially citrus."

The Arab population of Palestine has doubled in less than a generation. It has been almost stationary in all other Arab countries. The reason lies not only in the raising of the standard of living; it is in part due directly to Jewish improvement of the land. The Peel Report goes on:

"The reclamation and anti-malaria work undertaken in Jewish colonies have benefitted all Arabs in the neighborhood. Institutions founded with Jewish funds primarily to serve the National Home have also served the Arab population . . . *The Arab charge that the Jews have obtained too large a proportion of good land cannot be maintained. Much of the land now carrying orange groves was sand dunes or swamp and uncultivated when it was purchased.*"

What more, then, could the Jews have done "to win over the Arabs"? Presumably they could have increased these benefits. They could have brought more money into the land, founded more colonies, extended their institutions, drained more swamps, provided an even larger market for Arab cultivators. But this implies greater, not smaller, Jewish immigration. The argument cannot be worked both ways; it does not make sense to assert that the Jews should have refrained from coming into the country in considerable numbers, but should nevertheless have lifted the country out of its condition of backwardness and neglect.

Perhaps the Jews might have done more than they did in organizing the Arab workers. But the little they did — it included the formation of Arab unions and the publication of the first Arab labor newspaper in the Near East, the *Itahad el Amal* — only infuriated the Arab ruling class the more. Further, it should be remembered that the Arabs are predominantly peasants and shepherds, and even a comparatively strong urban labor movement would represent only a small fraction of the general Arab population.

I have pointed out, in connection with the riots of 1929, that the attempt to inflame the masses of the Arabs against the Jews was in effect a failure. The great majority of the peasants and workers wanted to be left alone. They did not participate in the game of power politics pursued by the Nazi-Fascist leadership. On the other hand, they did not have the strength to fight it. The revolt against the Jewish Homeland has remained the affair of an unrepresentative though stubborn and ruthless minority.

But even this minority cannot be considered exclusively as an Arab phenomenon. The history of the problem takes us into a study of the British role in Palestine and, later, of the interplay between the British, the Arabs and the totalitarian-democratic world struggle.

The intention of England's leading statesmen toward Palestine was expressed in the Balfour Declaration in 1917. Between that intention and its implementation something intervened — a mixture of incomprehension and hostility on the part of the British colonial administrative class which constituted the implement. Very likely the hostility was to a large extent the result of the incomprehension. Admittedly the enterprise was unique, ideologically and technically. Englishmen who had been trained in the classic tradition of colonial administration were sent out to manage a country which had been set apart for an unprecedented purpose: reoccupation and reconstruction by a people which had been absent from it for nearly twenty centuries. The center of gravity of the problem did not lie in the usual managerial technique of colonial government; it lay in an imaginative anticipation of new situations. The "man on the spot" had to think of millions of Jews waiting to make Palestine their Homeland. The ordinary static principles of administration, which take into account the factors at hand, did not apply. The Balfour Declaration had been issued to the Jewish people throughout the world, not to the handful of Jews in Palestine. It was between the Jewish people throughout the world and the Arabs of Palestine that the problem was focussed.

A specially trained class of administrators was needed. It did not exist, and it was not created. With a few exceptions, like Sir Arthur Wauchope and Sir Wyndham Deedes, the Englishmen sent out to Palestine were merely good, run-of-the-mill civil servants, who simply did not understand what was afoot. They were bewildered and irritated by the dynamic aspect of the task.

They had not even a touch of the world vision which was implicit in the restoration of the Jewish Homeland.

If well begun is half done, badly begun is half ruined. When Dr. Weizmann came out to Palestine early in 1918, at the head of the Zionist Commission which was to institute the new policy, only Judaea was in British hands; Samaria and Galilee still had to be conquered. The military men were concerned with winning the war; they were not interested in winning the peace. (That has a familiar sound, no doubt.) The Balfour Declaration had scarcely reached the ears of the English generals in Palestine, certainly not their consciousness. No effort was made to impress upon the Arab population of Palestine the character of the decision taken by the Allied and Associated Powers. When the Balfour Declaration was brought to their attention, the generals could answer with a show of reason that this was not the time to alienate the Arab population.* Actually it would have been nothing more than a show of reason; for the Arab population, supine against the Turks, whom it had reason enough to hate, incapable of an effort toward self-liberation, would have made no trouble, with a powerful British army in the country. When the war came to an end, the military administration continued for some time. It still followed the path it had chosen; the proclamation of the Balfour Declaration, in unmistakable terms, as the fundamental constitution of the country, was delayed. The succeeding civil administration inherited the policy of inertia,

* As I read proof on this book, I am struck by the painful similarity of the situation today — 1944. The anti-White Paper Resolution before the Foreign Affairs Committee of Congress is running up against the identical military opposition (M. S.).

though it was headed by a Jew — Sir Herbert (afterwards Lord) Samuel.

The agitation against the fulfilment of the Balfour Declaration had already begun. In 1920 there occurred the attack of the Halsa tribe on Tel Hai, and a riot in Jerusalem, in which six Jews were killed. In May 1921 disturbances occurred in Jaffa; forty-seven Jews and forty-eight Arabs were killed. These outbreaks cannot be regarded as national risings against the project of the Jewish Homeland; had they been such, it would be impossible to explain the long interval of peace (1921–1929) already alluded to, during which the foundations of the Jewish Homeland were securely laid. Certainly they were connected with incitement to riot; and in the post-war days of restlessness incidents of this kind were to be expected in a country with a high record of criminality. But here the first fatal blunder (if it was a blunder) occurred. The British temporarily suspended Jewish immigration into Palestine. Whatever had been the motives of the rioters, the British Administration imposed upon the situation a nationalist and anti-Jewish character by the suspension of Jewish immigration.

It was the beginning of a steady retreat from the purpose of the Balfour Declaration. In June, 1922, the Colonial Office (Mr. Winston Churchill was then Colonial Secretary) issued a White Paper, the first of a series which was to reduce, item by item, the implementation of the Jewish National Home. The first paragraph read:

"His Majesty's Government did not contemplate either the creation of a wholly Jewish Palestine or the disappearance of or subordination of the Arab population, language or culture in Palestine."

This was in effect a reiteration of the guarantee clause of the Balfour Declaration. But the second paragraph was something more — it was a limitation on the Balfour Declaration, such as had not, according to the statesmen who have been quoted, been intended by its formulators:

"The terms of the Balfour Declaration did not contemplate that Palestine as a whole should be converted into a Jewish National Home, but that such a Home should be founded in Palestine."

The fourth paragraph, seemingly in contradiction to the third, read:

"For the fulfilment of the policy, the Jewish community in Palestine should be able to increase its members by immigration, it being understood that such immigration should not exceed what might be at the time the economic capacity of the country, that the immigrants should not be a burden on the people of Palestine as a whole and that they should not deprive any section of the present population of their employment."

It was, I repeat, a seeming contradiction of paragraph three. If Jewish immigration was to be permitted up to the limit of the absorptive capacity of the country, the Jewish Homeland would emerge according to the economic possibilities, and not according to a political formula. In effect, though, the formula of "absorptive capacity" was introduced as a step in the diminution of the force of the Balfour Declaration. When, after a decade and a half of building, it became evident that Palestine's absorptive capacity was constantly being increased, and that economic grounds could not be invoked against the Jewish Homeland, a flat political decree was issued.

258

But the stages in the whittling down of the Balfour Declaration are instructive. In October, 1922, the British government arbitrarily divided Transjordan from cis-Jordan, withdrawing it from the application of the Balfour Declaration, and closing it to Jewish immigration. Transjordan was set up as a separate kingdom under the rule of the Emir Abdullah, as a counter-weight to King Ibn Saud of interior Arabia. Thus an area three times the size of cis-Jordan, with a population of less than 300,000, was lopped off, by administrative decree, from the territory originally contemplated in the Balfour Declaration.

After the riots of 1929, the British government sent out a Commission to Palestine, under the chairmanship of Sir Walter Shaw, to investigate the nature and the causes of the disturbances. The Commission issued a report which admitted that the Arabs had been the attackers, but placed the blame on Jewish immigration.

But what did that mean? That Jewish immigration had been a burden on the Arabs? That there were genuine economic grievances traceable to the newcomers? An expert, Sir John Hope Simpson, was sent out to Palestine the following year, to make another investigation. His report contained the following paragraph:

"The development which has followed on Jewish immigration during the last nine years has provided additional openings for Arab labour . . . In many directions Jewish development has meant more work for the Arabs, and it is a fair conclusion that the competition of imported Jewish labor is equalized by those increased opportunities." Oddly enough, the following conclusion was reached: "So long as wide-spread suspicion exists, as it does exist, among the Arab population, that the economic depression, under which they undoubtedly suffer, is largely due to excessive Jewish immigration, and so long as some grounds exist on which this suspicion may plausibly be represented to be well-founded, there can be little hope of any improvement in the mutual relations of the two races." "Arab unemployment is liable to be used as a political pawn."

By whom? Certainly not by the Arab leaders alone. If Jewish immigration did *not* diminish the labor opportunities of the Arab population, but was being represented as doing so, it was not a particularly high level of statesmanship which fell in line with such misrepresentation. Yet the report recommended that "in estimating the absorptive capacity of Palestine at any time, account should be taken of the Arab as well as Jewish unemployment in determining the rate at which Jewish immigration should be permitted." All this taken together amounts to the following: "If there is Arab unemployment, Jewish immigration shall be limited, though Jewish immigration has been shown to help in solving Arab unemployment."!!

Sir John Hope Simpson went further. He asserted categorically that there was not room in Palestine for more than 20,000 new settlers, without crowding out the Arabs. This was in 1930, when the Jewish population was about 170,000, the Arab 750,000. Since that time, the Jewish population has grown to nearly 600,000 and the Arab population to over 1,000,000! And in 1936 the Peel Report, already summarized, exposed the Simpson Report as completely unreliable.

However, 1930 saw the publication of another White Paper, signed, this time, by Lord Passfield (Sidney

Webb). It accepted, in large measure, the conclusions of the Hope Simpson Report. Dr. Weizmann resigned from the Presidency of the Jewish Agency in protest, whereupon the Prime Minister, Ramsay MacDonald, softened the effect of the White Paper in an official letter which actually left matters pretty much where they were.

It may seem to the reader that altogether too much space has been given here to the element of British policy. But it is impossible to understand the problem of Arab-Jewish relations unless the background of the British attitude is given with some degree of fulness. It is not unfair to say that the situation was muffed from the beginning, and that, a wrong turn having been taken at the outset, the course continued awry. Much worse was to follow, for after the riots of 1936, described in the next chapter, Palestine became a focus of German and Italian intrigue, much as Spain became one at the other end of the Mediterranean. England entered then on the melancholy "appeasement" period immediately preceding the Second World War. The fantastic retreat from principle which halted only with the outbreak of the war, and which saw one country after another sacrificed to the hope of "peace in our time," pulled the Jewish Homeland along in its wake. But in Palestine the groundwork had been laid for a futile surrender long before Manchukuo and Abyssinia and Spain were attacked. It had been laid by the systematic evasion of the issues implicit in the creation of the Jewish Homeland, and by the consequent encouragement, intentional or unintentional, of destructive elements in the Arab population.

The criticism of British policy implicit in this chapter is incidental rather than purposive. Perhaps it is some mitigation of the criticism to add that the period between the two wars was one of general confusion. Not a single one of the great democratic peoples can congratulate itself on having made a timely stand against the forces which were preparing to prevent an ordered solution of international problems. And perhaps the concept of a reconstituted Jewish Homeland in Palestine, and its role in the solution of the Jewish problem, made a special call on imaginative statesmanship at a time notably lacking in it. The purpose of this chapter is, however, to set forth the correlation of all factors in the Jewish-British-Arab problem. The solution can still be found, but only if we cease to consider the constituent elements of the problem in isolation, and attack it as a whole.

CHAPTER TWENTY-THREE

Toward the World Abyss

❁

To SAY of the years 1936 to 1939 that they were a time of "general confusion" is almost a euphemism. The period was unique in history. It must be described as the time of mankind's supreme humiliation; its unforgettable hideousness did not lie so much in the threat of aggression which hung over the world — that is an old story in human experience; it lay in the character, thoroughly representative of the movements they headed, of the men who dominated the scene and cowed the leaders of western civilization into something compounded of fear, loathing, horrified admiration and shifty acquiescence. An ascetic Rasputin in Germany and a slick thug in Italy entered into an alliance and on a career of conquest, the central technique of which was the debauching of the intelligence and morality of the nations. They owed part of their success to a headstart in armament, part of it to the moral and intellectual defection of the leadership of the democratic countries.

It is not easy to recapture the spirit of that long nightmare of cowardly hopes and cumulative concessions.

Nor is this the place for an extended study of the general effect of that experience on the tone of our political life. But the subject of this book calls for mention of one feature of the period, and a somewhat more detailed examination of another. The first was the emergence of anti-Semitism as a cohesive world force, stripped of all moral timidity or hesitancy, and integrated with the general plan for the undermining of the human character. Its consequence, or at least one of its consequences, was to extend the front of Jewish self-defense over the entire globe. A second was to precipitate an intensified assault on the Jewish Homeland, and this at a time when the disastrous collapse of the Jewish position at large made it impossible for the Jews to concentrate their energies at any one point.

We can see far more clearly today than we did in 1936 to what extent the Arab riots of that year were a part of the general scheme of piecemeal assault on the world order. Not that we were wholly blind to the total issue then, either in respect of the direct anti-Semitic policy of Germany, or of the special Axis conspiracy against Palestine. Today the record is complete. The Grand Mufti of Jerusalem, and his closest collaborators, are publicly committed to the cause of Hitler. The resistance offered in Iraq and Syria to the armies of the United Nations fits into the pattern. But even in 1936 and 1937, when the Italian Arabic-speaking broadcasting station at Bari was encouraging unrest in Palestine, we knew that Italian money, as well as Italian and German directives, had no small share in the attack on the Jewish Homeland. We knew also, and vainly proclaimed it to the world, that the Italian adventure in Abyssinia had given the signal to the Arab terrorists in Palestine; and, further, that these activities were but part of the far-sighted plan for the dislocation of all international regulation, prior to the grand assault.

The 1936 disturbances in Palestine were very different from those of 1921 and 1929. They were not sharp bursts of violence subsiding in the course of a few days. They were not the work of local agitators alone. They had behind them the encouragement of an international restlessness, and the immediate collaboration of European governments. Beginning in Jaffa on April 19, when an Arab mob launched a pogrom on groups of defenseless and unwarned Jews pursuing their regular business in that city, they spread throughout the country and were exacerbated by the calling of a general strike by the Arab Higher Committee. The strike, and the disturbances, lasted for six months. A wave of terrorism against Arabs who were disinclined to participate in the boycott and the bloodshed was maintained throughout that period. It was clear on the face of it that such an extensive and prolonged campaign of planned disorder could not have been carried out with local means only.

Before touching on the government attitude toward the disorders, I shall stress the resistance of *Arabs* to this brutal intrusion on their daily life, and describe the reaction of the Jewish settlement. As to the first: the prosperity which the development of the country was bringing to large sections of the Arab population had reconciled them to the building of the Jewish Homeland. The country had never before known such well-being; and the interruption in the mutually beneficial intercourse between the two peoples was bitterly resented by tens of thousands of Arabs. That this was the case was proved by the anti-Arab terror which the rebels were compelled to initiate. But in the nature of the case, the peaceful part of the population was not prepared to resist the interruption. It could only carry on surreptitiously, though it did this effectively enough to break the back of the rebellion.

I was a firsthand witness of the continuous passive resistance of peace-loving Arabs. My house stood on the northwestern outskirts of Tel Aviv. Less than a mile away, across empty fields, was the Arab village of Sumael. For years past the Arabs of Sumael had come into our section of Tel Aviv with their fruits, vegetables, eggs, chickens and fish. They had grown prosperous. The adobe and rough stone huts which they had once inhabited had yielded, as in many another Arab village in the vicinity of Jews, to neat, red-roofed houses. Sumael was busy and contented. Debts had been paid off, fields redeemed. Sumael did not want to fight the Jews of Tel Aviv; it wanted to do business with them.

For the first few weeks of the strike and terror, Sumael suspended connections with us. No laden donkeys came across the fields, no Arab women balancing their baskets on their heads. Fruits, vegetables and eggs rotted. The men did not go down to the seashore by the Yarkon to fish. Sumael began to feel the pinch; but the men of Sumael did not dare at first to break the strike and boycott. Every day members of the terrorist groups visited the village, to check up. It was more than a man's — or woman's — life was worth to resume business relations with the Jews.

The fear of death by knife or bullet, and the fear of death by starvation, fought it out. Then, when a few weeks had passed, a curious ritual began to be enacted in the nights at our end of the city. Two or three shots would be heard suddenly; then came an interval of quiet, during which figures could be dimly seen stealing across the fields. There was a whispering and scurrying in empty lots. Then two or three shots again — and silence for the rest of the night.

What was happening? Business was being done in a novel way. Arab farmers and fishermen came sneaking at night toward Tel Aviv. When they were close to the boundary, they fired a few shots, to make it appear that they were attacking the Jewish city. Jews came out to meet them; goods and money were exchanged; the groups parted, and a few more shots were fired. The terrorists were thrown off the scent, and the old connections were resumed in a weird setting.

In one way or another, a similar activity was maintained in other parts of Tel Aviv and in other parts of the country. But it need hardly be said that this was no adequate substitute for the normal conduct of business.

If the riots of 1929 failed spectacularly to arrest the growth of the Jewish Homeland, those of 1936 and the subsequent years were equally futile in their intended effect on the determination of the Jews to go on building. But now larger forces were at work — and more insidious ones — against which it was more difficult to make headway. The Arab terror of 1936 lasted six months, and then collapsed; but only temporarily. We must take the full period of the world decline from 1936 to 1939 as the background to this part of our survey; we shall then understand more clearly the nature of the cumulative opposition which confronted the Jewish people, and the character of its resistance on the Palestinian front.

Palestine was advancing in the midst of a receding

world; it was constructive in the midst of disintegration. The contradiction could not long be maintained. The "appeasement" phase of world politics, that phase of continuous retreat and surrender which did not even serve to delay the cataclysm, threw as dark a shadow over Palestine as over Abyssinia and Spain. At the beginning of the new Arab terror there was a certain degree of firmness — marred by delays and confusion — on the part of the Palestinian government. But before long the echo of the far deeper confusion reigning in London reached the Palestinian Administration. For the years 1936 to 1939 the total official Jewish immigration in Palestine was in the neighborhood of fifty thousand, about one-half of it in 1936 — in the very midst of the terror. There was also some "unofficial" immigration. But both official and unofficial immigration tapered off as the Imperial Government became more and more deeply compromised to the policy of appeasement. In 1936 the Jewish Agency asked for some 22,000 labor immigration certificates, but received a little over 5,000, of which 1,000 were held back to "cover" illegal immigration. In 1937, 14,000 were asked for, 2,500 granted, of which some 400 were withheld. It must be remembered that these were the years during which the mounting agony of European, and especially of German, Jewry was making itself heard through the world. The "illegal" immigrants into Palestine were literally in flight from death. The smallness of the number of certificates granted, the cancellation of some of these as an offset against the men, women and children who managed to smuggle their way into the Jewish Homeland, as the last desperate refuge, must be counted as a victory of the forces which were dedicated to the

destruction of the Jewish people. Concerning the tragedy of this "illegal" flight from death into Palestine
more will be said in the sequel.

Within the country the Jews carried on with unshaken
determination. For months on end the roads were not
safe. Travellers were ambushed and convoys attacked.
Landmines were planted on the routes between Jewish
colonies. The drivers of the Jewish cooperative bus
lines sprang into sudden prominence as heroic figures. Colonies suffered direct attacks; harvests were
burned; fruit trees uprooted; robbery increased. Still
the Jews carried on. They were determined on two lines
of action; self-defense and *Havlagah*.

This last word became very familiar to the Jewish
world. It means "patience," "self-restraint," "refusal
to be provoked." As in 1929, the Arab leadership hoped
to sting the Jews into indiscriminate reprisals, setting
off a civil war; and, as then, the Jews were on guard
against this *maneuver*. It will be remembered that very
early in the *Shomrim* movement the anti-vendetta tradition had been established. As far back as the first decade
of the century Jews had foreseen that, if they let themselves be dragged down to the moral level of feuding
tribes, they would never achieve understanding with
their neighbors. There had always been provocation;
and it had always been resisted; but in the years 1936
to 1939 the provocation became systematic, subtle and
unbearable. A grim spirit of endurance took hold of
the *Yishuv*. It was determined that, among the casualties, the sense of balance and justice should never
appear. In the main it was successful. The policy of
Havlagah was fiercely denounced, particularly by the

Revisionist Party. And there were a few isolated instances of reprisals. But in the main the *Havlagah* policy triumphed until the end — that is, until the outbreak of the Second World War brought compulsory peace within the borders of Palestine.

The iron self-restraint of the Jews was all the more remarkable when we consider that provocation was accompanied by opportunity. The longer the terror lasted, the more skilful the Jews became in guerrilla tactics. Moreover, from 1936 on, the government armed an increasing number of Jews, enrolling them as supernumerary police, or *Gaffirim*, as they were called. These men became adepts in the use of arms. They worked side by side with the British troops who were sent to put down the Arab terrorists; and the relations between the *Gaffirim* and the British soldiers were very friendly. Unfortunately the relations between the British Administration and the Higher Arab Committee, which had instigated the strike and the terror, were not *unfriendly*. Official negotiations were carried on continuously between the Administration and the directors of the assassins and arsonists who were making war on women and children; by these negotiations the Administration conferred on the Arab Higher Committee the status of legal and, as it were, respectable belligerents! Not until the war broke out were these employers of thugs rounded up and deported to an island in the Indian Ocean. But not the Mufti! Somehow he escaped, and, fleeing the country, allied himself openly with the men who had been his secret abettors — Hitler and Mussolini.

About 500 Jews were killed in those three years; but the founding of colonies went on. A new technique arose; the technique of sudden and complete occupation of a piece of territory by a completely organized group. It was another demonstration of the remarkable adaptability of the Jews; it was also, in its application, one of the most thrilling phenomena in the history of the Homeland.

One day, in the spring of 1937, I was able to witness the carrying out of such an occupation. I passed the night in the old, established colony from which the "foray" was to be made. Long before the dawn, I was awakened; the convoy of builders was ready to set out. Some fifteen trucks were lined up. In three of them the men assembled, among them a dozen armed *Gaffirim*. The other trucks carried *walls*. Section by section these wooden walls had been prepared, according to specifications; walls for a stockade, walls for huts and barracks, and walls for a watchtower. Our objective was a stretch of Jewish-owned land at the eastern end of the Valley of Jezreel; our purpose to set up the colony in its completeness before any attack could be made.

We set out by moonlight; and when the first streaks of light were coming up over the Jordan Valley, we were at our destination. The trucks drew up in a circle, the *Gaffirim* stationed themselves about the perimeter of the field. Swiftly, systematically, the pioneers began to set up the walls of the stockade: wooden walls, consisting of a front and back separated by a distance of six inches, the interval filled in with *hatzatz*, a mixture of earth and pebbles. In the center of the square was erected the criss-cross framework of the watchtower, fifty feet high, and crowned by a searchlight. All day long the work went on, without interruption. By the time the sun was sinking toward the Carmel range, the work was completed, and there was still time for a celebration. The *Gaffirim* maintained their guard; all the others assembled about the watch-tower; speeches were made, songs were sung, and the representative of the Zionist Office (it was Jacob Hartzfeld on that occasion) presented the colony with a set of the works of Theodore Herzl, in Hebrew.

There was no attack on the new colony that day. The action had been too well organized; the front was too formidable. Later on, when the men were in the fields, there were stray shots and casualties. In the nights the searchlight on top of the tower threw its powerful beam in slowly moving circles to the farthest end of the colony. It was thus not only in the new settlements, but in many that had long been established. The period was one of intense and racking strain for the workers; between spells of labor in the fields there were spells of sentry duty. Everyone was on double shift. Yet there was no talk of retreat. "This too will pass," I heard people say. And one man, whom I met in Zurich at the Zionist Congress of August, 1939, a few days after the Russo-German pact, and a few days before the outbreak of the war, summed up for me the attitude of his fellow-workers in one of the colonies.

They had made, he said, a brief calculation. "Between 1919 and 1939, that is, in twenty years, about a thousand Jews have been killed while building the Jewish Homeland. In that time we have increased our numbers by nearly 500,000. We will say, then, that for every five hundred Jews we bring into the country, one must be killed. Is that a very high price? Or put it this way. For every Jew so killed, we have saved five hundred. How many Jews are saved by the death of a Jew in Germany?"

If it had only been so simple! They were ready enough to die, those builders in Palestine; but neither heroism, nor the creative will, nor the justice of their claim could avail against the deterioration of purpose, foresight and principle which had set in like a furious malady among the democratic governments and peoples. Manchukuo, Abyssinia, Spain, Austria, the Sudetenland, Czecho-Slovakia, Palestine — not to mention, because it was a continuous theme, a sinister background of more and more lurid significance, the anti-Semitic fury — were the milestones of what seemed then to be an endless Via Dolorosa. In a sort of fascinated helplessness we moved from catastrophe to catastrophe; and that universal paralysis of the civilized nations was to many the precursor of the end of our civilization.

Palestine was only one tiny episode in the vast, macabre drama, but it mirrored perfectly the satanic motif of the whole. And it had, perhaps, a special significance; for the idea of the rebuilt Jewish Homeland was symbolic of the larger purpose which inspired the founders of the League. Its four outstanding artificers — Woodrow Wilson, of America; Lord Cecil, of England; Jan Smuts, of South Africa; and Leon Bourgeois, of France — advocated this special act of restitution warmly. Lord Cecil said, on one occasion, that for him the two great gains snatched from the calamity of the First World War were the League of Nations and the Jewish Homeland in Palestine. The drive to compel the abandonment of the Balfour Declaration and the Mandate was only a part of the political strategy of the Axis; ideologically it had a value disproportionate to the number of human beings directly involved.

273

The year 1935 was the dividing line for the Jewish Homeland. Until then the difficulties with the Mandatory Power had stemmed from the hostility or indifference of *Englishmen* to the policy of the Jewish National Home. The bungling of 1921 and 1929, the White Papers of 1922 and 1930, had expressed contradictions between *British* policy (itself suffering from internal contradictions) and the purpose of the Mandate. But we have seen that these difficulties were in a sense manageable. For after 1929 there came the great upswing of 1933, 1934, 1935. After 1935 the difficulties stemmed, not from specific British opposition to the purpose of the Mandate, but much more from England's ever deeper involvement in the frantic policy of appeasement. The protests addressed to England on the subject of Palestine, before 1935, had been heard and considered. After 1935 neither England nor the rest of the democratic world heard them. They did not seem to register. The nations were engaged in watching, in dread mingled with a sort of fascination, the cataclysmic advance of the totalitarian power. The words "justice," "law," "order," "humanity," were losing their content. The panic and stupefaction which seized the world were overlaid with admiration for the demonic efficiency of the naked power-principle. "To get by" was the hope of each individual nation. Who could listen, then, to arguments concerning the interdependence of moral and political values?

For the larger part of 1936 the Palestine Administration held out against the pressure to restrict Jewish immigration. In the fall of that year the Royal Commission, better known as the Peel Commission, from the name of its chairman, Lord Peel, came out to investigate the causes of the riots. It says much for the blindness which reigned then in high places that such an investigation was confined to conditions in Palestine, and had no reference, even the most tacit, to Berlin and Rome, Abyssinia and Spain. The Peel Commission produced a splendid document, sections of which have already been quoted. It vindicated the Jewish position in its complete disproof of those economic complaints which the Arab leadership alleged as the cause of the riots. It took the stand that a Jewish Homeland had definitely been promised to the Jewish people. But in effect it pronounced that promise to be unredeemable and the Mandate unworkable. One could just as well have said that the freedom of Czecho-Slovakia and the independence of the Philippines were "unworkable." It depended on the point of view. In a world going to pieces in the moral stampede of those days, nothing was workable; and the implication that the Jewish Homeland was unworkable in a special sense could come only from the terrorized "statesmanship" of that time, which did not even dare to name the enemy.

In 1921 and 1929 Arab rioting had produced temporary suspensions of immigration. The riots of 1936–1939 produced permanent restrictions followed by the last White Paper, and total suspension after 1944. The report of the Peel Commission set in motion an attempt to answer the problem by partitioning Palestine into a tiny Jewish Homeland, an Arab State and an internationalized zone administered by England. The proposal was hotly debated throughout the Jewish world. In effect it was meaningless; for the root of the trouble did not lie in Palestine; and no ingenuities of management could safeguard the tranquillity or progress of a given country when all sense of order was disappearing from the world. The partitioning of Palestine was as futile a suggestion as the surrender of the Sudeten area of Czecho-Slovakia.

In July 1937 the British government openly abandoned the principle of economic absorptive capacity, and launched upon a policy of *political* restriction of immigration. The Mandates Commission of the League of Nations declared this to be a "departure from the spirit of the Mandate." But by that time the League of Nations counted for very little, and its pronouncements were simply ignored. Immigration, which had been nearly 30,000 in 1936, in spite of the unsettled state of the country, was held down to 10,500 in 1937. Yet there was practically no unemployment, and tens of thousands of the refugees of Germany and Austria could have been usefully admitted. The situation went from bad to worse. In November, 1938, the British government proposed a general conference between the leaders of Palestinian Jewry and the Arab leaders of Palestine and neighboring states. The Jews had requested a conference with the Palestinian Arabs alone. The Arabs of Iraq or Syria had no moral competence in the matter of the Jewish Homeland in Palestine, or rather, they had only the same moral competence as all the other nations. But the consensus of the nations on the subject had already been uttered through the League — and it was being ignored. The calling in of neighboring Arab states had actually no relation to the problem of Palestine; it had much more to do with England's attempts to win Arab support generally for the time of stress to come. Like all concessions made under compulsion, this one compromised the offer morally without producing any practical results. The Arab leaders were convinced that England, like the other democracies, was no longer a power to be reckoned with.

In February and March, 1939, the "Conference" was held in London. It was in reality two conferences; one a British-Arab, the other a British-Jewish, for the Arabs would not sit with the Jews. Well might they refuse! They anticipated the complete collapse of French and British power in the Mediterranean, the disappearance of the League of Nations, the reapportionment of spheres of influence, in short, "the new order." What had they to gain from any concessions to England or the Jews? Already Jewish immigration into Palestine had been practically stopped. There remained only the formal repudiation of the Balfour Declaration and the proclamation of Palestine as an independent state, in which the Jews would be a permanent minority. If the Arabs did not get this from England, they would get it from the Axis.

This was the setting in which the Jews of Palestine continued their constructive work in 1936 and on. New colonies sprang up, old ones were extended; factories opened; the University expanded; cooperatives multiplied; the Palestine Symphony Orchestra gave a hundred concerts annually, four of them in Egypt, two in Syria; the Technical School of Haifa was turning out graduate engineers; the citrus industry boomed, so that Palestine oranges ranked next to Spanish and Italian in the world market; the Palestine Electric Corporation sold sixty million kilowatt hours per annum; the Haifa harbor approached completion; the Tel Aviv harbor, built as an offset to the Jaffa harbor, became an important factor in the country; the deposits of the Anglo-Palestine Bank rose to thirty-five million dollars; Tenuvah, the co-operative of the Labor Federation, did a business of nearly $3,000,000 in 1937.

The world was rushing toward the abyss; Palestine was thrusting in the opposite direction. There could not be any doubt about the outcome in such an opposition of forces. The White Paper of 1939 was the expression of the resolution of this strain.

In the spring of 1936 I came across old Joshua Chankin, that marvelous survivor of the *Bilu* days. He was, I think, nearly eighty years of age, but still erect, still touched with the spirit which had brought him to the country some sixty years before. This was the man who had bought the first land for Tel Aviv, for most of the colonies of the Valley of Jezreel, and for many of those of the PICA. The famous stick was still part of him; and as of old, he went about the country unarmed. But now he was attended by two ferocious dogs. He would not carry a revolver, which he regarded as an implement of aggression. The dogs were, however, something new. Old Joshua Chankin did not mind so much if he were shot from ambush. He feared only one thing—being kidnapped and tortured, as had happened to some Jews in those years. The only alternative was, of course, to stay at home. "That," he said, "is naturally out of the question. I must go about my work."

CHAPTER TWENTY-FOUR

White Paper and Black Days

⚙

THE record shows, I believe, the fateful difference between the quality of British opposition (more exactly, the opposition of certain British groups) to the Jewish Homeland in Palestine before and after 1935 or 1936. In the first period that opposition was sporadic; it was effective in varying degrees; it was largely overcome during the years 1933 to 1935. In the second period it was consistent and successful. It then resembled Arab opposition in not being indigenous and free, for it was fed by external sources. The genuine opposition among Englishmen (and such always existed), like the genuine opposition among Arabs (and that too always existed), got the upper hand. It was the time of appeasement.

This much must be understood, lest the false conclusion be drawn that a Jewish Homeland in Palestine is by its essence contrary to British or Arab interests. What the factual record shows is borne out by the utterances of a group of extremely influential Englishmen on the subject of the White Paper of 1939.

The contents of this document, issued in May, 1939, and known officially as *Command 6019*, may be summarized as follows. It takes up the view expressed by the Peel Commission that the Mandate is "unworkable." But it also takes up the view that the promises contained in the Balfour Declaration have already been fulfilled, and that the Jewish Homeland, originally contemplated by the framers of the Balfour Declaration, is already in existence. However, as a concession to Jewish need, the British government would permit some 75,000 Jews to enter Palestine in the five-year period following the publication of the White Paper. Thereafter "no further Jewish immigration will be permitted unless the Arabs of Palestine are prepared to acquiesce in it." Further: the British government will do "everything in their power to create conditions which will enable the independent Arab State [of Palestine] to come into being within ten years."

Before summarizing the attack on the White Paper in the House of Commons, I think it proper to make two observations. It is impossible to state, at one and the same time, that the Mandate is unworkable, and that the Mandate has been fulfilled. What Malcolm Mac-Donald sought to imply, through this untenable statement, was that the Mandate had gone beyond the intended purpose of the Balfour Declaration. He could not state this explicitly, since Britain had accepted the Mandate, and he knew that the Mandates Commission would not stultify itself by ratifying his illogical thesis.

The White Paper went on to say that "to seek to expand the Jewish National Home indefinitely by immigration, against the strongly expressed will of the Arab people of the country" would mean "rule by force." Here several contradictions spring to the eye. If a Jewish National Home is already in existence, as promised, and the Jews seek, not its establishment (that

280

having already taken place, according to the argument), but its "expansion," we must ask: "What kind of expansion?" If we mean growth, development, increase of population, within the accepted boundaries, then the Jewish National Home has the right to engage in that promotion, or else it is not a National Home. The only limiting factor is the economic absorptive capacity of the country, which operates as a natural law, without British intervention. The protection of the putative minority is taken care of in the very constitution which guarantees the Jewish National Home. Again: it is clear to everyone, and was repeatedly stressed in the House of Commons, that *it was the suspension of Jewish immigration into Palestine under pressure of Arab riots and Axis intrigue which represented "rule by force."* Third, and in the same line, the phrase "unless the Arabs of Palestine are prepared to acquiesce in it [Jewish immigration]" assumes tacitly that the Arab masses of Palestine are free to express their will. The assumption is unwarranted, and will remain so for a long time. And fourth — this being the most striking contradiction — the question of the Jewish Homeland in Palestine was *not* referred to the Arabs of Palestine, but was made the football of the Near East political game by bringing in Arabs of other countries to have a say in the matter.

The opponents of the White Paper, in the House of Commons, were the opponents of the appeasement policy; they regarded the White Paper as part of the useless retreat of the Chamberlain Government; they opposed it on grounds of national honor, and as enemies of the Nazi-Fascist advance. That the foremost opponents of Nazi-Fascism should have been friends of the Jewish Homeland in Palestine is significant in the extreme; and it is particularly heartening to those who believe in the moral significance of the Jewish Homeland that its supporters should be of that political and moral mould which could not tolerate the appeasement policy of the Chamberlain Government.

When we consider the attitude of the Mandates Commission of the League of Nations on the White Paper, we are confronted with a totally different analysis. The Mandates Commission asked, not whether the White Paper was appeasement, or derogatory to British honor, or harmful to British interests, but simply whether it was legally and morally defensible from the point of view of international law. The answer was in the negative. It is true that the voice of the League of Nations was lost in the tumult of the pre-war days; but the record is of importance. We must not assume that law and order and morality have come to an end, exactly as if Hitler had won the war. Nor must we be misled into extreme statements like: "England never wanted to build a Jewish Homeland; from the beginning she set out to undermine the Balfour Declaration and the Mandate." I have tried to show that a confusion of outlook and a conflict of purposes always existed in England on the subject of Palestine; and it is only through this objective evaluation that we can explain both the successes and failures of the enterprise.

The debate on the White Paper took place on May 25th, 1939. Mr. Tom Williams (later Parliamentary Secretary to the Ministry of Agriculture and Fisheries under the Churchill Government) presented the counter-resolution, the essence of which reads:

"The proposals of His Majesty's Government relating

to Palestine as set out in *Command 6019* are inconsistent with the letter and spirit of the Mandate and not calculated to secure the peaceful and prosperous development of Palestine." Mr. Williams declared that the White Paper was "in fact tantamount almost to the abrogation of the Balfour Declaration." Criticizing the speech of the Secretary for the Colonies (Mr. Malcolm MacDonald), who presented the White Paper, Mr. Williams said: "When the Right Honorable Gentleman [Mr. MacDonald] refers to fear on the part of the Arabs, is he thinking in terms of the peasants, farmers, or the few overlords? I suggest that the so-called fear of the Arabs being dominated by the Jews refers to a comparatively small number who have been encouraged by the enemies of this country, and to whom this country has at long last surrendered . . . I ask the Right Honorable Gentleman why he thinks in terms of an independent Arab State. Can he visualise the possibility of that independent Government rising above the Jewish tide of economic prosperity, or is there a possibility that they may descend to the economic swamps of Irak, Transjordan and the other Arab States? The Right Honorable Gentleman is not only responsible for the rich landlord Arab, or the High Churchman Arab, but for the hundreds of thousands of Arab workers who stand to gain most if economic prosperity is developed in that country . . . The fear argument is a mere excuse. It is another victory for Hitler and Mussolini and those who think as they think, and those who have been guiding the terror into activities during the past three years."

Leopold Amery, a life-long friend of the Jewish Homeland, one-time Secretary for the Colonies and later, under the Churchill Government, Secretary of State for India, was equally outspoken. He said: "We have this White Paper which, from beginning to end, is a confession of failure, a direct negation of the principles on which our administration in Palestine has been based, and, in my view at any rate, a repudiation of the pledges on the strength of which the Government of Palestine was entrusted to our hands . . . The White Paper is a direct invitation to the Arabs to continue to make trouble. As for the Jews, they are now told that . . . all the pledges and promises that had been given them are broken."

Mr. Amery adverted to the misrepresentations with which Mr. MacDonald sought to bolster his defense of the White Paper:

"It is somewhat misleading for my Right Honorable friend to give the impression that it is the policy of the Mandate which has driven the whole Arab population into three years of sustained revolt, as if it were the whole Arab population which had risen against some intolerable oppression. The trouble has come from a different class of the community, a class animated increasingly by the intolerant totalitarian conception of race . . . What is the watchword now? The watchword is, 'appease the Arabs, appease the Mufti.' Appeasement at all costs; appease them by abandoning the declared policy of every Government for twenty years past. Appease them by breaking faith with the Jews. Appease them at the cost of sacrificing all the prestige which we might have gained from either Jews or Arabs by consistency, by firmness, by justice to both sides."

Mr. Noel Baker, later Parliamentary Secretary to the Ministry for War Transport under the Churchill Government, regarded the policy of the Chamberlain Government in regard to Palestine not merely as a breach of the Mandate, but as an indefensible innovation of principle. "For him [Mr. MacDonald] the primary purpose of the Mandate is no longer the establishment of the Jewish National Home but the protection of Arab rights; and not the rights of the Balfour Declaration — political freedom and civil justice in a free state — but a new right which he has invented, the right that the Arabs shall be a majority for ever. By inventing this new Arab right to be in a majority, he has utterly destroyed the purpose and meaning of the Mandate and has violated its spirit in every possible way."

Among those who achieved new prominence when the Chamberlain Government was swept out of office there were three men of exceptional ability, Herbert Morrison, Sir Archibald Sinclair and Sir Stafford Cripps. Morrison, like the others, saw the issue in a wider setting than that of Palestine. "If we do this thing today," he said, "we shall have done a thing which is dishonorable to our good name, which is discreditable to our capacity to govern, and which is dangerous to British security, to peace and to the economic interest of the world in general and of our own country . . ." And again the real source of the troubles was uncovered: "Knowing that most of the trouble in Palestine has been created, not by the masses of the Arab people at all, but through a minority of certain classes of the Arabs, probably mostly by the agents of Herr Hitler and Signor Mussolini; knowing that this was so, and it began in the days when the Prime Minister [Mr. Neville Chamberlain] had a particular friendship with Herr Hitler and Signor Mussolini — knowing that this trouble was largely the creation of foreign intervention and the activities of foreign agents, the Government were nevertheless not aware, in the early days, of these difficulties . . . We regard this White Paper and the policy in it as a cynical breach of pledges given to the Jews and the world, including America. This policy will do us no good in the U. S. A."

Sir Archibald Sinclair was equally perturbed about the effects on Britain's reputation: "The good name of Great Britain will be tainted if Parliament accepts this White Paper and endorses it before obtaining the impartial judgment of the Hague Court and the Mandates Commission." He was aware, however, that the times were not propitious for right action. "If I say that this restriction of immigration within arbitrary limits, unrelated to the economic absorptive capacity of the country, and the undertaking to make its continuance dependent on Arab sufferance, this restriction of Jewish immigration, thus having swept away the obligations imposed by the Mandate to facilitate Jewish immigration, introducing into the immigration policy, contrary to the terms of the Mandate, an element of discrimination against the Jews on grounds of race and religion, the reduction of the Jews to the status of a permanent minority — all these things, whether justified or not in the existing circumstances in Palestine — this is not a question which I am arguing for the moment — are all grave departures from the terms of the Mandate, and they call in question our moral right to continue to hold it. They are not matters within the sole jurisdiction and responsibility of His Majesty's Government, or even of Parliament, but require the most careful study and examination at the hands of the Mandates Commission."

Again and again the distinction between the terrorist gangs of Palestine and the welfare of the masses was brought to the fore.

Sir Archibald Sinclair said: "When I think of the Arab people I want to help, I don't think of those powerful feudal families, and of the Mufti and the Nashashibis. I think of the fellaheen living by the hundreds of thousands on the land, and living there more prosperously, as the Royal Commission reported to us, than they were before the Jews came to establish their National Home ... I think of the fellaheen, of those people who are working in industry and improving their position, of the villagers terrorized by the bands of the Mufti, and working where they can in close cooperation with the Jews ... These are the Arabs whom the House ought to protect against the feudal Arabs and the foreign agitators, and protect them against the loss of the spring of their own happiness which is the Jewish National Home."

Sir Stafford Cripps spoke from the viewpoint of Labor: "I am sure that the Palestine problem is in its essence very largely an economic one. The real problem is the problem of the peasant and the worker. It is not the problem of the landlords and the moneyed class."

But the most powerful utterances on the subject of the White Paper came, as might have been expected, from the man who was to succeed Chamberlain in power — the man who has made his name synonymous with England's greatness. The style and accent are unmistakable. It is Winston Churchill speaking:

"I come to the gravamen of the case ... There is

287

much in this White Paper which is alien to the spirit of the Balfour Declaration, but I will not trouble about that. I select the one point upon which there is plainly a breach and repudiation of the Balfour Declaration — the provision that Jewish immigration can be stopped in a five years' time by a decision of an Arab majority. This is a plain breach of a solemn obligation . . .

"I cannot understand why this course has been taken. I search around for the answer. Is our condition so parlous and our stock so poor that we must, in our weakness, make this sacrifice of our declared purpose? . . . If the Government, with their superior knowledge of the deficiencies in armaments which have arisen during their stewardship, really feel that we are too weak to carry out our obligation, and wish to file a petition in moral and physical bankruptcy, that is an argument which, however ignominious, should certainly have weight with the House in these dangerous times. But is it true? I do not believe that it is true . . . What will our potential enemies think? What will those who have been stirring up these Arab agitators think? Will they not be encouraged by our confession of recoil? . . .

"We are now asked to submit — and this is what rankles most with me — to an agitation which is fed with foreign money and ceaselessly inflamed by Nazi and Fascist propaganda . . . Surely it would be only prudent and decent for the Government . . . to ascertain the view taken by the Mandates Commission of the League of Nations before whom these proposals are to go before claiming a parliamentary decision in their favor."

But the Chamberlain Government could not wait to consult the Mandates Commission. Parliament was in the midst of the moral stampede which goes by the name of "Munich." Even so, the White Paper was adopted by the narrow margin of 89 votes; and there is not the slightest doubt that many of those who voted for it did so in the deep conviction that they were yielding a principle in the face of mortal danger.

The Mandates Commission of the League of Nations met in June, 1939, and considered the White Paper during five sessions. Before it appeared Mr. Malcolm MacDonald, as the "accredited representative" of the British government, to defend the action. I have said that the Mandates Commission was not concerned with the effects of the White Paper on England's political fortunes or on the course of world events. But whatever the leaders-to-be of England could offer against the moral blemishes of the White Paper was repeated by members of the Mandates Commission. One additional point was raised by Miss Dannevig, the Danish member. She asked: Did the "accredited representative" think that the Jews would have gone to Palestine in such large numers — 500,000 in fifteen years — if they had known that after twenty-two years their immigration was to be stopped and made dependent on Arab agreement? The point was answered indirectly in the White Paper itself, which states that it is not concerned with what the Jews were thinking when they were given the Balfour Declaration and the Mandate. But the point must be pressed home, for a contract is constituted by the understanding of the parties as to the the meaning of its terms. It is true that tens of thousands of Jews entered Palestine because they could not go elsewhere, and that they did not look into the terms of the Balfour Declaration; but tens of thousands of

Jews preceded them on a very express interpretation of
the Balfour Declaration. The foundations of the Jewish
Homeland were laid by men who *could* have gone to
other countries and joined Jewish minorities already ex-
istent there. And since without these pioneers the later
tens of thousands would not have followed, it is proper
to say that practically all the Jews in Palestine are there
because of the Balfour Declaration and of the promise
of a Jewish Homeland.

Mr. MacDonald's plea that the White Paper was in
harmony with the terms of the Palestine Mandate was
rejected by the Mandates Commission. It was the last
utterance of the League on this question. The war
broke out in September.

One of the paragraphs of the White Paper reads:
"His Majesty's Government are determined to check
illegal immigration [into Palestine], and further preventive measures are being adopted. The numbers of any
Jewish illegal immigrants who, despite these measures,
may succeed in coming into the country, and cannot
be deported, will be deducted from the yearly quota."

If the Palestine administration had brought to the
repression of the Arab terrorists the determination and
vigilance which it brought to the task of preventing
Jews from saving their lives by illegal entry into Palestine, one of the most revolting chapters in modern
history would have remained unwritten. Long after
Germany had revealed, in the shamelessness of insanity,
the fullness of her program toward the Jews, namely,
complete extermination; long after the passage of the
Nuremberg Laws, after the burning of the synagogues,
after the overrunning of Austria and Czecho-Slovakia,

after the conquest of Poland and France, the White Paper continued [and at the date of writing continues] in unabated force. The story of its application is so ugly that to recite it coldly would be an unforgivable affectation. In Palestine over half a million Jews waited with open arms for their tormented and homeless kin (in most cases literally their kin, their brothers and sisters, their parents, grandparents, parents-in-law, uncles, aunts, cousins), while over the Mediterranean and Black Seas unclean and unseaworthy little cargo boats crept from port to port, or tossed about on the open waters, waiting in vain for permission to discharge their crowded human cargoes. Hunger, thirst, disease and unspeakable living conditions reigned on those floating coffins. Before the outbreak of the war the scandal attracted some attention even in the midst of the general confusion and uncertainty. After September 3rd, 1939, it was pushed out of the public prints. The innocent thousands of men, women and children who, living, had been thrust out of the world of the living, were completely forgotten, except by the Jews — and the Palestine administration.

Some of the illicit traffic in salvation was successful — Jews were actually landed, by stealth, along lonely stretches of the Palestine coast. Most of it was not. There is a list of mass tragedies already available; incomplete though it certainly must be, it is sickeningly long.

In November, 1939, the tiny tramp steamer, *Salvador*, which no captain should have taken out to sea, and which no passenger should ever have boarded, set out from Roumania for Palestine, with some five hundred refugees, most of them children. Good ships were not available for an enterprise of this kind, but the refugees had no choice. The *Salvador* sank in the Sea of Marmora, and between two and three hundred refugees were drowned.

In March, 1940, the *Darien* reached Palestine with eight hundred refugees from the Bucharest pogroms, plus the survivors of the *Salvador*. The boat made port in a sinking condition, and no other boat was available for the deportation of the refugees. They were taken off under escort and placed in an internment camp.

In November, 1940, two vessels, the *Pacific* and the *Milos*, reached Palestine with 1,770 Jews who had escaped from Nazi-occupied lands. They had neither visas nor immigration permits for Palestine. The boats were stopped at Haifa, the refugees taken off and transferred to the *Patria*, for deportation to Africa. On November 25th an explosion occurred on the *Patria*, and 250 of the passengers were killed. The origin of the explosion is unknown. It has been attributed to the refugees themselves, *reproachfully!* Jewish victims in flight from Nazism to their National Homeland must not commit suicide if their last hope is snatched from them on the threshold of realization. The survivors of the *Patria* were taken ashore, and still held for deportation, until vigorous protests from the United States to Great Britain caused the order to be withdrawn.

The maddest touch in this mad story was to follow. One hundred and fifty of the *Patria* survivors subsequently joined the British armed forces in the Near East, and the first British soldier to fall at Tobruk was a Czech Jew taken off the *Patria*.

About the time the *Patria* was sunk, a 400-ton boat, the *Atlantic*, arrived in Palestine with 1,800 refugees.

What conditions on the *Atlantic* were like may be gathered from the fact that the normal *full* passenger capacity of a 20,000-ton liner is much less than 1,800. The *Atlantic* could not put out to sea again; it was in a sinking condition. The 1,800 men, women and children were removed to shore and interned. The ancient tradition, that a slave who sets foot on British-ruled soil becomes free, did not apply to the Jewish slaves of Hitler. These, having reached Palestine, were rounded up in the night, forced aboard another vessel, and deported to the island of Mauritius in the Indian Ocean.

In December, 1941, the steamship *Struma*, of 180-tons burden, arrived at the port of Istambul with 750 Jewish refugees on board. Permission to set foot on Turkish soil was refused unless the passengers could produce visas for Palestine. Repeated pleas addressed to the Palestine Administration for such visas were totally rejected until February, 1942, when the ruling of the White Paper was so far relaxed as to give admission to all children under sixteen on the *Struma*. But this concession arrived too late, for on February 24th the Turkish authorities ordered the *Struma* to leave Turkish territorial waters. The captain protested, asserting that the vessel would sink. His protest was ignored. The *Struma* was towed out of port, and fell apart when it reached the open sea. All but five of the 750 refugees were drowned.

"I cannot understand why this course has been taken. I search around for the answer," said Churchill of the White Paper, when it was submitted to Parliament. What shall we say now, when the results of the White Paper are before us? Shall we ask how many soldiers the armies of the democracies lost, in a time of desperate need, with the sinking of the *Salvador* and the *Struma*, with the blowing up of the *Patria* and the deportations to Mauritius? And how many more with the final discouragement which these incidents meant for those who waited on the shores of Europe? If, of 1,500 survivors on the *Patria*, 150 joined the British armies, 100,000 Jews admitted into Palestine would have yielded 10,000 soldiers. Were 10,000 fanatical anti-Nazi fighters, added to the other thousands Jewish Palestine supplied, of no account in the days when Rommel stood at the gates of Alexandria?

We, too, search around for the answer. Why did the Churchill Government, the leaders of which had denounced the White Paper in such unmeasured language in 1939, retain it after they had taken office? Certainly, once a course is begun it may be easier to continue than to reverse it. But on this point, too, Churchill had spoken with his usual statesmanlike insight. He had said, in the course of the debate: "Long before these five years are passed, either there will be a Britain which knows how to keep its word on the Balfour Declaration and is not afraid to do so, or, believe me, we shall find ourselves relieved of many overseas responsibilities other than those comprised within the Palestine Mandate ... I warn the Conservative Party — and some of my warnings have not, alas, been ill-founded — that, by committing themselves to this lamentable act of default, they will cast our country, and all that it stands for, one more step downward in its fortunes, which step will later on have to be retrieved by hard exertions. That is why I say that upon the larger aspect of this matter the policy which you think is a relief and an easement, you will find afterwards, you will have to retrieve in suffering and greater exertions than those we are making."

The opposition group, as it then was, did not fear the Arabs, or it considered the danger from this source to be increased rather than diminished by the White Paper. They were right. Neither Iraq nor Syria were softened toward the democracies by the White Paper. So much the record tells us. They were "won over" by the decline of Nazi-Fascist fortunes. The Arabs of Palestine were silenced by the sudden and obvious determination of England to brook no interference with the war effort; and they were silenced, too, by the presence of over half a million Jews eagerly — in spite of everything — on the side of England.

What, then, is the answer? It can only be what I have suggested, that the policy once initiated was easier to continue than abandon. The "men on the spot" were set in this policy of repression; a change would have meant a drastic revision of personnel, for these men had compromised themselves by the hard, ruthless efficiency which they had brought to their odious task. Less than any group of British officials ever sent to administer Palestine were these able to understand the moral implications of the Mandate and the Jewish Homeland. They had, on the contrary, a peculiar fitness for the burking of the Mandate, springing in some instances from innate opposition to the idea, in others from a strong anti-Jewish bias.

More Jews have been killed by the White Paper than in all the Arab riots of the last twenty-three years. I am not speaking of those who were prevented from setting out for Palestine, and perished in Poland, in Germany, in Roumania, but only of those who managed to reach shipboard and went down in the waters of the Mediterranean and Black Seas. Their tragedy is surely not greater, in itself, than the tragedy of thousands of civilians who have been killed in Allied air-raids over France and Belgium and Czecho-Slovakia; perhaps they suffered longer, physically and morally, before the end came; perhaps they were less reconciled to the meaninglessness of their fate. The tragedy lies in the peculiar moral issue, focal to this war. They need not have died. The policy which sentenced them to death did not bring nearer the end of the war; and they did not die, even against their will, that others might live. The tragedy is, then, one of miserable and perverse error; and if restitution cannot be made to the dead, penance can be done by the living.

I cannot bring myself to close this chapter on such a negative note. Life and death, hope and despair, have been closely intertwined in the recent history of Palestine, as in the history of all the world. For the tens of thousands who failed to reach Palestine, and are no longer in need of an earthly homeland, there are thousands who have been permitted to reap the harvest sown there in the last sixty years; and among them none makes a quicker appeal than the boys and girls of the Youth *Aliyah*, the Ascent of the Children. Of these, too, many died a needless and purposeless death, at sea, or on the roads of Europe and Asia. But many came home. By devious routes, from Germany and Poland and Czecho-Slovakia, across the Carpathians and the Caucasus, by way of the Caspian and of Persia, they trekked into Palestine — hundreds and thousands of them, in a new children's crusade. The story of their

296

Odysseys, their endurance, their arrival, their reception, their integration into the life of Jewish Palestine, is told in the *Sefer Aliyat ha-No'ar*, "The Book of the Youth *Aliyah*," presented to the mother of the Youth *Aliyah*, Henrietta Szold, on her eightieth birthday; or rather, it is told in part, for it still continues. In the midst of the terror of this war, in the midst of the Jewish tragedy, the voices of these children sound a continuous note of redemption. For their sake much will be forgiven.

CHAPTER TWENTY-FIVE

The Homeland Vindicates Itself

❁

Against the background of the White Paper, of the sinking ships and drowning refugees, emerges the brilliant protest of Jewish Palestine's record in the war against the totalitarian powers. The brief review which follows is not offered in a spirit of competition; and not even, for the moment, by way of rebuke to the British officialdom which has meanly played down the contribution of the Jewish Homeland toward the victory of the democracies. On the other hand, there is a sense in which that contribution must not be taken for granted. It is true that Jewish Palestine is the concentration of the general Jewish democratic will, the distillation of its historic democratic character. It is also true that against all Jews, against every manifestation of Jewish life, Nazism had directed a special and significant hatred. Yet, in the bitterness of their frustration, the Jews of Palestine could have chosen *not* to fight on the side of democracies. They could have argued: "Our little effort will not determine the outcome of the war. If Germany wins, we are done for. If the democracies win, we still have the White Paper to fight. We will conserve our energies."

There were other peoples than the Jewish which had motive enough to fight the Axis, but did not lift a finger. What freedom would have been left to Egypt, Iraq, Turkey, Syria (to name only Palestine's neighbors) if the democracies had been defeated? But Egypt and Turkey remained neutral; Iraq and Syria played the Nazi game until the tide turned; the Arab masses did not flock to the United Nations armies. It was otherwise with Jewish Palestine.

No sooner was war declared than the *Yishuv* mobilized, entirely of its own accord. In five days 136,000 men and women had enrolled for service at the stations set up by the *Va'ad Leumi*, the National Jewish Council of Palestine. The Palestine Administration made no response at first. (It will be remembered that this was the period of the "phony war.") The offer of the Jews to raise an army serving as a unit was rejected — and is still rejected. But on October 12th, 1939, the government asked for 1,360 men between the ages of 20 and 32, for a service corps. It was proposed that Jews and Arabs be enrolled in equal numbers; but, since the Arabs were slow in responding, this would have meant that the requisite force would not have been raised. Jews and Arabs were therefore enrolled as they came forward. They were enrolled as "Palestinians." They were practically always referred to under that name, so that the disproportionately high contribution of the Jews actually served to mask the discreditable record of the Arabs.

The first batch of "Palestinians," 700 in number, arrived in France on February 28th, 1940. Three-quarters of them were Jews, although the Arabs constitute more than two-thirds of the population of Palestine, and they had just been given the White Paper. For the first few weeks the "Palestinians" did only transport work. Then they were armed, and were among the troops which covered the retreat of the Second British Expeditionary Force from St. Malo.

In September, 1940, the unit returned to Palestine. When France went down, the Near East became the focus of attention. The British forces were badly in need of mechanics and technicians. The Jewish Agency was asked for 1,200 specialists, and at once responded with 1,500, for service outside Palestine. Within the country barracks had to be built in a hurry for 18,000 troops. In six weeks the job was completed by 8,000 Jews, working day and night in three shifts. On February 28th, 1941, the British Colonial Office issued the statement that 6,000 Jews were serving with the British armies in the Near East, side by side with 3,000 Arabs. It omitted 1,500 Jews enrolled in the Royal Air Force. The figures were, then, 7,500 Jews, 3,000 Arabs. The Arabs had the entire Near East to draw on, the Jews only Palestine. By the summer of 1942 the Jewish contingent in the British armies had risen to 12,000, the Arab contingent lagged below 5,000. If we consider only Palestine, the Jews were contributing five times their proportion of volunteers for service *outside* of Palestine.

During the first advance into the desert west of Egypt the "Palestinians" were in the front line, and were mentioned in despatches by General Sir Richard O'Connor, who stated that the first capture of Tobruk would have been impossible without the help of those pioneers. General Wavell's report of them was: "They performed fine work, prominently at Sidi Barrani, Sollum, Fort Capuzzo, Bardia and Tobruk. Despite frequent bombing, their morale is excellent, and they were eager to help in the overthrow of the dictators." And again: "They showed remarkable courage and a splendid spirit of self-sacrifice." The British major in immediate charge of one unit reported: "Never in my life have I seen such keen and gallant soldiers. I am proud of them."

The "Palestinians" fought in Eritrea. In the advance on Keren they covered the left flank of the British army, cutting off an Italian attack. They fought in Abyssinia. One unit of three hundred was divided up into "suicide squads," and was assigned to the most dangerous missions. They fought in Greece, with the ill-fated expeditionary force. General Sir Henry Maitland Wilson reported of them: "The Palestinians worked well in Greece. They stood up in a satisfactory manner to the large-scale attacks to which they were submitted. Their severe losses are a matter of great regret." They fought in Crete. Mr. Peter Frazer, Premier of New Zealand, having toured the Near East front in those days, stated: "The Palestinians fought admirably in Greece and Crete, shoulder to shoulder with the New Zealanders and Australians." Among the 10,000 prisoners taken by the Germans in Greece and Crete, there were 1,444 Palestinians, of whom 1,023 were Jews, 421 Arabs.

They fought in Syria, in the days when the Vichy Government had decided to resist the British advance northward from Palestine. "Palestinians" familiar with the locality paced the British troops and helped in the capture of Kuneitra, the key position on the road to Damascus. On this occasion the reticence of the British on the identity of the Palestinians broke down, and General Sir Henry Maitland Wilson stated officially that he "much appreciated the assistance rendered by the Jews in this campaign."

They served on the sea. Hundreds of young trainees of the Jewish Maritime Service enrolled in the Royal Navy. They are still serving at various marine stations in the Near East.

And all this leaves out of account 20,000 Jews enrolled in the Home Guards of Palestine — one of the reasons, perhaps the main reason, for the failure of the Palestinian Arabs to follow the treacherous example of the Arabs of Iraq and Syria.

Of the 12,000 Palestinian Jewish volunteers in action outside of Palestine, 2,000 had fallen by the middle of 1942. It would be well, in this connection, to remember Mr. Churchill's report that during the Libyan campaign *there were never more than 45,000 men in action.*

So much for the work on the battlefront. Behind the fighting units stood a Jewish Homeland determined to score a comparable record in production. In the First World War, as we may remember, the Jewish economy was completely broken up by the end of the first year; almost half the Jewish population was uprooted, so that of nearly 100,000 Jews only 55,000 were to be found in the country when hostilities ceased. In this war the Jewish population suffered an initial shock, recovered, then geared itself to war production. Instead of a decline, there was a swift rise in the output of all commodities, and a remarkable exhibition of inventiveness and adaptability. The fishing yield doubled; milk and egg production increase from month to month. Palestine was providing 50% of its wheat needs, all of its vegetable needs. But the most significant work was done in the industrial field.

There are, at this writing, over 2,000 Jewish industrial

establishments in Palestine, 300 of them created since 1939, employing 45,000 workers. They are turning out textiles, metals, leather, machine parts, canvas for tents, boots, heavy harbor equipment, armored cars, fire-extinguishing apparatus, hospital equipment, ambulances, kitchen utensils and concrete ships. The saving in transportation from England and America is only one aspect of the achievement. Perhaps of greater importance is the production, by Jewish scientists of Palestine, of critical chemicals like ether, sulfanilamide, benzoic acid, nicotine acid, vitamin B complex, insulin, alkaloids, pyrethrum, thymus, digitalis and menthol. Atabrin and plasmochin, substitutes for quinine, are being produced at the Daniel Sieff Research Institute of Rehovoth. The research facilities of the Hadassah Hospital in surgery and tropical diseases have been placed at the disposal of the United Nations armies. Hundreds of thousands of tons of potash are being taken out of the Dead Sea and transported to Britain. New military roads in Syria were built by Jewish contractors, and when, with the fall of Rostov to the Germans, there was a sudden need to extend the oil refineries of the Anglo-Persian Oil Company, several hundred Jewish technicians and skilled workers were drawn from Palestine. Palestinian Jews are working in the war effort as far afield as India and Ceylon.

The cash value of the Jewish war effort in Palestine can easily be stated; $20,000,000 in 1941, $40,000,000 in 1942. (I have not been able to obtain the figures for 1943.) America spends four times as much in one day as Palestine can create in a year. But the Polish soldiers in Russia who received 70,000 phials of anti-typhus serum from Palestine did not stop to make any calculations. And the soldiers of all democratic countries who have been treated by the Jewish physicians of Palestine, and all its Jewish institutions, know that some of them owe their lives to this little enclave of democracy.

The record would have been higher, more lives would have been saved, if the Jewish Homeland had been given the encouragement it was promised, or even the simple right of way. In any case, apart from the toll of Jews who have fallen in all the democratic armies, the two or three thousand dead of Palestinian Jewry stack up well (God forgive the phrase) with the dead of any other people in the war for world freedom.

CHAPTER TWENTY-SIX

The Life Struggle of Palestine

❀

$\mathbf{T}$HERE are many ways of considering the future of Palestine, and of the Jewish role therein. We may speak of the possible function of a certain area in the general structure of a civilization; and it is not too fanciful — especially in connection with Palestine — to speak of that area as engaged in a life-and-death struggle to fulfil its function. The land is capable of doing a special job in the world of tomorrow. The question is: Will it be permitted to do that job, or will it be held back among the functionless areas of the world?

In the Commons debate on the White Paper of 1939, Leopold Amery told of the affirmative intentions which had moved the framers of the Balfour Declaration in 1917. He said: "We believed that it was Britain's mission to restore prosperity and civilization to that ancient land that had once been the very center of the civilized and prosperous life of the world and its creative thought. We knew ... that real regeneration could only come from some more intimate and directly quickening influence. It seemed to us that the Jews alone could supply that influence. They alone could bring western civilization to the East with an instinctive understanding of its outlook."

Much of this book has been devoted to indicating, in descriptions of everyday life, the character of that "more intimate and directly quickening influence" which the Jews alone could supply in the regeneration of Palestine. I have been more concerned with that special relationship — the hinge of the whole problem — than with any other single factor. If we ignore it, we shall understand neither the primary source of Palestine's potential strength, nor the special relationship of the land to the Jewish problem.

The vista which now opens before Palestine dwarfs everything about the old *Halutzim* except their moral stature and their significance as indices of history. The plans and hopes for the future differ in the quality of their conception from those which were projected by the beginners of the enterprise. Not even Herzl foresaw what the conjuncture of Palestine and the Jews could mean for the land, the people and the Near East, under the aspects of physical and moral productivity.

We recall that somewhere in the early nineteen-thirties the rebuilding of Palestine passed from the episodic to the statistical. The new stage sees the statistical sublimated into the organic. The land is now considered as a physical personality, a personality compounded of all its peculiarities of soil, climate and topography; and it is being treated as an organic unit from which, in its completeness, the maximum of economic advantage must be drawn.

Let me warn the reader against any suspicion of mysticism in my approach. The larger part of my facts, at this point, are drawn from the scientific work of W. C. Lowdermilk, Assistant Chief to the Soil Conservation Service of the United States Government Department of Agriculture. His study of Palestine is the same, in character, though more extensive in detail, as the studies he has made of other great reclamation projects, like those of the Yellow River, in China; of the Zuider Zee, in Holland; of the *Landes*, in Southern France; of the T. V. A., Boulder Dam and the Grand Coulee in America. In Lowdermilk's view the Valley of the Jordan offers a combination of natural features and a concentration of resources which "set the stage for one of the greatest and most far-reaching reclamation projects in the world." He sees Palestine affording room, under such a program, for five million Jews, without displacing any Arabs. The Jordan Valley Authority plan, which is well advanced in the blueprint stage, integrates the physical personality of Palestine in a harmony of all its features.

At the present time the pure waters of the Jordan empty uselessly into the heavily chemicalized waters of the Dead Sea. Instead of being permitted thus to run to waste, they are to be diverted for irrigation. But not for ordinary irrigation alone, as we shall see. To replace the water needed to maintain the level of the Dead Sea, a canal, part of it open, part running through a tunnel, will be cut from the Mediterranean to the Dead Sea. The salt waters of the Mediterranean are more useful for the Dead Sea than the pure waters of the Jordan. In their fall of thirteen hundred feet between the Mediterranean and the Dead Sea, these waters will be utilized in transit, by hydroelectric plants stationed at various levels. The electricity thus generated will be turned to several purposes, among which not the least important will be the extraction of the minerals contained in the concentrated salt solutions of the Dead Sea. For the Dead Sea is actually nothing more than an immense drying pan, in which are to be found unparalleled quantities of chemicals, for the extraction of which much power is needed. That power, then, will be supplied by the very agency — the canal — which helps to maintain the salinity of the Dead Sea.

There was a time when Jewish pioneers contemplated the reclamation of Palestine as a piecemeal job; Petah Tikvah in the old days, Neuris and Nahalal in the middle period; the Huleh — more ambitious, this — in the latter period. Today the organic approach to the land contemplates the total interrelation of resources, in a manner which differs in kind from the groping of the *Bilus* and the fierce, uninstructed idealism of the *Halutzim*.

Here is an instance of the new method: In the lower Jordan Valley alone there are nearly 100,000 acres of land which was considered irreclaimable. Here and there a few wild plants grew in the soil, which is so heavily impregnated with salts that it will not tolerate cultivation. What is to be done? Shall this area be marked for ever, "Uninhabitable"? Such was the prospect until the new view emerged. Today there is an answer: Get the salt out of the soil! How? By "leaching," or flushing. Once that is done, the soil is as fertile as the soil of Daganiah. How shall the leaching be done? By diverting the waters of the Jordan, which will thus cleanse the soil of its salinity as it once cleansed the leprosy from the flesh of Naaman, captain of the hosts of Syria.

The agricultural research station of Rehovoth undertook the first experiments in 1936. An area, one of the most saline, was staked out. A pipe, two kilometers in length, brought water from the Jordan to wash the boxed-in plots. At the end of four months the salts were flooded out. Manure and fertilizer were applied. Young pioneers — Youth *Aliyah* graduates of Germany and Austria among them — carried on the work in that hot region, below sea-level. Today, on the land that was once man- and God-forsaken, they produce most of their own food, tomatoes, potatoes, corn and bananas; they sell milk and eggs to the employees of the Potash Company, next door. They "export" to Jerusalem. They also grow rich, clean crops of clover, maize, and sunflower for the dairy herd and the poultry.

The lower Jordan Valley is only an instance of the new method. Once the implications of the vision come home to us, we perceive that all the old talk about shortage of land, about the struggle of two populations, has become utterly meaningless. It is a lesson in the passage of mankind from the primitive-competitive, with its hatreds and fears, to the advanced-cooperative, with its new foundation of relationships.

Lowdermilk sees further. Palestine can and should set the pace for the reclamation of that enormous area of the Near East which today suffers from under- not over-population. He sees, moreover, the reconciliation of the two immemorially hostile elements of the ancient world, the settled farmer and the wandering shepherd, the *Bedouin* and the *Fellaheen*. Though he does not put it thus, he sees — at long last — the reconciliation of Cain and Abel. For grazing lands will no longer be dependent on irregular rainfall, and hungry shepherds will no longer wander in search of pasture. Still other lands, unsuited for grazing and farming, will be good for forestation, giving timber for fuel and construction. The land was once rich in forests; it lost them, not through the action of nature, but through the indifference or ignorance of man, through the cutting down of trees without systematic replacement.

So much for one part of the picture. There is another, equally exciting. Just as science is teaching us to take full advantage of the topographic personality of a land, so it is teaching us a complementary lesson in the independence of man from the personality of the land. More and more clearly we realize that, in respect of both lessons, the basic economic assets of a country must be sought in the abilities, vigor, imagination and inventiveness of its inhabitants. While they have learned to make the most of what nature provides — and this is part of the fruit of their character — they supplement or replace the inadequacies of nature by their ingenuity. Is there any intrinsic reason why Amsterdam should be the diamond-cutting center of the world? No, there is only a historic reason — the Dutch interest in South Africa. Today there are nearly three thousand expert diamond-cutters working in Palestine. Is there any reason why Palestine should not produce textiles, clothes, surgical instruments, precision instruments? There was a reason once — the people were not there to carry on these industries. That reason no longer holds good. As transportation becomes less and less of a problem, the location of raw materials becomes less and less of a determinant factor in the economic life of a country. The factor will, of course, never disappear.

But the tyranny of its hold is broken; and whatever of it remains can be mitigated, too. The shift from heavy metals to light metals and plastics, from raw fuels to fuels obtained by fermentation, means a shift, also, in the centers of gravity of production, an equalization of opportunity. Coal and oil are fixed in the earth, and in definite quantities. The grain for plastics and for fermentation can be grown anywhere, and renews itself every year.

I have spoken hitherto of the reclamation of physical Palestine, which changes fundamentally the terms of the populational problem. Ancient Babylonia, with its twenty-odd million inhabitants, is modern Iraq, with its less than four million. Modern Iraq can become as fruitful as ancient Babylonia. What is lacking is the approach, and that alone — the willingness of the West to repay its debt to the East. The problem undergoes another change, already referred to at the beginning of this chapter. We see the reluctance and hostility of various forces in a new light. The imperialisms of western powers, and the connivance in them of old and reactionary local aristocracies, take on the aspect of a conspiracy to prevent the Near East from coming to life again, or rather, to keep it suspended between life and death, to hold it back from acquiring a modern civilization and taking its place among the other productive world areas. Inertia and prejudice unite with special interests; the savage obstinacy of the long outlived feudal system works hand in hand with the equally savage exploitative impulses of the last phase of freebooter capitalism; and against them Palestine leads in the struggle for a whole subcontinent.

311

We thus reach the larger meaning of the effort to hold down the Jewish Homeland. Had the Jews come to Palestine in the spirit of western masters seeking eastern servants, they would not have built a Homeland; they would have become the emissaries of investors, intent on securing the position of foremen among a docile laboring population. Such was not the spirit of their Return. In the belated industrial and scientific revolution of the Near East which they are initiating, they play a peculiar part. They seek to overleap the now unnecessary, wasteful and inhuman stages through which the earlier industrial revolutions have passed. The uncontrolled scramble which the early theorists of capitalism saw as the perfectly balanced system of self-interest versus efficiency, the consequent exploitation of the weak (weak, that is, in acquisitive strength, not in social usefulness), the concomitant evils of child labor, starvation, frustration, ugliness, need not be the price for the development of a rational system of production. I have been careful to indicate that what I call the predominant outlook of the Return was not common to all Jews seeking Palestine as a Homeland. But I believe that the character of the enterprise as a whole tallies with the purpose I here ascribe to it. Certainly at the beginning, dreamers like the *Bilus* and the first *Halutzim* were in the minority. But the popular support behind the Zionist movement, and the general spiritual purpose in the majority of the "founding fathers" — the builders who fixed the character of the enterprise — crystallized into this new method of colonization.

The social structure of the Homeland is dominated

by two institutions or organizations — the Jewish National Fund and the General Federation of Labor. Both of these have had to struggle against adverse internal forces. The purely capitalist colonization outlook of the Rothschild period saw the Jewish National Fund as a minor — and futile — experiment. Today the Jewish National Fund holds nearly one-half of the colonized land. The early capitalist colonists looked upon the labor ideals of the early immigrants as, at best, a passing revolutionary aberration. Today the General Federation, or *Histadruth*, with a membership of over 150,000, is the strongest single force in the actual *constructive* complex of the country.

The *Histadruth*, as a labor organization, is an altogether peculiar institution. There is nothing like it anywhere in the world, simply because nowhere else was a labor organization created under such conditions and with such a purpose. It is at once a colonizing agency, an instrument of industrialization and a moulder of social forms. Its outstanding peculiarity is that it seeks more labor immigration without being hostile to industrial enterprise. I have never heard of a national labor federation, anywhere, which has, at the head of its program, "More Immigration." But then, I have never heard of a labor federation which is dedicated, not simply to the improvement of the status of the working class, but to the development of a land and the redemption of exiles.

The *Histadruth* operates within the framework of the Jewish National Homeland but seeks to give that Homeland a special form, less by fighting the uncontrolled capitalist tendency — though it must do that too —

313

than by setting up its own economy. It has certain unique historical advantages. It does not have to change a vast, rigid mould already gripping a totally developed land. It was on the scene, if not from the beginning of developments, then at least early in the process. It has the support of the rebuilding movement as a whole, though not without opposition. It has the backing of a diffused tradition which regarded a Jewish Homeland as the expression, in part, of an ethical purpose. This tradition is very old, and has a strong religious tinge. Whatever the actual historical facts of the beginnings of the Jewish people, the earliest formulated purpose of the exodus from Egypt and the ascent to Palestine, as accepted by the people, told of a destiny couched in spiritual terms. As they put it then, they had come to Palestine to be a holy people. The outlook is echoed strongly in the present Return. They have come to Palestine to be an ethical and social people. Hence, at least in part, the consistently sympathetic attitude of the external supporters of the Return toward the social philosophy of the internal executors of the Return.

The *Histadruth* has its colonies, on Jewish National Fund land, its cooperatives, its cultural enterprises, its theater, newspapers, banks and sport organizations. It is basically constructive, not combative. It collaborates with capital wherever capital is cooperative. It will go into partnership with employers, wherever these will meet it half way. It seeks a special form of revolution in the social system — revolution by construction and cooperation.

Nothing like it has been attempted before. The

effect on an emergent Near East is of incalculable value. For this is not propaganda of social values by the written and spoken word alone. It is the infectious example of a successful embodiment of principles in the daily life of a people. Certainly this does not fit in with what the Arab leaders are dreaming of in connection with a future Palestine or a future Near East. The landowners, moneylenders, muftis and incipient capitalists cannot see a future for themselves among Arabs who learn from the Jews the idea of an Arab National Fund, of an Arab *Histadruth*, of Arab cooperative shops and factories, bakeries, canning, preserving, clothing and shoe factories. And it is a question how far this suits the book of capitalists of the West interested exclusively in the oil resources of the Near East.

But there are forces in the western world which will understand this larger significance of the Jewish Return, and theirs must be the last word. They are the forces on which the progress of mankind as a whole depends. They must see that the opening of Palestine to millions of Jewish refugees has a greater purpose even than the saving of so many lives: it is part of the world's reconstructive program, operating in an area which cannot be left derelict lest it serve again, as it is bound to do if it remains unregenerated, as a center of infection for the reactionary disease.

Many great collaborative episodes in history have begun with misunderstanding and friction. The friction and misunderstanding were born of narrow views and small egotisms. History overrode them in the end because the creative impulses of life as a whole were stronger. A collaborative episode between Arab and

Jewish life is not a new thing. For centuries Jewish and Arab genius kept alive a brilliant civilization when Europe was a human jungle "inhabited by beasts of burden and beasts of prey." The episode can be repeated, this time in the setting of a world vision common to all intelligent men in all parts of the world. It is to this level that the ambition of the Return has now been lifted.